Never

Too

Late

To

Learn

The Adult
Student's Guide
to College

THE PRINCETON REVIEW

Never
Too
The Adult
Student's Guide
to College
Late
To
Learn

by Vicky Phillips

Random House, Inc.
New York
www.randomhouse.com/princetonreview

FNG/ 1/17/2003 /631 54/ 11.00/ 448X /

Princeton Review Publishing, L.L.C.
2315 Broadway
New York, NY 10024

E-mail: comments@review.com

Published in the United States by Random House, Inc., New York, and simultaneously in
Canada by Random House of Canada Limited, Toronto.

ISBN 0-375-75478-4

Editor: Laurie Barnett
Designer: Stephanie Martin
Production Editor: Kristen Azzara
Production Coordinator: Stephanie Martin

Manufactured in the United States of America.

9   8   7   6   5   4   3   2   1

116302

CONTENTS

INTRODUCTION

What's it like to head back to college at midlife? It's incredibly exciting . . . and scary as all hell.

This book contains wisdom gleaned from my work with more than 10,000 adult learners: older college "kids" who decided that getting a higher education was a dream worth chasing. These gray-haired college kids have been kind enough to teach me, step-by-step over the last twenty years, what returning to college has honestly felt like to them.

Many people helped formulate the structure and ideas in this book. Moreover, almost all of them helped without realizing it, because it took me twenty years to go from learning these ideas to actually writing about them.

Carol Arner, once with Student Services at DePauw University, now with the Vermont Student Assistance Corporation, first gifted me with the notion that should always be treated like people in all ways. Her genuine concern for students helped ignite my own relentless passion in this field and the field of psychology.

Rick Eckel, once Director of Student Services for the Electronic University Network, now active in experimental adult education and distance learning with Oregon State University, taught me how to pioneer and sustain electronic learning communities for adult learners.

Gretchen Bryant of Speak Up Press in Denver, Colorado, was kind enough to remind me while I was writing this book, that old dogs can learn amazing new tricks if a few tasty bones get tossed their way.

I welcome any comments or ideas about this book. You can reach me at the contact address below, or visit me at our Adult Education and Distance Learner's Resource Center on the World Wide Web.

Vicky Phillips
geteducated.com
170 South Main Street
Waterbury, Vermont 05676 USA
vicky@geteducated.com
http://www.geteducated.com

1 BACK IN COLLEGE AT MIDLIFE: REAL FEARS AND EMERGING HOPES

College is more than a physical place. It is an opportunity to fulfill personal dreams and career aspirations. Traditionally, American colleges offered educational opportunity only to the young: 18- to 21-year-olds. In earlier times, only a tiny percent of the population attended college because most of the children were needed to work on farms. In addition, few young people had the the time or money that would allow them the luxury of leaving home for a few years to learn new skills. The only people who attended college in Colonial America were those who needed to learn how to read and write Greek and Latin so that they could pursue one of the few professions that required literacy: medicine, the ministry, or law.

LIFELONG LEARNING: THE NEW IMPERATIVE

In 1870, after the Civil War, less than 2 percent of Americans attended college. By 1970, a century later, half of all Americans went to college after high school. In 1999, two-thirds of high school graduates will attend college. We live in a society where college has become the rule rather than the exception. Americans who do not hold college degrees or career credentials are finding they are a minority— and they have difficulty changing jobs or careers.

These days, many people change careers three to five times during their lifetime. That's careers, not just jobs. We live in a time when technological advances can make knowledge obsolete overnight, and shifting local economies can lead to sudden job extinction. In 1970, only 12 million Americans held college degrees. By 1997, 41 million held college degrees. In 1998, a new record number of young people packed their bags and went off to give college a try.

> *N*ever in the history of the world have so many people been so well educated.

COLLEGE: A NEW AND IMPROVED ADULT-FRIENDLY INSTITUTION

It was bound to happen. America is an aging society. Along with every other institution, the college campus is going gray. It's not just the professors who are looking older. A record number of students are showing up on campus at midlife or beyond. A new generation of adult students is seeking to remain career competitive by completing long-delayed degrees or earning new career credentials.

Today almost half the students on college campuses are over the age of twenty-four. Students over the age of forty comprise the fastest growing population pursuing post-high school education and training. From 1970 to 1993, older students (40 years or more) who enrolled in higher education increased by 253 percent: Their numbers skyrocketed from 477,000 to more than 1.6 million. Forty percent of Americans over the age of 16 participate in some form of continuing education each year.

> *S*tudents over the age of forty comprise the fastest growing population pursuing post-high school education and training.

The good news is that there has never been a better time to attend college than right now—regardless of your age or income. Because so many older students have begun relying on colleges to provide them with lifelong learning, many colleges have changed to become more adult-friendly institutions.

ADULT-DEGREE PROGRAMS (ADPS) FOR MATURE LEARNERS

College courses used to be taught 9 to 5, Monday through Friday because the assumption was that the students were young, unemployed, and able to attend college full-time. These days, many colleges have expanded their hours as well as the programs they're offering. Many campuses now offer weekend college or evening university programs that welcome older, employed students who must study part-time to reach their educational goals. Unlike even a decade ago, most colleges now offer special Adult Degree Programs (ADPs). ADPs serve older students by providing services such as college preparatory courses, counseling, day care, special grants, and programs that allow them to earn credit for their career experience.

WHY RETURN TO COLLEGE AS AN OLDER STUDENT?

GREATER CAREER CHOICE

The Department of Labor estimates that at least 75 percent of all jobs require some kind of post-secondary education or specialized training. Your chance of being interviewed for a new job or career will be greatly enhanced by any degree or certification that helps differentiate you from the crowd of well-educated job seekers.

> *B*usiness is the number one major sought by students today.

People attend college to earn all types of degrees. Though business is the number one major earned these days, people also continue to earn degrees in things that may seem impractical: subjects such as English literature, feminism, philosophy, or pottery. These people may or may not enter careers that correlate with their degrees.

One of my best friends in college was a music major. She still plays in a band and teaches music from time to time, but her day career is as a stockbroker. Has she wasted her music degree ? No. She needed a college degree to be accepted into the stockbroker training program. They did not care what kind of degree she had, only that she had a degree.

Another one of my best friends has two bachelor's degrees. She earned her first one in psychology. When she decided to be a special education teacher, she also had to earn a second degree in education to meet state teacher licensing requirements. She also holds a master's degree in education. Today she does not teach. She works as a computer network specialist.

The important thing to remember is that holding a degree—any kind of degree—will give you greater career flexibility and keep doors open should you decide to change jobs, or even careers, as you grow older.

CAREER ADVANCEMENT

If you began your career twenty or more years ago, the people whom you competed with were much less educated. It was easier then to move ahead without holding a formal degree or career credential. But today, many people are finding that companies have ceilings on career advancement for those who do not hold a college degree. In many large companies you must hold a degree if you hope to be considered for in-house management training.

Not holding a degree can mean that you will be automatically passed over for promotions or more desirable assignments even though you may have the experience and the skills to excel at an advanced level.

One of the most common reasons adults return to school is because they feel that they will not be promoted or placed in advanced training programs unless they hold a degree. A college degree has become the golden key that unlocks the first level of possibility in an increasing number of occupations and industries.

PERSONAL SATISFACTION

Not everyone who attends college does so to boost their career. Some people attend college simply because they love to learn or because they wanted to attend college when they were younger but were held back by things such as shortage of funds, a lack of understanding about how colleges work, or marrying young and having children. Any reason you have for returning to college is a valid one.

Some people attend college simply because they love to learn.

Many who enter college at midlife have doubts about their intelligence. And there are many who enter college later in life to help quell these nagging doubts. You may feel in your heart that you are smart, yet seek the satisfaction of having your innate intelligence validated. Colleges are perceived as the institutions that put the stamp of approval on intelligence these days.

A highly successful 62-year-old man explained that he wanted to complete college because he had always felt ashamed that he had dropped out to help support his family after the first year. This man had gone on to become a very successful business executive, a self-made millionaire. His colleagues generally assumed that he had a college degree because he was a nationally known expert in the area of business finance. Over time the man had stopped correcting his business colleagues when they assumed he had a college degree. Facing early retirement with all his financial goals met, the man wanted to earn his degree as a way of proving to himself that he was indeed as smart as people thought.

A 52-year-old woman wanted to earn her art degree at long last. She has always loved art but had not attended college because her family had warned her that it was impractical and would be a waste of money. It was only after her children were raised and gone, and she had been through a difficult divorce, that this woman returned to college to realize the dream that she put on hold thirty years earlier.

HEIGHTENED EARNINGS

While earning a college degree will not automatically entitle you to a raise, the Census Bureau has consistently found that the more education you have, on average, the higher your annual wages will be.

> College graduates with four-year bachelor degrees can expect, on average, to earn about $15,000 more per year than those who hold only a high school diploma.

Within these averages you have to remember that not all people who earn college degrees make more than those who stop their education at high school. Much depends on the kind of degree you earn and the kind of job you take after earning that degree. An experienced electrician who does not hold a college degree may earn more than a kindergarten teacher or a librarian who have graduate degrees. While a college degree or career credential may not boost your earnings automatically, chances are they will improve your odds at bringing home a better paycheck as the years roll by.

Annual Average Wages by Educational Level
1996 Census Data

No High School Diploma	$14,013
High School Diploma	$21,431
Some College	$22,392
Associate's Degree	$27,780
Bachelor's Degree	$36,980

COMMON FEARS AND CONCERNS

I'M TOO OLD TO LEARN NEW TRICKS

If you think you're too old to compete for a seat in the very best colleges in the nation, think again. Harvard University has operated an evening extension university for older students since 1909. Today, Harvard's average evening division college "kid" is 32 years old.

> The oldest person to graduate from the Harvard Extension Program is Mary Fasano. Mary earned her associate's degree from Harvard in 1997 at the age of 89.

Mary's advice to students who think they are too old to cut the intellectual mustard: "Don't stop—Keep going. It will be worth it in the end. To have knowledge is to have power."

Research shows that only certain, limited intellectual features actually change with age. For example, it does take people slightly longer to retrieve information as they age, but a person's ability to learn and understand remains undiminished. Moreover, the more you use your mind—at any age—the more agile and capable your mind becomes.

> The great news: Studies show that older students tend to earn better grades and receive better evaluations from their instructors.

This is because older students enter college with more life experience, hence more information to draw upon. Also, older students tend to take their studies more seriously than younger students. As it is a conscious and deliberate decision to return to school, older students tend to work harder and spend more time on their homework and out-of-class assignments than their younger peers, who often go to school because of others' expectations.

I'M NOT SURE WHAT TO STUDY

Many people procrastinate from applying to college or taking courses because they are not sure what kind of degree they may want to earn. Do not let this stop you. You can take a few classes without worrying about the formal admissions process. If you eventually decide that you want to earn a degree, you can complete a more thorough application process. Colleges call this process "degree matriculation." This just means that after taking a few courses you have decided that you want to earn a degree and are ready to declare your major area of study and the kind of degree you want to earn.

It is always a good idea to take a course or two just to see how you like college or how you like certain subject areas. Maybe you have always imagined you'd like computer programming, but you are not sure. If so, register to take a beginning course in computer science and see how you like it.

Let college be a time of exploration and learning new things. Remember that most colleges have career and testing services that you can use for free, or for a small fee. If your college has a class in career choice or career planning, and if you are unsure about your goals, make that class your first one. Campus career centers can help you understand the types of jobs and careers that you would find the most satisfying. You will also learn more about these careers, salary levels, and what will be required of you in terms of education.

MY SPOUSE OR FAMILY WILL THINK I'M SILLY

Going back to college is a big step. It is a big step both for the person who decides to return to college and the spouse, kids, or significant others who have to adjust to a new routine. More women than men return to college later in life because, traditionally, women have been more likely to drop out of college to raise families. Younger men have tended to continue to attend college for career and financial reasons.

In the best of cases, spouses and significant others will be supportive of your college plans. However, we do not live in an ideal world: Support for college is not always forthcoming. In some cases significant others may be threatened by plans to return to college and belittle any and all attempts at higher education.

Why would anyone be threatened by your returning to college? Going back to college may signal all sorts of things to a spouse or a parent, even to your grown children. Spouses may fear that they will be left behind. This is especially true if the spouse does not have a college education. Children may feel that it is silly for their "old" parents to be toting around textbooks and taking final exams. We discuss the personal side of returning to college and dealing with new feelings, both yours and those of your family and employer in chapter 8: The Personal Juggling Act.

There Is No Campus Near Me

Attending college used to be a problem if you live in a rural area. We say "used to be a problem" because in the last decade a new generation of campus-free colleges or "virtual universities" have been built. These new distance learning colleges use the internet, mailed lessons, cable TV, videotape, CD-ROMs, phone conferencing, and other technology to make college accessible to students who cannot physically get to a campus because of time or lifestyle constraints. If you have been unable to attend college because you can't afford a sitter for your kids or home health care for your disabled older parents, a distance-learning college may be the best option for you.

Many adults find virtual campuses the ideal way to learn because all the emphasis is placed on the studies themselves with no competing interests such as Saturday night football games, fraternity parties, or joining the right college social clique. The average age of the distance-learning college "kid" is around 40. We cover accredited distance-learning colleges in chapter 4: Distance Learning.

My Skills Aren't College Level

As the number and types of learners who attend college have increased so has the need for remedial training for new students regardless of whether they enter college at the age of 18 or 68. More than one-third of today's college freshmen need to take remedial coursework in English or math. If your math or English skills are rusty, rest assured you will have plenty of company when you arrive on campus.

> Don't put off college because you fear that you can't do college-level work.

Give the college a chance to make a realistic assessment of your current skills and to help you bring your skills up to speed. Look for a college that offers a college-preparatory program that can assist you in building your basic skills. In chapter 2: Preparing for College Admission at Midlife, we deal with issues like working with your academic weaknesses, dealing with poor academic performance in the past, and preparing to take college admission and placement exams.

I Can't Afford College

Most adults do not realize that colleges charge widely varying amounts for their services. Publicly supported colleges charge less than private colleges because publicly supported colleges receive tax dollars. If you choose to attend a public college rather than a private one you can often cut your tuition expenses in half. What's more, even the price of attending a publicly supported college can vary drastically from state to state. If you reside in California, you can attend the state community college system and earn your associate or two-year degree for about $1,000, whereas the same degree earned at a publicly supported community college in Vermont can cost you more than $6,000.

If you comparison shop among colleges you will find that no two colleges charge the same amount for tuition and fees. You will also discover that each college varies in how much money they are willing to give to students in the form of grants and scholarships.

Many adult learners are able to cut their college costs significantly by getting degree credits from their careers and even life experiences, or by taking specific standardized exams to test out of courses where they already have experience. We cover the trend of getting credit for life experience programs to accelerate college while simultaneously cutting tuition costs in chapter 6: Earning Credit for Career and Life Experience.

College Cost Is an Elusive Creature

It is impossible to determine up front how much a college education will eventually cost you. Bear in mind that few students end up paying the sticker price for their college degree. Receiving financial aid is a complicated process, and is determined by your financial ability to pay for your college education. Financial assistance will depend on everything from your gross income and your academic grade average, to the number of dependents you list on your tax forms.

One of the best financial aid strategies is to cut your college costs up front. If you have any college credits—the majority of adult students do have transfer credits—you need to understand the college transfer process so you can get the most transfer credit for your academic dollar. We cover this process in detail in chapter 5: Saving Time and Money.

The only way to really know how much a college education will cost is to actually apply to college. You must submit all the paperwork that the government requires so the college can determine your ability to pay and award you additional support in the form of loans, grants (free money), or tax credits. We cover the complicated ins and outs of financing your college education in chapter 9: Money Matters.

WHAT'S IT REALLY LIKE TO GO BACK TO COLLEGE?

What's it really like to be in college at midlife? Ask any adult student and you will most likely get a two-edged answer: It's as exciting as anything . . . and scary as all hell. In the last two decades almost everything about college has changed. Libraries have fewer books and more electronic learning and information retrieval systems. Students no longer sit in neat rows taking down what the professor says verbatim. Students are more likely to work on team projects than they are to be asked to stand up and recite unapplied facts and theoretical suppositions. Your class may have a web site where you are required to participate in discussions or lab sessions between face-to-face class meetings.

If you're an adult student, you are about to arrive at the foot of the collegiate Ivory Tower with all sorts of things other than your textbooks stuffed into your backpack. Unlike the traditional 18- to 21-year-old learner, you probably have a mortgage to pay, kids that need attention, parents that are aging and in need of special care, and maybe even a boss that has made it clear that you'd better get a degree of some kind . . . or else.

Because going back to college can be stressful as well as exhilarating, we include not one but two chapters to help you deal with the psychology of returning to college. chapter 8: The Personal Juggling Act assumes that you will be emotionally squeezed trying to keep up with all your obligations. Use this chapter to understand how to better manage your time, overcome procrastination, and use your college's resources to deal with stressful issues like the competing demands of your significant other.

To succeed in college, you will need to understand the student role, how to act in class, and how to deal with time-honored stresses like test-taking and performance anxiety.

In chapter 7, we outline the complex process of learning to be a student again. Most adults, accustomed to ruling their own lives, find that adopting the student role can bring up unexpected stresses.

2 PREPARING FOR COLLEGE ADMISSION AT MIDLIFE

College admission once required a high school diploma with honors and letters of lush praise from your Latin teacher. Some colleges still honor this traditional approach, but most have altered their admissions process to suit the needs of older students. After all, even if your high school Latin teacher is still available to write a recommendation letter, how you performed in high school twenty years ago is probably not the best indicator of your intellectual ability today.

How do you prepare for the back to college experience? Where do you begin? Your first step is to locate the colleges that offer what you want to study. Your second step is to successfully apply and gain admission to the college of your choice. This chapter is designed to show you the ropes of getting ready for your return to college. Ready? Set? Let's crack the books!

FINDING A COLLEGE

First question: How do you know where the colleges are, and which offer what you want to study? This is a very good question because not all colleges offer all types of degrees and majors. For example, let's say you want to become an architect. First off, few colleges even offer an architectural degree. Then, if your goal is to become a registered architect, you will need to earn a special five-year bachelor's degree from a college that holds several types of special accreditation. Accreditation is important, because it tells you that the standards have been met in the education that you are about to purchase. (See chapter 3 for a full discussion on accreditation.) If you want to earn a unique professional degree (for example, architecture) you need to be prepared for the fact that there may not always be a college within commuting distance of your home that offers the particular type of degree you are looking for. On the other hand, almost every college offers degrees in three of the most popular career areas: business, psychology, and computer science.

Almost every college offers degrees in three of the most popular career areas: business, psychology, and computer science.

USING COLLEGE GUIDES

The best way to find a college within your commuting area is to check one of the standard guides available in your public library. Two popular guides are the *Complete Book of Colleges* and *The Best 331 Colleges*, both published by The Princeton Review. Two other such guides are *Peterson's Guide to Four-Year Colleges* and *Peterson's Guide to Two-Year Colleges*, both by Peterson's Guides.

It is worth noting that not all college guides are created equal. If you are looking for a four-year college, or one that awards bachelor degrees, you will want to consult a guide to four-year colleges. Both The Princeton Review's *Complete Book of Colleges* and *Peterson's Guide to Four-Year Colleges* catalog about 1,400 four-year colleges that operate across the United States and Canada. If you are especially looking for two-year colleges, or colleges that offer associate degrees, you will want to consult a guide like *Peterson's Guide to Two-Year Colleges*, which focuses on two-year schools.

A good college guide should give detailed profiles of each college and list them by geographic area, as well as by the academic area that you want to specialize in, for example, business administration or computer science. A good college guide will also index colleges by the type of academic credential they offer: certificate, associate, or bachelor's degree. By consulting the index of a good college guide you will be able to quickly locate all the colleges in your home state or commuting area that offer the type of credentials you seek, in the subject area that interests you.

One additional way to locate colleges is to read your local paper and listen to the radio. These days many local and small colleges advertise in newspapers, on TV, and on the radio. This is particularly true of private colleges and state colleges that offer special evening or weekend college programs for working adults. Many programs that cater to the needs of adults and older students advertise during commuting time on local radio stations. If you have access to the internet, you can also visit the web sites of local colleges to learn more about their degree programs and admission procedures.

Once you locate the colleges that offer what you need in terms of both location and degrees or certificates, your next step will be to contact the admissions office and ask them to send you an application package.

USING THE INTERNET

In addition to consulting printed guides in your local library, you can utilize college search engines and databases on the web. These databases allow you to input information about the kind of college and degree you are seeking. For example, a good college database allows you to specify that you are looking for colleges in California that offer bachelor's degrees in history. The database should search for these types of colleges only and return with a list of possible colleges for you to explore.

> *A* good college database should sort any of your data input—things such as tuition cost and type of degree—and return a list of colleges nationwide that fulfill your needs.

Unfortunately, many internet college database sites are not fully developed. The data they contain may often be spotty, dated, or inaccurate. Most are geared toward the traditional 18-year-old student and provide grand coverage on things like college sports and the best party schools, but they provide little if any information of interest to adult students, such as weekend or evening college programs. There are few free internet databases as comprehensive as the printed guides that you'll find in your public library. You can begin your search online, but don't stop there! The addresses of some of the more popular internet web sites are listed below:

Money Magazine's Best College Buys
http://www.pathfinder.com/money/colleges99

Comparative data on 1,346 traditional four-year colleges in the United States. Includes recommendations on selecting a college from the editors of *Money* magazine. This is a great beginning resource but provides no data on two-year colleges, trade schools, or nontraditional programs for older adult learners.

CollegeNet
http://www.collegenet.com
Search and apply to colleges nationwide by using this system. Includes two-year, four-year, and vocational technical schools. A nice system but far from comprehensive. More colleges are missing than are included in this data system.

CollegeEdge
http://collegeedge.com
A search system for two-year and four-year colleges, complete with career guidance information. The most comprehensive, free college search system on the Internet. No data or information is provided on special college programs for adults, however.

CollegeSource
http://www.collegesource.org
A collection of college catalogs from two-year, four-year, and graduate schools. You can download local college catalogs to check on items such as tuition costs, degree requirements, credit for life experience, and transfer credit policies.

WHAT DO ADMISSIONS PEOPLE REALLY WANT FROM ADULT STUDENTS?

Admissions officers are the gatekeepers of higher education and opportunity. Traditionally, the job of the admissions advisor was to make sure that ill-prepared students did not end up in the college classroom. To some degree this is still true. However, only a handful of America's more than 3,000 accredited colleges practice truly competitive admissions. The majority of colleges are willing to open their intellectual gates to anyone who demonstrates an aptitude and eagerness for higher education.

Harvard University, for instance, has operated an evening university for older learners since 1909. You do not have to be a genius to be admitted to Harvard's evening university. In fact, you do not even need a high school diploma. The only admissions requirement at Harvard's evening university is that you show up for classes. After that, you must pass at least three courses with a grade of B- or higher. Your classroom performance, and your performance alone, decides whether or not you will ultimately earn a Harvard degree.

> *Y*ou do not have to be a genius to be admitted to Harvard's evening university. In fact, you do not even need a high school diploma!

Admissions officers are really looking to see that you are prepared to succeed at a college level. If your skills are not yet at college-level—perhaps you never took algebra at all in high school—most colleges will gladly assist you in preparing for college. Preparation is commonly offered in the form of tutoring or special classes. If English is not your native language, colleges will want to see that you can read and write well enough in English to comprehend the textbooks and lectures, which will be in English. If you are not a native English speaker and want to attend college to earn a degree, you may need to take a course or two in English as a second language (ESL) to enhance your vocabulary and ability to write papers in English.

Many colleges have in-house college preparatory (prep) programs dedicated to helping older students brush up on basic skills in math, English, and the life sciences. This is especially true at two-year or community colleges, but also increasingly true at four-year colleges that operate special evening and weekend programs for adult learners. We discuss the option of using college prep programs in this chapter and in more detail in chapter 7: Back in College.

DEALING WITH PREVIOUS ACADEMIC DISMISSAL

One of the greatest myths of higher education is that only geniuses attend college. Having been both student and teacher at several colleges, I can assure you that people of varying levels of intelligence can—and do!—earn college degrees every year.

We have seen people flunk out of high school, yet graduate from college with highest honors three decades later. We have also seen academically gifted individuals who sailed through high school attend college only to flunk all essential subjects.

If you did poorly in high school or previous colleges, be honest with yourself about the reasons for your poor academic performance. We have seen extremely intelligent adults come slinking into our offices with previous records marked "Academic Probation" semester after semester, followed by one final red mark of "Dismissed for Inadequate Grades." (To earn any college degree you must maintain a C grade average!)

One 50-year-old man had to laugh at himself as he pointed at his last semester of Ds and Fs and said: "That was thirty years ago. College wasn't important to me. I was majoring in P&P (Party and Pizza). I know I can do better this time." And he did. He graduated at the top of his class two years later. Not bad for a guy who flunked out of college the first time around!

Another common misconception is that if you were ever dismissed from a college for poor grades, you can never be admitted to a good college again. Practically every college will consider admitting a student who has been dismissed from another college, and will admit students on a provisional or probationary basis. Probationary admission will give you a chance to show your new college that you are serious this time around.

IDENTIFYING AND WORKING ON YOUR WEAKNESSES

If you received poor grades in your previous academic work, ask yourself what caused these low grades. If you can identify what contributed to your poor performance, you can then develop a plan to address these specific weaknesses this time around. Did you take your studies seriously when you were younger? If not, are you ready to take them more seriously? Did you need tutoring or refresher courses and fail to take them? Were you trying to major in an area that seemed like a good career choice but failed to engage you?

On this last point we have seen people try to force themselves to major in subjects that their spouses or parents thought were a good choice but they themselves did not enjoy. If you've already tried to earn a degree in nursing three times only to drop out of your nursing courses time and time again, you should rethink your major area of study! If you dropped out of college because you were unsure of your career, or what you wanted to be when you grew up, make the campus career counseling center your first stop for academic success.

The important point—and one that we cannot stress too strongly—is that you must identify and work on the factors that made college an unsuccessful experience for you the last time around. Work honestly with your admissions advisor to make sure that you get the help you need at the beginning of your academic program.

Four of the most common deficiencies that quickly lower college GPA if not dealt with up front are:

1. Poor research and writing skills
2. Poor time management
3. Poor study skills
4. Poor test-taking skills.

Each of these four skill areas can be worked on and improved as a part of your new college program.

> Today, unlike even a decade ago, most colleges have student support centers where you can get help with your skills in everything from test-taking to career choice and time management.

If poor skills in one or more of the above areas previously held you back, make it a priority to address these issues in the very first semester of your back to college plan, before you start taking formal courses. Ask your college advisor to help you locate the campus resources that will help you deal with your trouble areas. We talk more comprehensively about using all the support services that college has to offer you as an adult learner in chapters 7: Back in College and chapter 8: The Personal Juggling Act.

USING COLLEGE PREP PROGRAMS TO GIVE YOURSELF A BOOST

The two most dreaded words to an adult about to return to college are *algebra* and *essay*. These words have the power to make grown women and men weep. Unfortunately, almost every college will require you to take at least one course in math, and one or two in English composition or writing to earn a degree. So, sharpen that pencil and put some batteries in that calculator. You'll need basic math and English skills to succeed at almost any college endeavor.

> At least one-third of all college kids need some type of refresher course in either math or English, often both.

If high school is a decade or more behind you, do not be surprised if you need a refresher course in how to multiply fractions or prepare a bibliography. This can be true even if you always did well in English or math. Skills grow rusty, especially when not used. Community colleges are especially strong in offering remedial and tutoring services to adult students. However, more and more, four-year colleges have developed special college-prep programs for older learners.

If you think you might need remedial courses or special assistance for things like learning disabilities or English as a second language, ask your admissions advisor to explain the options. Colleges differ in the special services they offer. The presence or absence of these special services can make the difference between two colleges that otherwise appear equally attractive.

For example, Sinclair Community College, in Dayton, Ohio, offers adult students a variety of services to help them prepare for college-level work. Like many community or two-year colleges, Sinclair has what is called a Developmental Studies Program. First, all full-time incoming students are given placement tests to assess their skill levels in reading, writing, and math. Academic plans are then individualized to make sure that students who need tutoring or remedial coursework receive it. Sinclair also offers a tutoring service. So, if you need a little extra help in biology, you can drop by Tutorial Services, in Room 10444, and receive one-on-one help with that, or any other subject that troubles you.

Trinity College, a small Catholic liberal arts college in Burlington, Vermont that offers two-year and four-year degrees, offers an array of special services for adult students. Trinity's Program for Adult Continuing Education (PACE) sponsors several free evening workshops for older learners. These workshops include Polishing Study Skills and Basic Writing Review, among others. Students who feel unsure about their math skills can start with a math workshop that reviews high school basics. After that, they can graduate to a full-length, noncredit course called Fundamentals of Math, a course for those who need a solid introduction to basic algebra before trying a regular college algebra course.

Like many colleges these days, Trinity offers these special courses and services because they know that many adults will hesitate before returning to college for fear that they are inadequately prepared. At Trinity, as at many colleges these days, a vital part of the college admissions process involves helping older learners to honestly identify their weaknesses. Once identified, weaknesses can be addressed as a vital part of the degree-planning process.

Again, ask the admissions advisor at your selected college if they offer a college prep program. If your selected college does not offer a college prep program, ask for a referral to the nearest college that does. Contact your local community college for the most complete array of college prep programs.

HOW COMPETITIVE IS ADMISSIONS?

Most programs for adult college students practice what is termed "open admissions." An open admissions policy will allow you to register for classes without having to meet many, if any, special requirements. For example, Central Texas College, a typical two-year college in Killeen, Texas, is an "open door" institution. Anyone in the community who feels like they are ready to take a college course is welcome to register.

Open admissions has become popular for older adults because traditional indicators of academic success, like your high school GPA (grade point average), become invalid over time. A high GPA from high school is a good thing to have, but if your high school records were poor do not let it keep you from considering college.

In assessing older students, i.e., those over the age of 25, colleges will almost always look at indicators other than high school performance. Admissions advisors want to know if you are willing to attempt college-level work. Therefore, an advisor may request and review a number of items. The most commonly requested materials include:

> High School Transcripts
>
> Transcripts of Past College Work
>
> Letters of Recommendation
>
> Written Application Forms
>
> Results on Standard Academic Tests

Different colleges may require different materials from you. Additionally, not all colleges will use these materials in the same way. We cover each of the above five items in detail later in this chapter. Remember that individual colleges may have some completely different requirements for admission. Always read the admissions packet that your selected college sends you. Pay particular attention to the items required for admissions. Your admissions advisor can help you understand and obtain any documents or test results that will be required for admission to any specific academic program.

GETTING YOUR ACADEMIC RECORDS IN ORDER

HIGH SCHOOL TRANSCRIPTS

The college of your choice may require a copy of your high school transcript, which you will need to obtain yourself. A high school transcript is an official copy of your old grade reports. High schools have traditionally kept these records on file. However, these days many older high school records have been transferred to central microfilm or computer files. It is increasingly common for older records to be kept on file not at your high school but at the offices of county educational officials or State Superintendents of Education.

If your high school still exists—many have been torn down or consolidated into other schools—call or write the principal's office. It is usually preferable to call because you can speak with someone in the records office. They can then inform you about the status of your records. If your old high school no longer exists, look in the phone book for your county or state department of education. Someone in the records department of a county or state government education office can assist you in locating your high school records.

Getting a copy of your high school records may take a while. You will need to allow at least four to six weeks for a transcript request to be processed. Start now to locate your records and learn how to order an official transcript. You will eventually need to make a written request to your high school or a government education officer to have official copies of your transcripts forwarded to your college of choice.

TRANSCRIPTS OF PAST COLLEGE WORK

If you've already attended college, and you intend to seek a degree at a new college, your new college will require a grade transcript from all of your old schools. The college registrar is the person who keeps your collegiate grade records. You will need to write the registrar at every college you have attended and request that they send official copies of your old grade reports to your new college.

Many colleges charge a fee of about $2 to $5 to have an official transcript sent to a new college. Call the registrar at your old college to find out what information they need to process a transcript request. Most colleges will not process an official transcript request on the phone. In order to protect the confidentiality of your records, they will require you to submit a written request with the necessary fee.

You'll Need a Transcript from Every College

You will need to request official transcripts from every college that you have attended. If you have attended three colleges, you probably already have had your credits from the first two colleges transferred to the third. So why can't you just have the last college you attended send a cumulative transcript to your new college? Because every college has different rules about how they handle transfer credits. It could be that the last college you attended did not accept all your previous credits in transfer. For this reason, you will need to contact each college you have attended and request an official transcript of your work be sent to your new college.

For admission purposes, most colleges require an overall or cumulative transfer Grade Point Average (GPA) of 2.0. A 2.0 is a C grade average. More competitive colleges may require you to have a transfer GPA in the range of 2.5 to 2.75 (C+ to B–). If you do not have a transfer GPA in the range of 2.5 to 2.75, most competitive colleges will still consider your application, but you will probably be admitted "provisionally." For example, you may be allowed to take courses only for a semester so they can then see how well you do. If you do well in your first semester, earning grades of C or above, you may then be officially admitted to a degree program. If you do not perform well your first semester your application for admission may be denied.

Dealing with Foreign Transcripts

If you attended a university that was not located in the United States nor accredited by an agency recognized by the United States Department of Education, you may need a special assessment of your old transcripts. This will always be true if English was not the instructional language of your former university.

The registrar at your new college can check on the accreditation status of any foreign institution for you. The admissions advisor at your new college will tell you if you need to have a formal assessment of your foreign college records. These assessments may include a translation of your old transcripts into English and a listing of how your old college credits convert into the credit system used by American colleges.

If you need a course-by-course translation and assessment of foreign college records, the following companies perform assessments for a fee. Contact them directly for information on their services. However, before using a foreign translation and assessment service, make sure the college you plan to attend will accept an assessment from the company. A few colleges may require that foreign assessments be done in-house, or through their own referral services.

Education Credentials Evaluators
PO Box 92970
Milwaukee, WI 53202-0970
414-289-3400

International Education Research Foundation
PO Box 66940
Los Angeles, CA 90066
310-390-6276

World Education Services
PO Box 745
New York, NY 10113-0745
212-966-6311

LETTERS OF RECOMMENDATION

Almost every college will require one to three letters of reference from people who can attest to your drive and educational ability. These letters can come from many sources: teachers, ministers, bosses, coworkers, volunteer leaders, local politicians, and professional colleagues. Anyone who is not related to you, and who can attest to your intelligence and character, would be a good person to ask.

Start now to think of at least three people who might write letters on your behalf. Pick at least one person who can speak about your talent to perform in your chosen academic area. For example, if you are going back to school to become a mental health counselor, it would be good to have at least one letter from someone who has known you in a counseling capacity. If you already work as a counselor, you should ask a professional colleague or supervisor to write a recommendation letter for you.

Remember that not everyone feels comfortable writing about other people. If someone does not want to write a letter for you, try not to take it personally. Thank them, and ask someone else. Writing a recommendation letter is not as easy as it may sound! It can take hours to write a good recommendation. Give people at least thirty days to write a letter for you. Also, since people tend to procrastinate, remind your references regularly that you will need the letter from them by a certain date. Late or missing recommendation letters are the most common items that delay college admission for older learners.

WRITTEN APPLICATION FORMS

If you are applying to a college to earn a degree or a professional certificate you will be asked to complete a written application form. Many two-year or community colleges use simple application forms. Simple application forms often ask for little information other than your name, address, date of birth, and other vital statistics. In some cases, you may also be asked to write an essay or a series of essays on why you want to return to college at this time. This is typical when applying to a four-year college to earn a bachelor degree but much less typical when applying to a two-year college to earn an associate degree.

Take the Time to Polish Your Application and Essay

The written application and admission essay are vital documents. They are also documents that you can prepare and polish at your leisure. Prepare these written documents carefully. If you are trying to be admitted to a degree program, admissions people will scrutinize your writing abilities. We have seen people denied admission based on poorly written admissions forms and essays. The first thing an admissions advisor will look at is your application and essay. She or he will be checking to see if you can express yourself well in writing.

If you are asked to write an essay, or to write brief answers to several questions about your interest in attending college, take this assignment seriously. Check your written materials for grammar, spelling, and for syntax, as well as clarity of the ideas you wish to express. Ask someone you trust to read over your writing and point out any errors.

It is a good idea to first make a draft of what you want to say and then set this aside for a few days. Come back to your draft and read it again in its entirety. Read it aloud to see how it sounds. Make changes until it reads exactly how you'd like it to read. Don't be afraid to give your second or third drafts to a friend to read over. Spell check all your documents. As with all things, you only have one chance to make a good first impression.

What kinds of questions might you be asked as a part of your admission application? This will vary. Traditionally, colleges have asked high school kids questions that relate to what they hope to be when they grow up. Most adults are already busy "being" a lot of things when they get around to going back to college, so colleges tend to ask older students different types of questions. Most of these questions are designed to figure out how well-read you are and if you are able to express yourself in writing at a college level.

For example, Eckerd College, a private four-year college in Florida, asks five questions of adults hoping to earn a bachelor's degree through their Program for Experienced Learners, a special program for older learners. The five questions are:

1. List three books you have read in the last year. Discuss why at least one of these books was important to you.
2. What publications do you read on a regular basis?
3. If you are employed, describe your responsibilities.
4. Describe volunteer activities in which you are involved; include any leadership responsibilities you have had.
5. Describe a significant personal or professional accomplishment.

In addition to these five questions, Eckerd asks adult students to write a 250-word essay about why an Eckerd degree is important to their professional and personal growth. Tough questions? You bet! These questions require thought. Your admissions advisor will be looking for clear evidence that you are able to think through complex questions and respond in writing with well-thought-out, grammatically correct answers.

STANDARD ACADEMIC TESTS

Four types of tests are frequently mentioned in admissions materials. These tests are the GED (General Equivalency Diploma), the SAT, the ACT (American College Test), and placement exams such as Asset or COMPASS (Computer Adaptive Placement Assessment and Support System).

If you're applying to college as an older student you may need to take some of these exams. All of these exams are nationally standardized and must be taken in special proctored (supervised) settings under controlled testing conditions. College advisors may use the scores on these exams to help determine your admissions status.

What Is the GED?

The GED, also known as the General Equivalency Diploma or the General Educational Development Test, has been around since 1942. More than 700,000 adult learners take the GED in the United States each year. It is taken by people who, for whatever reason, failed to complete their formal high school education.

GED-takers include older individuals who lived at a time when people did not routinely complete twelve years of compulsory education; younger teens who have dropped out of high school for various reasons; those in foster or institutional care; and people in the military who often take the GED as part of their basic training.

Anyone who did not complete a formal high school education may be asked to take the GED so that college admissions advisors can have evidence that the prospective student possesses the "equivalent" knowledge of someone who has been formally graduated from high school.

If you do not have a high school diploma, and you want to attend college, do not panic.

> The good news is that almost every college in the United States, including Ivy League colleges such as Harvard, will accept your scores on the GED in lieu of a high school diploma.

In fact, according to the developers of the GED, more than 95 percent of the colleges in the United States will accept scores on the GED in lieu of a high school diploma for admission.

Do not be alarmed if your local college asks you to take the GED. Naturally, colleges want to make sure that you are academically prepared to enter college. Many people think that you must possess either a high school diploma or a GED to attend college. This is not always true. The New York Institute of Technology, a regionally accredited four-year university, will, for example accept students who do not hold either a GED or a high school diploma provided that they have already completed at least 24 credits of college work with at least a C grade average.

Moreover, in some states, publicly supported universities not only accept older students who do not hold high school credentials but will actually award them a high school diploma after they have successfully completed a year of college study. Check with your local college for their policy on admissions without a high school credential. There is one possible downside to entering college without either a GED or a high school diploma: You may not qualify for all forms of government student aid. Check this angle carefully before embarking on your college career without a GED or high school diploma.

What's Inside the GED?

The GED tests your "General Educational Development," hence its name. The educational standards used on the GED are derived from testing actual high school seniors each year.

The bad news for those taking the GED is that the GED is not one test, but five of them. The good news is that according to the American Council on Education more than 60 percent of the 700,000 adults who take the GED each year are doing so to prepare for higher education. The GED is a multiple-choice test that consists of five sections and takes more than seven hours to complete. The five sections, which will be scored separately, are:

> Social Studies
>
> Science
>
> Interpreting Literature and the Arts
>
> Mathematics
>
> Writing Skills (Two Parts)

The second part of the Writing Skills section requires test-takers to write an essay. College admissions advisors often require both a minimum score on the entire GED, (all five parts added together), as well as a minimum score on the Writing Skills section. If your college of choice accepts the GED, check their minimum scores and compare these to your own. The University of Maryland, for example, accepts applicants whose GED score totals at least 225 on all five parts, with no one test at a score of 40 or below.

Preparing to Take the GED

You have several options for preparing to take the GED. You can obtain a book that will help you self-study. For example, The Princeton Review, publishers of this book, offer a self-study book called *Cracking the GED*. This book, as well as others like it, can be found in most public libraries. These self-study books explain the GED, provide sample tests and answers with explanations, and also give helpful study tips.

If you do not want to study alone, every state, each province of Canada, and many sites abroad support a GED program for people who want to attend formal classes and work with tutors. Local high schools, community colleges, and public libraries run these programs nationwide. Most provide free tutoring. In addition, many states participate in GED preparation via TV. Under this program, study sessions are broadcast to rural areas on public access cable TV. So, you can prepare for the GED by watching cable TV study programs at home.

To find out about GED study programs in your community, call the national GED hotline at 800-62-MY-GED, or call a career counselor at your local community college. If you have internet access, you can check the comprehensive GED directory online at the web site of the American Council on Education at http://www.acenet.edu.

Further Information on the GED

The American Council on Education's Center for Adult Learning and Educational Credentials oversees the GED program. Their web site, http://www.acenet.edu/programs/CALEC/GED/home.html, houses information on the GED, registration, passing scores, frequently asked questions, and special policies and procedures. The Center also has free publications to help you along. You can order their free pamphlets, *The ABCs of the GED*, *GED: The Key to Your Future*, and the *GED Information Bulletin*. The sixteen-page *GED Information Bulletin* contains sample test items and places to contact to get more help with the GED. You can order these free publications by contacting GED Fulfillment Services, PO Box 261, Annapolis Junction, Maryland 20701; phone 301-604-9073; e-mail ged@ace.nche.edu.

Alternatives to the GED: Earning a High School Diploma

Some people do not want to take the GED because they feel a stigma is attached to having earned not a high school diploma but only the "equivalent" of one. This stigma is based on prejudice, not fact. Anyone who earns a GED has proven that they possess the very same level of knowledge as your average high school graduate.

If you'd still like to complete a formal high school course of study, contact the guidance department at your local high school and ask if coming back into the classroom is an option at your local school. The problem with taking formal classes is that most adults feel out of place in the social environment of high school. High school is not, after all, all books and exams. High school is also a hotbed of adolescent social development. The hallowed halls of high school ring not just with knowledge but with the concerns of what to do about your acne and the fact that you have no date for the Saturday night football game.

However, some urban high schools do operate special night schools for adult learners. Check with the guidance counselor at your local high school to see if high school via night school is a possibility.

High School Diploma via Home Study

If you do not want to sit through formal classes, or if formal classes are not available in your area, you can still earn an accredited high school diploma by taking classes in the comfort of your own living room. Consider attending an independent study high school. In these programs, counselors will help you to select the courses that will allow you to pick up your high school education exactly where you left off. You can, for example, start with the last semester of your senior year, if that is in fact where you left off.

High school by independent study works just like regular high school. You work with a counselor to determine what grade you last completed. The counselor then advises you on which courses to take at what grade level to earn your diploma.

After your counselor and you have determined what courses you need to complete your high school education, you select your courses from a course catalog. You can register by mail, phone, fax, or e-mail. The course materials and your textbooks arrive in the mail. Sometimes videotapes and computer learning software are also a part of your course package. Your course materials will include reading assignments and weekly homework. You do your lessons and mail, fax, or e-mail your homework back to your instructor. The instructor grades your lessons. The diploma you get at the end is a regular state-accredited high school diploma, not a GED.

High school by independent study is a good option for anyone who seeks a structured approach to building basic skills prior to entering college. Even if you decide to take the GED, you can still take a high school course or two by independent study to help you brush up in trouble areas. Many adult learners who have high school diplomas or GEDs have enrolled in "refresher" high school courses through home study before attempting college courses.

The following universities offer inexpensive home study options for earning an accredited high school diploma from the comfort of your couch and VCR, or your computer and modem. Visit them on the internet or call to request a detailed program catalog.

Brigham Young University
Independent Study High School
205 HCEB
PO Box 21514
Provo, UT 84602
Phone: 801-378-2868
E-Mail: indstudy@byu.edu
URL: http://coned.byu.edu/is

North Dakota Division of Independent Learning
High School Independent Study
Box 5036
State University Station
Fargo, ND 58105-5036
Phone: 701-231-6000
E-Mail: stone@sendit.nodak.edu (Robert Stone)
URL: http://www.dis.dpi.state.nd.us

University of Nebraska—Lincoln
Independent Study High School
Division of Continuing Education
269 Clifford Hardin Nebraska Center for Continuing Education
Lincoln, NE 68583-9800
Phone: 402-472-4321
E-Mail: unldde1@unl.edu
URL: http://www.unl.edu/conted/disted

The SAT I

The SAT I is a test taken each year by high school juniors or seniors who want to attend college. It is the test most commonly used by colleges to screen incoming freshman who are recent high school graduates. The SAT I tests high school students abilities to reason in mathematical and verbal terms.

Though you may be asked to take this test as an adult learner, the SAT I is rarely used for admissions purposes with students who are older than 25. When it is used, it is not typically used for college entrance decisions, but instead to help college advisors decide where to place you in math or English composition classes.

For example, if your math scores are low on the SAT I (as is common for those who have not had a math course for a decade or more!), your admissions counselor may assign you to a refresher or remedial math course in your first term of study. If you do well in your refresher course, you'll then be permitted to continue on in your education. The next semester you will take a regular college-level math course. Check with your selected college to determine the availability of remedial courses and services. If your college does not offer these services they will usually refer you to another local college or two-year community college nearby that does offer these special college prep services and courses.

> **A**lthough the SAT is the most commonly used test to screen incoming freshmen, it is rarely required for students over the age of 25.

If your college requires the SAT I, your advisor or college counseling and testing center will assist you in registering for the test and in interpreting the score report that you will receive after the exam. As with all standardized exams, your library will have several guides that contain sample tests that will help you self-study for the SAT I. The Princeton Review offers one such guide: *Cracking the SAT*.

You can find out more about the SAT I, which is offered several times a year at high school sites across the United States, by contacting Educational Testing Services, SAT Registration, PO Box 6200, Princeton, NJ 08541; phone 609-771-7600. You may also visit the Educational Testing Services online at http://www.ets.org or e-mail them at etsinfo@ets.org.

The American College Test (ACT)

The ACT assessment is another traditional college entrance exam offered at five different times a year to high school juniors and seniors. The ACT is a multiple-choice, proctored exam that tests your abilities in math, reading, writing, and science. It costs $21 to take this test. Like the SAT, it is rarely required for adult learners. Check with the college of your choice to see if they require the ACT. Again, while the ACT is often required of recent high school graduates, it is rarely used to determine admissions for students over the age of 25.

Unlike the SAT, the ACT is not a general test of your aptitude. Instead, it is an actual test of the knowledge you should have learned in high school in various subject areas. Over 1.7 million high school kids take the ACT each year.

As with all standardized exams, your library will have several guides that contain sample tests to help you self-study for the ACT. The Princeton Review offers one such guide with a computer CD-ROM, called *Cracking the ACT with Sample Tests on CD-ROM*.

If your college of choice requires the ACT, you can obtain free information and a registration form from ACT Test Administration, P.O. Box 168, Iowa City, IA 52243-0168; Phone 319-337-1270. You can also find out more about the ACT by visiting the American College Testing site on the web at http://www.act.org.

Local Placement Exams

Most adult learners are not required to take the traditional SAT I or ACT exams. In place of these exams, most colleges use what are called "local placement exams." These exams are called local because they are given on demand at a local college's own testing center. Your academic advisor may give you these exams in his or her office with pencil and paper or a computer terminal.

These exams are called placement exams because they have been designed to test your level of knowledge in the basic college skill areas of math, reading, and English composition. Your scores on these exams will determine your initial placement in math, English, and writing courses. The most commonly used local placement exams are Asset and COMPASS, though your college may use others.

You will not need to worry about placement tests unless your college specifically requires them. If your college requires them, they will schedule you for the exams and administer them to you. You will be asked to take these placement exams either when you apply, or after you have been accepted. The results of your placement exams will be used by your academic advisor to help place you in the best beginning sequence of courses.

3 COLLEGE ACCREDITATION AND DEGREES

The questions that adult students tote around before they set foot on campus are complex. How do you find a reputable college? What's the difference between an associate degree and a bachelor's degree? Do you really need a bachelor's degree or would a professional certificate or diploma be a better buy? Do you need to attend an accredited college? Is it a good idea to earn an associate's degree at a community college, then transfer to a four-year bachelor's degree program? What's an "accelerated" degree? What is a CEU credit, and why can't you just combine all 100 of yours from work into a single college degree?

If you've just begun looking at colleges and are feeling overwhelmed, we guarantee you are not alone! Selecting the right college and kind of degree or educational program is such a crucial issue that we have dedicated an entire chapter to it.

STEP 1: UNDERSTANDING COLLEGE ACCREDITATION

College shopping is a task that should come with the warning label "Buyer Beware!"

You've found a college that appears to meet your career needs, and they are pressuring you to enroll. Telemarketers are calling late at night, urging you to sign up now! Something feels wrong. You begin to wonder if your chosen college is on the up-and-up. Are you right to be suspicious of a college? Maybe. While most colleges are trustworthy, well-managed, nonprofit institutions, not all are as trustworthy as others. In addition, many colleges these days are in the education business to turn a profit. Their drive to make a profit should sometimes put you, the consumer, on red alert. Moreover, some "colleges" are not colleges at all but unaccredited degree mills: schools that specialize in taking your money and giving you a paper degree without bothering to include much in the way of an education.

The most common complaint from adult students is that they attended a college that was not accredited; or they attended one that was accredited but by an unrecognized agency. Worse still, some students attended a college that was accredited but by the wrong agency for their long-term career needs. In this situation, a student may have invested several years and thousands of dollars to earn a degree or certificate, but, alas, that degree or certificate does not meet the professional requirements that an independent licensing agency has established for their chosen profession. Finding the best kind of college is not easy.

What Is College Accreditation?

College accreditation exists to protect you, the consumer, from fly-by-night, substandard schools.

College accreditation exists to make sure that the quality of an education offered at one college is on par with the quality of education offered at another college. To be accredited, colleges must meet the standards set forth by other colleges. Accreditation is important because it tells you that clear standards have been met in the design and delivery of the education that you are about to purchase.

Who Is a Recognized Accreditor?

You have considered several colleges and narrowed your decision down to three of them. The three colleges that you like are all accredited. You relax! But wait: They are all accredited by different agencies. You feel a headache coming on. Are all three of these agencies recognized accreditors? Does it make a difference if you select one college over another one? To answer these questions, let's look at your hypothetical choices in more detail.

- College A is accredited by a regional accreditation agency, the Western Association of Schools and Colleges (WASC).

- College B is accredited by the National Association of Accredited Institutions (NAAI).
- College C is accredited by the Accrediting Council for Independent Colleges & Schools (ACICS).

Your question: Are these all recognized accreditors?

The answer: No.

Of these three accreditors, the second one, the National Association of Accredited Institutions (NAAI), is a bogus agency. How do we know it is bogus? Because it is not recognized by the United States Secretary of Education, Office of Postsecondary Education (OPE), or by the Council on Higher Education Accreditation (CHEA).

The United States Secretary of Education, Office of Postsecondary Education, is the government agency that recognizes college accrediting agencies in the United States. Each year, the Office of Postsecondary Education publishes a free "List of Nationally Recognized Accrediting Agencies," recognized by the United States Secretary of Education. The list is available on the internet at http://www.ifab.ed.gov/csb_html/agency.htm. A free list may also be obtained from the United States Department of Education, Office of Postsecondary Education, 600 Independence Avenue, SW, Washington, D.C. 20202.

The Council on Higher Education Accreditation (CHEA) is the national, nongovernmental agency recognized by the Office of Postsecondary Education (OPE) to oversee and recognize new accrediting agencies. CHEA lists recognized college accrediting agencies on its web site at http://www.chea.org.

CHEA also works with the American Council on Education to publish the annual book, *Accredited Institutions of Postsecondary Education*. A listing in this annual guide entitles a college to honestly advertise as an accredited educational institution. OPE and CHEA recognize many different accrediting agencies. Later in this chapter we cover the major accrediting agencies recognized by CHEA and the Office of Postsecondary Education.

If you ever feel uncomfortable with a college, check their accreditation with the Office of Postsecondary Education and the Council on Higher Education Accreditation before you enroll. Also, don't hesitate to contact your local Better Business Bureau. If other consumers have had problems with a college or training institute you will most likely find unresolved complaints on file with the Better Business Bureau. Never buy education blind. Be forewarned that crooked colleges do exist.

Why Attend an Accredited College?

Two compelling reasons exist for attending an accredited college. The first is that it can help protect you from getting ripped off. Attending an accredited college is like buying a used car with a warranty. Because the school is accredited, you have some assurance that standards are in place and being followed when it comes to issues as diverse as academic appeals, tuition refund policies, and national recognition for your degree or career credential.

The second reason for attending an accredited college has to do with your long-term career and educational goals. Colleges that are accredited by the same agency recognize each other's courses and degrees as valid. This means that if you attend an accredited college to earn your two-year associate degree now, and ten years from now you want to go back to another college and earn your four-year bachelor's degree, your old courses will be accepted in transfer toward your new degree.

Accredited colleges recognize courses and degrees from other accredited colleges. They do not recognize courses and degrees from unaccredited colleges.

Do All the Accreditors Recognize Each Other?

The sad answer to this question is no. Several accrediting agencies are recognized by CHEA and OPE. Each accrediting agency reviews and accredits slightly different types of colleges, and for this reason, they do not recognize each other as offering the same kind of education.

For example, regional accreditation, the most widely recognized college accreditation, covers traditional universities that offer what is called a "liberal arts curriculum." These types of curricula are less career oriented and practical. More than half of most liberal arts degrees consist of general knowledge subjects like reading, writing, philosophy, and critical thinking. Regional accreditation covers established private universities like Yale University, as well as all large, established state university systems, like the University of Massachusetts.

Another agency, the Accrediting Commission for Career Schools/Colleges of Technology (ACCS/CT), was developed to review and accredit colleges that offer a more practical, applied, career-oriented course of study. The ACCS/CT is more likely to accredit colleges that offer short-study career certificates or two-year applied degrees that are tied to specific careers like heating and air conditioning, technology, or bookkeeping.

Regionally accredited colleges rarely recognize the courses and degrees earned at ACCS/CT accredited colleges or any college that is not also regionally accredited. For this reason, *you need to be very careful about the type of accreditation that your selected college holds.* You should be very careful that the degree or credential you earn today will be accepted for your career and college needs later on.

TYPES OF RECOGNIZED ACCREDITATION

Regional Accreditation

Regional accreditation is the most widely recognized and respected form of college accreditation in the United States. Harvard University is regionally accredited, for example. So too are Princeton, Yale, and Stanford, as well as every member of the traditional Ivy League system. By the same token, most publicly funded state and county college systems are also regionally accredited. For example, in the State of Indiana, Indiana State University, Indiana University, and Ivy Tech State College are all regionally accredited colleges.

The six regional accrediting agencies are:

1. Middle States Association of Colleges and Schools (MSACS)
2. New England Association of Colleges and Schools (NEACS)
3. North Central Association of Colleges and Schools (NCACS)
4. Northwest Association of Schools and Colleges (NASC)
5. Southern Association of Colleges and Schools (SACS)
6. Western Association of Schools and Colleges (WASC)

Each agency oversees colleges that operate in its geographic area. No one regional agency is better than another. For example, there is no academic distinction between programs that are accredited by the Southern Association of Colleges and Schools (SACS) and ones that are accredited by the Western Association of Schools and Colleges (WASC). The important point is whether or not the college you attend is accredited by one of these regional boards.

Regionally accredited colleges recognize each other's degrees and credits. For example, if you attended the Community College of Vermont, a regionally accredited two-year college system, the degree you earned there will be accepted in transfer for entry into the University of Vermont, a regionally accredited four-year college system.

From a consumer's perspective, the power of regional accreditation lies in the fact that regionally accredited colleges recognize each other's courses and degrees. By the same token, regionally accredited colleges do not routinely recognize credits and degrees earned at colleges that are accredited by one of the other recognized agencies listed below.

Distance Education and Training Council

The Distance Education and Training Council (DETC) used to be called the National Home Study Council. The DETC accredits schools that offer distance education or home-study programs. Distance education programs are programs that can be completed at home by mail, the internet, videotape, or other noncampus means.

Most of the schools accredited by the DETC are proprietary or for-profit schools that offer career-oriented studies. Most of the schools accredited by the DETC do not offer campus-based college studies. Most offer only home-study programs. For example, ICS Learning Systems, also known as International Correspondence Schools, a founding member of the DETC, offers a variety of career certificates and courses through correspondence studies. ICS also offers a few specialized career-oriented associate degrees in areas such as accounting and computer programming. ICS, which has operated for more than seventy-five years, maintains an administrative and enrollment headquarters in Pennsylvania. ICS does not, however, operate a teaching campus. You cannot physically attend ICS and take courses. You can only take ICS courses via home or correspondence study.

Many regionally accredited colleges also offer distance-learning or home-study degree programs. We cover this trend in chapter 4: Distance Learning. However, regionally accredited colleges do not commonly seek DETC accreditation for their distance degrees. This is because regional accreditation is more widely recognized than DETC accreditation. Regional accreditation boards have their own separate set of standards that they ask their member colleges to apply in developing regionally accredited distance-degree programs.

Accrediting Association of Bible Colleges

The Accrediting Association of Bible Colleges (AABC) was founded to help Christian Bible colleges develop standards of educational quality. Bible colleges are nonprofit colleges, run by Christian agencies. Baptists, Lutherans, and Seventh Day Adventists are a few of the denominations that operate Bible colleges in the United States.

Degrees offered by Bible colleges include study of the Bible and the doctrines of the church that operates the college. To attend these colleges you may have to sign a declaration of faith that attests to your belief in the religious principles of the college. Examples of AABC-accredited Bible colleges include The Mid-America Bible College, operated by the Church of God in Oklahoma City and the Clear Creek Baptist Bible College in Pineville, Kentucky.

Not all church-operated colleges are accredited by the AABC. Many are regionally accredited instead. For example, Kentucky Wesleyan College, associated with the Methodist Church, is regionally accredited by the Southern Association of Colleges and Schools (SACS). The Southern Baptist Theological Seminary, located in Louisville, Kentucky, is also accredited by SACS, not by the AABC. Most Catholic universities are regionally accredited.

Accrediting Commission for Career Schools/Colleges of Technology

Many proprietary or for-profit schools that teach the trades are accredited by the Accrediting Commission for Career Schools/Colleges of Technology (ACCS/CT). The Oklahoma State Horseshoeing School, located in Ardmore, Oklahoma, is accredited by the ACCS/CT. Similarly, the Titan Helicopter Academy, in Millville, New Jersey, and the French Culinary Institute, in New York, New York, are ACCS/CT-accredited schools. A selection of California colleges that are ACCS/CT accredited would include such institutions as the Institute of Computer Technology, ITT Technical Institute, and the Interior Designs Institute. ACCS/CT-accredited colleges specialize in offering career credentials or certificates and two-year applied associate degrees in career areas such as electronics technology, the culinary arts, and the industrial arts.

Accrediting Council for Independent Colleges & Schools

The Accrediting Council for Independent Colleges and Schools (ACICS) accredits many proprietary, or for-profit business schools. For example, New York schools that are ACICS-accredited included the Blake Business School, the ASA Institute of Business and Computer Training, and the Computer Career Center. A small selection of ACICS-accredited colleges in California would include the National Hispanic University, the Southern California College of Business and Law, and Valley Commercial College.

Specialized Programmatic Accrediting Agencies

In addition to the above accreditors, who accredit whole universities, you may need to attend a program that holds special programmatic accreditation. Academic departments within a college may need to be accredited by special agencies. For example, if you are considering a career as a registered nurse (RN), you may need to attend a nursing school that is accredited by the National League of Nursing (NLN). The college you attend may be regionally accredited, while the nursing program within that college is accredited by the NLN.

Specialized or programmatic accrediting may be crucial if you are entering a career that requires you to meet state or national certification or licensing standards. Such careers include engineering, financial planning, social work, some counseling fields, pharmaceutical work, most medical technology fields, and public school teaching.

For example, public school teachers who teach children in kindergarten through grade 12 are often required to earn a four-year bachelor's in education from a regionally accredited college. In addition, that regionally accredited college may need to operate a state-approved education department that is accredited by the National Council of Accreditation for Teacher Education. We mention that the education department might need to be state-approved because each of the fifty states has the right to determine the type of credential needed to teach in a public school that operates within state boundaries. Earning a teaching degree that has been approved by the state of Alabama may or may not qualify you to teach in a school in New York.

If you are not sure if your chosen career requires a certification or licensing accreditation, visit the career counseling center at your college, or speak directly with an academic advisor at the college you are considering. If you do not have access to a career counseling center, research your chosen career at your local library. One excellent book for researching the educational requirements for any career is the Occupational Outlook Handbook. The *OOH*, as it is called, is an annual guide published by the government. The *OOH* details hundreds of occupations. Details found inside the OOH include the working conditions for hundreds of careers as well as any special educational requirements that must be met to enter or advance in most professional careers. If you have internet access you can read the *OOH* for free at the web site of the Bureau of Labor Statistics at http://www.bls.gov/oco-home.htm. If you are uncertain what kind of education you need to enter a new career take the initiative now to research this issue. If you fail to do this now, you could end up with a great degree—but one that will not qualify you to practice as a professional in your chosen career area.

WHAT ABOUT STATE-APPROVED OR LICENSED SCHOOLS?

Some technical and trade schools are not accredited by any agency. Instead, they are reviewed and approved by State Boards of Postsecondary Vocational and Technical Education. State approval, or school licensing as it is sometimes called, is more popular in some states than others. California, for example, boasts a variety of state-approved training institutes that teach everything from dog grooming and massage therapy to radiology, airplane piloting, and computer electronics.

If a college is state approved then it has been reviewed, found to be a sound operation from a business perspective, and granted a license to deliver career-relevant education at a post-high school level. A state-approved school may meet your needs, especially if you are looking for training programs tied to specific career skills. However, state-approved schools are not eligible to offer government student aid programs such as student loans. *From a consumer's perspective, the primary problem with attending a state-approved college is that degrees earned at nonaccredited, state-approved colleges are not as widely recognized as those earned at accredited institutions.*

STEP 2: MATCHING COLLEGE CREDENTIALS TO CAREER CONCERNS

You may be certain that you need a college education yet remain unclear about the type of degree you need to earn. If you are the typical adult learner, you are fairly clear on what you want to do with your degree. For example, you may know that you want be a computer programmer or that you want to be a financial planner. The question is what kind of degree will help you meet that career goal? Would a certificate help you? Do you need an associate's degree? Or should you earn a bachelor's degree? To help you answer this question, let's look at your educational options in detail.

UNDERSTANDING TYPES OF COLLEGE CREDENTIALS

Certificates

A certificate, or diploma education, is the shortest course of study. A certificate program is any concentrated course of study in one subject area. A certificate generally indicates that you have completed anywhere from three to twelve courses, all within a year or so of your enrollment. Certificates consist of courses that help you develop career competencies in one subject area. Most people earn certificates in order to qualify for entry into a new career or to learn specialized skills within an existing career area. For example, you might earn a certificate in C+ computer programming, one in paralegal studies, or one in direct marketing.

People who have already earned college degrees and seek new knowledge to change or expand their careers often use certificate programs. For example, you might already hold an associate's or bachelor's degree in business administration. You earned that degree several years ago. Since then you have begun working in marketing. You now want to specialize in the area of direct marketing. In this case, earning a certificate in Direct Marketing might be a wise career move.

What would a certificate look like? Below is an outline of a six-course certificate offered by Mercy College, a private, regionally accredited college, located in Dobbs Ferry, New York. Notice that like most certificate programs, this one offers a straight, no-nonsense approach to learning about one career field—in this case the field of direct marketing.

Mercy College
Certificate in Direct Marketing

Introduction to Direct Marketing
Creative Basics for Direct Marketing
Strategic Media Planning for Direct Marketing
Database Development and Marketing
Fulfillment
Customer Services in Direct Marketing

Certificate programs are becoming very popular with adult learners who attend evening universities and community colleges. New York University, a college that operates one of the largest continuing education programs for adult learners, offers many professional certificates through their evening, weekend, and summer divisions. Their most popular certificate programs teach computer science and programming and special business skills. Below are examples of two popular certificates offered by New York University.

More and more colleges are offering certificates to help adult learners quickly acquire the basic skills they need to enter new careers or to specialize within their current careers. More and more colleges are also offering certificates that can be applied later toward an associate's or bachelor's degree. If college is new to you, and you have no transfer credits, you might consider beginning your college studies by earning a certificate rather than a whole degree. Certificates can be earned more quickly than degrees because they require fewer courses. After you earn your certificate you might decide to go on and transfer the credits you have earned for your certificate toward an associate's or bachelor's degree.

When to Consider a Certificate

1. I need to acquire basic career skills to change my career quickly.
2. I already hold a degree and now want to specialize in a new career area.
3. The career I want to enter requires a certificate for licensing purposes.
4. I don't have a degree, and may want to earn one later, but I still want to acquire specific career skills quickly.

If you answered yes to any of these questions, a certificate may be your quickest and least costly educational choice.

Associate's Degrees

An associate's degree is a two-year degree. It typically takes two years of full-time study to earn an associate's degree. In earning an associate's degree you will complete your freshman and sophomore years of college.

To earn an associate's degree you will need to complete sixty semester credits of study, or about twenty college courses. Most associate's degrees are awarded by private career colleges or by publicly funded community or junior colleges. However, an increasing number of four-year colleges are giving students the option of earning an associate's degree when they complete the first two years of their four-year bachelor's degree.

Associate's degrees have been popular for the last twenty years. Increasingly, people are looking at the associate's degree as a shorter, less expensive route to career entry than the traditional four-year bachelor's degree, which takes twice as long to complete.

What does an associate degree look like? Every college will have its own degree plan that includes both required courses—courses that you must take—and elective courses, courses that you can elect or choose to take to earn an associate degree. If you decide to major in a special area, such as business management or psychology, then your associate's degree will include a requirement that you take a certain cluster of courses in your major area. Your degree will also include required courses in general critical thinking or what is called "the liberal arts." The liberal arts include courses such as English, humanities and arts, the social sciences, and science and math.

Below are two sample associate's degree courses of study from two different colleges. Again, different colleges will have slightly different degree programs. In selecting the right college, compare the degree requirements at different schools carefully.

Brevard Community College–Cocoa Beach Florida

Associate of Science in Electronic Engineering Technology
General Education/Liberal Arts Courses:

First Aid
College Algebra
Fundamentals of Speech
General Psychology
English Communications
American History
Spanish I

Major Area Required Courses:

Digital Fundamentals
Microprocessor Fundamentals
Analog Devices
Analog Circuits

High Reliability Soldering
Schematic Captures, Modeling and Simulation
Electronic Communications Systems
Instrumentation and Control Systems
Microcomputer Design

Elective Support Courses:

Basic Programming
Pascal Programming
C Programming
Fortran Programming

Community College of Vermont—Burlington, Vermont

Associate Degree in Business
General Education/Liberal Arts Courses:

English Communication I
English Communication II
Speech
College Algebra
Biology
Chemistry
Introduction to Computers
Microeconomics
American Government
Business and Professional Writing

Cross-Cultural Inquiry
Seminar in Educational Inquiry
Major Area Required Courses:

Introduction to Business
Principles of Accounting I
Business Law
Business Finance
Introduction to Marketing
Personnel Management
Small Business Management
Management of Information Systems

Elective Supportive Courses:

Principles of Accounting II

When to Consider an Associate's Degree

1. I already have some college experience, but less than 60 semester credits, and would like to add to this to quickly earn an associate's degree.

2. I already have about 60 semester credits of previous college experience and would like to find a college to consolidate these credits into an associate's degree for me.

3. I have been told that the associate's degree is the right degree for my immediate career needs.

4. I have no college experience but am certain that I want to begin by earning a degree of some kind.

Bachelor's Degree

A bachelor's degree is a four-year degree with typically a schedule of full-time study. In these four years, you will complete 120 semester credits, or about 40 college courses. In most cases, more than half of a bachelor's degree consists of general education or liberal arts courses in areas such as English, critical thinking, psychology, history, and mathematics. Typically only 30 to 36 credits, or 10 to 12 of your courses will be in the area of your major. Regionally accredited, liberal arts colleges award most of the bachelor's degrees in the United States.

Historically, the term "college degree" meant a bachelor's or traditional four-year degree. The bachelor's degree remains a required stepping-stone into many professional careers. In most cases, you cannot attend a professional graduate school in law, medicine, or teacher education unless you hold a bachelor's degree.

What does a bachelor's degree look like? Basically, it's like an associate degree doubled. We include below two sample bachelor's degrees so you can see the type of curriculum that might be included. Again, colleges will vary slightly in their exact degree requirements. Compare colleges carefully on the courses they require you to take to earn your bachelor's degree in any one major area

University of Wisconsin—Platteville, Wisconsin
Bachelor of Science in Business Administration
General Education/Liberal Arts Courses:

English Composition I
English Composition II
Speech Communication
College Algebra
Calculus I
Math of Finance
Art History I
Spanish I
German I
American History I
American History II
Political Science
Introductory Psychology
Organizational Psychology
Consumer Psychology
Astronomy
Physics I
Physics II
Physical Geography
Race and Gender Issues
World Geography

Major Area Required Courses:

Introduction to American Business
Introduction to Marketing
Business Law I

Financial Management
Administrative Policy
Introduction to Computers
Interpretation of Business and Economic Data
Elementary Accounting I
Elementary Accounting II
Managerial Accounting
Organization and Management
Principles of Microeconomics
Principles of MacroeconomicsCross-Cultural Inquiry

Elective Supportive Courses:

Business Law II
Human Resource Management

Elective Supportive Courses:

Business Law II
Human Resource Management
Government Regulation of Business
Labor-Management Relations
Quantitative Analysis and Decision Making
Gender Issues in Management

New York Institute of Technology—Old Westbury, New York

Bachelor of Science in Computer Science
General Education/Liberal Arts Courses:

College Success Seminar
English Composition I
English Composition II
Technical Writing I
Technical Writing II
Speech Communications
Introductory Japanese
Intermediate Japanese
Engineering Chemistry I
Calculus I
Calculus II
Linear Algebra
Math Gaming Theory
General Physics I
General Physics II

Economics
American Government
Introduction to Philosophy
Sociology of Family
German Philosophy
Science Fiction Literature I
Advanced Science Fiction Literature

Major Area Required Courses:

Introduction to Computer Science
Computer Programming I
Computer Programming II
Discrete Structures
Data Structures
Database Management
Seminar Project
Computer Organization
Computer Architecture
Operating Systems Business Law II

Elective Supportive Courses:

Microprocessors
Artificial Intelligence I
Artificial Intelligence II
Software Engineering
COBOL Programming
C and UNIX
Digital Communications
Communication Theory
Telecommunication System Design

When to Consider the Bachelor's Degree

1. I have been told that a bachelor's degree is required for my chosen career.

2. I have already attended college and earned more than 60 semester credits or an associate's degree. I would like to quickly add to these to earn my bachelor's degree.

3. I have been told that a graduate or professional degree might ultimately be required in my career area.advisor. Many students draw up learning contracts or undertake independent study units with Trinity faculty members. They then study independently to complete these learning contracts.

4. I have already earned one or more associate's degrees.

5. For reasons of personal fulfillment, I want to earn my bachelor's degree.

Master's Degree (Graduate and Professional School)

Graduate and professional schools may be attended after you have earned a bachelor's degree. Some professions require that you attend graduate school. For example, most states will let you begin teaching in the public schools with a bachelor's degree but many will require a master's degree (graduate degree) in order to renew your teaching license or allow you to qualify for pay raises.

Many states require mental health therapists to earn a master's degree if they want to open a private counseling practice. The same is true of social workers. Many states require students to earn a bachelor's in human services or social work, then attend a graduate school to earn a master's in social work if they want to see clients in private practice and accept insurance payments.

To practice law in most states you will need to earn a bachelor's degree before attending a three-year graduate-level law school. In business circles, the Master's in Business Administration (MBA) is a very popular graduate degree for those who want to have a competitive edge. A master's degree generally consists of 18 to 24 months of full-time study. This study is concentrated in your professional area.

Another type of graduate degree is the doctorate. The doctorate generally requires over four years of full-time study after you have earned your bachelor's degree, or two to three years after you have earned your master's degree. A doctorate is also known as a "Ph.D.," or Doctor of Philosophy degree.

STEP 3: UNDERSTANDING AND SELECTING THE RIGHT COLLEGE FORMAT

In addition to understanding the kind of accreditation and credentials that a college offers, you will need to understand the types of formats that are used to help adults earn their degrees. Special formats have been developed to make college a more accessible place for older learners.

COMMUNITY OR JUNIOR COLLEGES

Historically, the four-year bachelor's degree has been the most sought after and awarded degree in the United States. About half of any liberal arts bachelor degree typically consists of courses taken in critical thinking areas, such as classic literary works, political science, the arts and humanities, and cultural awareness.

Bachelor degrees in liberal arts were not originally meant to prepare one for a career.

They were meant instead to prepare scholars to do critical research, and to prepare "gentlemen" for public service in the ministry, medicine, social work, and politics.

After the Second World War, especially after the Korean Conflict in the 1960s, Americans needed a different, broader type of college system, one that might teach liberal arts not only to improve everyday critical thinking but also, and more importantly, to offer shorter, more career-oriented college degrees. Instead of a bachelor of arts in philosophy one might earn an associate in applied science in heating and air conditioning technology. Instead of a bachelor of arts in psychology, a primarily theory-based degree to prepare one for graduate school, one might earn an associate of applied arts in human services/counseling to prepare one to counsel people on everyday issues, like parental stress, in community clinics.

During the 1960s, states and counties built systems of junior colleges or community colleges.

The mission of the community college has always been to teach a more applied and career-oriented curriculum.

Most community colleges are regionally accredited because they retain some of the study of the liberal arts, like English composition and critical thinking. Community colleges do not, however, offer four-year bachelor degrees. They offer the two-year associate degree, as well as short career-relevant certificates.

FOUR-YEAR BACHELOR'S COLLEGES

Traditional, regionally accredited colleges offer the four-year bachelor's degree. Think of the four-year degree as you would four years of high school. There is a freshman, sophomore, junior, and senior year. Whereas community or junior colleges specialize in offering the freshman and sophomore years of a degree, four-year colleges specialize in offering the junior and senior years of an undergraduate degree.

These days many traditional, four-year colleges also offer associate degrees and certificates. If you attend a four-year college to work toward your bachelor's, you may be given the option of earning your associate's degree after you have completed the first 2 years of your studies. This option allows you to have a degree that you can put on your resume while you continue to study toward your final bachelor's degree.

For example, Harvard University's evening program for working adults awards bachelor degrees, but Harvard also now gives students the option of earning their associate's degree en route to their bachelor's. These types of programs are often referred to as "2 plus 2" programs. You can attend for two years and earn an associate's degree, then continue two more years to earn your bachelor's degree. These programs are designed to ensure that you can use credits you earned for your associate's degree in full transfer toward your bachelor's degree without losing any credits in the process.

> **2** plus 2 programs allow the older student the option of earning their associate's degree en route to their bachelor's degree.

Is It a Good Idea to Begin at a Community College and Transfer to a Four-Year Bachelor's College?

These days many older adults begin their college careers at community colleges. Older learners have several great reasons for gravitating toward community colleges. Community colleges have their roots in the community. In some states, such as California and New York, practically every county boasts a community college campus. Community colleges have helped to make college physically accessible to older learners nationwide.

In addition, community colleges generally charge less in tuition than traditional four-year colleges. This is because community colleges are heavily funded by state and county tax dollars. Community colleges can also spend more of their money on teaching and supporting students rather than on expensive scientific research, sports, and sleeping dormitories, as is often the case at traditional four-year universities.

Compared to traditional four-year colleges, community colleges are also more likely to offer practical courses that translate into entry or advancement in specific career areas. For example, if you are looking for training in welding or electronics, you are more likely to find that at a community or junior college than at a four-year college.

Finally, community colleges are more likely to offer tutoring, career planning, college preparatory courses, and support services for older learners than are four-year colleges, which have historically dealt with a much younger student population.

Is a Community College Right for You?

Special features that a community or junior college may offer an adult learner:

- Open admissions and easy access with a local campus site or extension classrooms.
- Career counseling and job-hunting skills.
- Enhanced emphasis on job placement as part of your degree planning.
- Concrete training in skills that match your immediate job needs.
- Lower tuition and fees.
- Professional certificates or associate degrees.

A community or junior college cannot offer you:

- A bachelor's degree.
- Preparation for graduate school.

Will the credits you earn at a community college transfer easily to a four-year school if you later decide to earn a bachelor's degree? This question is important if you intend to complete your first two years of college and earn an associate's degree at a community college, then transfer to a four-year college to complete your bachelor's degree. Many older learners use the "2 plus 2" approach because it is often cheaper to complete the first two years of college at a community college than to attend a full four years at a four-year college.

If you do plan on using the "2 plus 2" approach, make sure you consult chapter 5: Saving Time and Money. Ask your community college advisor to outline how the credits you earn for your associate's degree will transfer later to a four-year college and degree. Many state-supported community colleges have special agreements with state-supported four-year colleges that outline which courses will transfer, and which will not.

WEEKEND AND EVENING COLLEGES

College classes have traditionally been taught 9 to 5, but the majority of adults who return to college are employed at 9-to-5 jobs. This time conflict has led colleges to offer special weekend and evening universities for working adults. Weekend colleges operate by offering Saturday courses that last about 3 to 5 hours—an entire week's worth of class time is condensed into one Saturday morning or evening. Weekend colleges are very popular, especially in urban areas where long commutes and 60-hour work weeks make evening classes impossible.

How does weekend college work? Trinity College, for example, a small private college in Burlington, Vermont, offers a model weekend college program for adult learners. Trinity, which also offers traditional 9 to 5 courses for the 18- to 21-year-old learner, has taken many of their majors and adopted the courses so that they are taught on-campus on Friday evenings, and Saturday and Sunday mornings.

At Trinity, adult students can even arrange to stay in campus housing Friday and Saturday nights if they live too far to comfortably commute to the weekend program. Moreover, the college operates a shuttle service that will pick up students from outlying towns and deliver them to the college and back again on weekends. This shuttle service ensures that those without cars, or families with only one car, can still attend the weekend program. Finally, the college offers both reduced tuition and an accelerated three-year bachelor's degree program to help adults earn their degrees faster at a lower price. The weekend college program at Trinity serves more than 700 students, ages 22 to 69, who reside in Vermont, New York, and Canada, just across the Vermont border.

Not all weekend colleges offer transportation and overnight housing, but most universities do operate weekend and evening colleges to help adults work around their time constraints. For example, the University of Vermont, a traditional, regionally accredited four-year university, offers regular 9 to 5 courses and degrees for young students. They also offer an evening university program with courses that begin at 6 to 7 in the evening.

Today, most colleges, once 9-to-5 operations, have made modifications so that those who work full-time can access their educational offerings.

ACCELERATED PROGRAMS

Accelerated degree programs became very popular in the 1980s. In an accelerated program, classes generally meet once a week or every two weeks for longer periods of time, commonly 3 hours, instead of meeting the traditional three times a week for 1 hour. Typically, the time it takes to complete a course is also condensed. Instead of a course lasting for fifteen or sixteen weeks, as is common for a semester, the course lasts only six to eight weeks.

For example, the University of Phoenix, America's largest private adult-learning college for those seeking business degrees, offers all its degrees in an accelerated format. Phoenix has "extension campuses," which are located across the United States and Canada. Phoenix extension campuses are not Ivory Towers but rented rooms in commercial buildings close to Interstate exchanges where commuting professionals can easily attend classes after work.

Of course, if you attend an accelerated degree program you still must complete the same amount of studying and homework, but you will do it at a faster pace. While accelerated programs are popular with adults, who tend to be in a hurry to earn their degrees for career reasons, you should consider if quickening the pace is a good option for you. This is particularly true if college is new to you, or if you feel that you need to complete some refresher work before going full speed ahead.

WORK AND CAREER CO-OP OPTIONS

Since you will probably stay employed while earning your degree, it makes sense that you might integrate your work with your degree studies. Doing an internship or cooperative work-study is a time-honored way to earn additional college credits and enrich your degree experience. For example, if you have returned to college to earn your bachelor's in marketing, and you currently work as a market researcher, it would make sense that you might arrange to have one of your work projects supervised by a faculty member for degree credit.

The junior and senior years of college are a great time to take textbook theory and apply it to the real work-world. For example, maybe you have just completed an advanced course in market research. In that course you learned new ways to survey people for product development. You want to try out some of these new methods, so you decide to undertake research on a product that your company wants to market. This is the perfect opportunity to talk to your degree advisor about earning credit for an applied senior project in market research. You can design and execute your study and report on the results under the supervision of a faculty member. In return, you may earn degree credit.

The University of Maryland is a good example of a large, four-year, public university system that allows for cooperative educational credit for new learning that occurs on the job. Adult students who work at least twenty hours a week in a job related to their degree major can work with their degree advisor to document new learning that occurs on the job. The Maryland bachelor's program allows for up to 15 semester credits (the equivalent of five college courses) to be earned this way.

Many adult-degree programs support cooperative work-study. A few even require that adult learners complete a senior project that showcases their ability to apply their learning to a career situation. A senior capstone project is used instead of the traditional research thesis in some adult-degree programs.

Individualized Study and Contract Learning

Many who return to college later in life do so with a clear idea about what they want to study and how they want to study it. Colleges can offer only so many courses and so many majors. What if the college you want to attend does not offer the kind of degree you want to earn? What if your local college offers a degree in business administration, but what you really want to study is entrepreneurship and how to incubate and launch a small business? Are you out of luck? Not necessarily!

These days many colleges support individualized degree options for older, experienced learners. The University of Minnesota, a large, public university system, supports a Program for Individualized Learning (PIL). Under this program, adults meet with specially trained advisors to design degrees that fit their personal interests or career needs. Students in the Minnesota program have designed bachelor's degrees in unique areas like women and the law, biomedical communication, and landscape design.

These individualized degrees are especially attractive to older learners who know exactly what they want to study. For example, an accomplished musician knew his music inside and out, but he wanted to learn more about music law, copyright, and intellectual property. He eventually wanted to attend law school and specialize in music law. To prepare for this, he decided to design and complete a bachelor's in "music law." He earned the only such undergraduate degree that has ever been awarded in the United States.

Trinity College, a top-notch private university in Hartford, Connecticut, also supports an Individualized Degree Program (IDP) for Adult Students. While younger students attend Trinity to earn traditional degrees, older learners are invited to design their own degrees with the help of a Trinity advisor. Many students draw up learning contracts or undertake independent study units with Trinity faculty members. They then study independently to complete these learning contracts.

The learning contract is a document that outlines exactly what the student will study and how they will study it. Typically, a learning contract will include a bibliography of books and articles to be read, a list of projects to be completed (such as creative works, written papers, or research projects), and a statement of when the learning will be completed and how many degree credits it will carry. Older students can attend regular 9-to-5 courses on campus at Trinity, but the majority of them complete learning contracts or independent study units that they can work on at home. Trinity supports study in many areas, ranging from the theater arts to neuroscience.

DISTANCE LEARNING AND EXTERNAL DEGREES

What if you're ready to go to college but there is no college near where you live or work? Or, what if no local college offers the kind of degree you need at a price you can afford? Maybe there is a college in your neighborhood, but you have to travel for your job and you cannot commit to attending classes in the evenings or on the weekend.

The answer may be to use a distance learning degree program or an external degree program. "Distance learning" refers to any learning that occurs with the student located at a distance from the college and its faculty. Many colleges now offer distance learning or external degree programs for adults that require little or no time on campus. These programs typically combine some classroom study with some independent study, or mentored study completed at home under the remote guidance of faculty members.

Hofstra University, in Hempstead, New York, operates a program for adult learners called the University Without Walls at New College. The New College allows older individuals to design their own studies using mentor-assisted learning contracts. This is a true external degree program because most of the study is done "external to" or outside the regular classroom. Students need to live within commuting distance to Hofstra to meet regularly with faculty mentors, but much of their New College bachelor's degree will be completed without their having to attend 9-to-5 courses.

An increasing number of colleges are offering entire degrees that can be completed without any campus visits or with a few days on campus at the beginning of each semester. Accredited distance-learning degrees can be completed by using mailed videotapes, computer software, surface mail, internet conferencing, and by other means, even cable TV.

More and more students are combining campus-free, distance-learning courses with on-campus classroom study to accelerate or enrich their degrees.

If you are interested in completing your degree via distance learning, see chapter 4: Distance Learning.

NONDEGREE CONTINUING EDUCATION AND TRAINING PROGRAMS

You may need a college education, but not necessarily a degree. Not everyone needs or wants a long, packaged program of study like a certificate, an associate's degree, or a bachelor's degree. There are quite a few older learners who start out thinking they need a degree when all they really need is a few courses, or a short program of nondegree study.

Many careers do not require college degrees. For example, to be a real estate agent, you may only need to take one or two courses in real estate from an approved provider. In most states, after you've taken a course or two, you are then eligible to take the required licensing exam to become a licensed real estate agent.

If your dream is to become a Certified Public Accountant (CPA), each state has its own requirements for the education and experience you will need to gain. While most states now require CPAs to earn bachelor degrees from regionally accredited colleges, this is not true in all states. Moreover, if you already hold a nonbusiness bachelor's degree, say a bachelor's in music, you will not need to earn a second bachelor's degree in accounting to qualify to be a CPA. You will probably only need to complete certain additional courses in accounting and business.

Requirements can vary from state to state for any licensed career. If you are undertaking education to meet a career need, make sure you understand the exact kind of education you will need.

*T*ry not to buy more education than you need.

In some cases, you may not even need to take courses that award degree credits. You may need to take shorter courses that award continuing education units or CEUs. A CEU is a special kind of academic unit. If you take a course that awards one CEU it means that you completed a learning activity that required at least 10 hours to complete. Each CEU you earn is equal to 10 hours of study time.

For example, the University of Florida's Division of Continuing Education offers a Dietary Manager Training course. This course is designed to help dietary managers or those who plan nutrition programs in places like hospitals or nursing homes to study the basics before taking the national exam to become a Registered Dietician. The University of Florida training course awards thirty CEUs, but it does not award any degree credits.

*D*ieticians, financial planners, real estate agents, paralegals, electricians, dental assistants, and auto mechanics are just a few of the professional groups that must routinely take short, nondegree CEU courses to stay current in their career areas.

Computers and information technology are career areas where many people seek professional continuing education in place of or in addition to their college degrees. Two computer companies, Microsoft and Novell, require people to take tests that they have designed in order to receive certification that they are competent to install, configure, or troubleshoot their specific computer network systems. Many colleges now offer special nondegree courses that help people master Novell or Microsoft computer networks and prepare for these independent certification exams.

New York University, for example, offers a bachelor's degree in many areas of computer science, including computer networks. But New York University also offers a special nondegree certificate in Local Area Network

Administration. This certificate is taught for twelve weeks on Saturday mornings. At the end of the program, students are considered ready to take the Certified Netware Administrator Exam (CNA) and the Certified Netware Engineer Exam (CNE) to install, configure, and troubleshoot Novell computer networks. Both those professional certifications are highly coveted in the computer world. This is a great example of how CEUs, rather than degree credits, can lead to an independent certification process that carries as much or more weight than earning a college degree.

Many colleges now offer nondegree, continuing education programs. These programs offer professional training courses in areas as diverse as gardening and computer skills, and generally cost less than degree courses. However, there is a downside to taking continuing education or CEU courses: They usually cannot be applied toward a college degree at a later time.

4

DISTANCE LEARNING:
EARNING YOUR DEGREE
WITHOUT LEAVING HOME

You want to return to college. You know what you want to study. You're ready to write that tuition check. Too bad that no college exists within commuting distance of your home. Or, maybe lots of colleges dot your commute route, but either they cost too much or do not offer the subjects that interest you. Perhaps you, like many working adults, travel too much for your career to attend weekly classroom sessions.

What you need is a college that will come to you. If that idea sounds far-fetched, think again. Distance learning, or education that is delivered via videotape, internet conferencing, surface mail, fax, CD-ROM, telephone, videoconferncing, as well as other means of technology, is a booming event. Distance learning is allowing older adults to return to college in record numbers via their VCRs and computer keyboards. Forecasters predict that by the year 2002, more than 2.2 million students, most of them in their thirties or forties, will be attending college via electronic and virtual means.

> By 2002, more than 85 percent of both four- and two-year colleges are expected to support distance-learning programs.

WHAT IS DISTANCE LEARNING?

Distance learning is any form of learning that occurs between the instructor and the student located at a distance from each other. Distance learning is not a new phenomenon.

> *B*ooks were the first distance-learning tools: They allowed experts to transport their ideas over time and space to students who lived even in the most remote corners of the world.

The University of London began offering distance degrees in the 1850s. British citizens who lived abroad in the Colonial Empire, which at that time included India and Australia, could not attend a university in London. However, they could study textbooks and materials on their own, then take written exams to demonstrate their competency and earn their degrees.

In the United States, distance learning has been used successfully for more than a hundred years by such colleges as the University of Wisconsin and Pennsylvania State University to reach rural learners. In the early years, distance-learning assignments were sent by rural post, hand-graded, and returned to students in the mail. Students took proctored or supervised exams to prove they had mastered the material. The system remains the same, but the delivery methods have diversified.

FREQUENTLY ASKED QUESTIONS ABOUT DISTANCE LEARNING

ARE ALL DISTANCE DEGREES DELIVERED VIA THE INTERNET?

No. Many distance-delivery platforms exist. Some programs still use surface mail to deliver courses. Other programs are broadcast only through local cable TV channels. Many programs mail weekly videotapes of classroom lectures to students. Some programs are delivered via special satellite broadcasts to corporate reception rooms or electronic classrooms. The internet is the newest delivery tool.

Programs that are delivered via the internet will require you to own a computer, a modem (a device that allows your computer to dial into the internet), and have internet access via a dial-up account like America Online. Even if a college program is internet-based, chances are it will still use surface mail to send some materials. It may also mail videotapes to enhance the instructional program. This is because video is difficult to send and receive over the open internet on home PC (personal computer) systems.

Most internet programs use online computer conferencing and chat rooms. Students go online weekly to post their questions and answers to special computer bulletin boards. Generally, all students log on once a week and read and contribute to classroom message boards. The message boards and live chat discussions help re-create a classroom environment. Students may also communicate with faculty and each other via e-mail and discussion lists.

Is Distance Learning a Valid Way to Study?

Yes. Dr. Thomas Russell, of North Carolina State University, has reviewed the scientific literature on independent study options as compared to classroom study. His review of 355 research reports, summaries, and academic papers shows that there are no significant differences in learning outcomes when face-to-face classroom instruction is compared to distance learning. In other words, most people can master most subjects just as well using books, videotapes, or online conferencing as they can by attending a traditional classroom lecture.

A recent study of California college students taking a statistics class found that some actually learn better online than they do face to face. When the performance of a group of classroom students was compared to that of a group of online learners, the distance-learning students scored significantly better on their statistics exams.

Will All Distance-Learning Programs Deliver to My Home?

No. One of the most common misconceptions about distance learning is that if a college offers a distance-learning program anyone can access it. This is not true. Many different technology systems are being used to deliver courses and degrees at a distance. Programs that use surface mail, videotape, phone conferencing, and the internet are usually publicly accessible. These programs can be completed from your home. You will need a computer and VCR, but you will not need any special satellite or videoconferencing equipment to receive course broadcasts.

Many distance-learning programs, especially those offered by state university systems, are delivered only by satellite, local cable TV, interactive educational TV, or videoconferencing. These types of delivery systems require students to attend specially equipped reception sites to receive and participate in weekly lectures. The weekly class lectures are broadcast from a main classroom to reception sites, which are located within a very limited geographic region. Reception sites are often installed in high schools. Increasingly, four-year universities are delivering their courses via satellite or interactive TV to specially equipped electronic reception rooms at two-year college campuses.

The Public Broadcasting System (PBS) sponsors a special cable TV college program called *Going the Distance* (GTD). PBS telecourses or television courses are broadcast to local markets over seventy public TV stations in thirty-eight states. Students enroll in local community colleges, then watch courses on their local PBS TV stations. An associate's degree can be earned by utilizing PBS's GTD through some community college systems, though many colleges offer only selected courses by TV, not an entire degree.

Typically, students who participate in PBS's GTD still attend some classes on campus. They also usually attend orientation sessions on campus and take their exams and lab sessions at their local campus. To find out if your local two-year or community college is a member of the PBS Going the Distance Network contact them directly. You can also search the PBS directory of member colleges and participating local cable TV stations online at http://www.pbs.org/als/gtd or call PBS Adult Learning Services at 800-257-2578 for a referral to a college near you that carries PBS telecourses.

Site-Based Statewide Networks

Many public university systems broadcast their own courses over private statewide TV networks. The Indiana College Network (ICN), for example, is a site-based distance-delivery partnership of Ball State University, Indiana State University, Indiana University, Ivy Tech State College, Indiana's private colleges, Vincennes University, and the University of Southern Indiana. The network delivers college courses to specially equipped interactive television (ITV) sites at high schools, community colleges, military bases, and corporate offices statewide.

The ICN is a part of the Indiana Higher Education Telecommunications System (IHETS). Students who reside in Indiana can earn a bachelor's degree in nursing, as well as many other degrees, via IHETS. The nursing degree is offered by Ball State University, in Muncie, Indiana. But students do not need to travel to Muncie to take courses. Instead, they travel to the nearest IHETS reception site. More than sixty IHETS reception sites operate across Indiana.

The Iowa Communications Network (ICN), an endeavor similar to Indiana's College Network, is a project of the state universities of Iowa.

College courses and degrees are delivered via two-way audio and video at reception sites at high schools, corporations, community colleges, and military bases across Iowa. If you live in California, however, you cannot access an ICN site. You cannot earn a degree via ICN unless you attend weekly course broadcasts at reception sites.

You should not assume that just because a program has a distance-learning option you will be able to attend that program from where you reside. You must inquire about the type of delivery platform used by the program. Ask if the program is publicly accessible or site based. If the program is only available via satellite or interactive cable TV, you will need to determine where the reception sites are located.

At the end of this chapter we include a special directory to state- and site-based distance-degree catalogs and clearinghouses. Check this directory for information on site-based delivery networks that operate within your geographic area.

Locating Publicly Accessible Distance Degree Programs
In the appendix we include a special master directory of more than one hundred regionally accredited colleges that offer publicly accessible, nonsite-based degrees and career credentials. The programs we profile in our directory are fully accessible to students in the United States *no matter where they reside*.

Some of these programs do, however, require weekend orientations or brief campus visits to complete degree planning. Use our special directory to locate colleges that offer the type of degree or career credential you seek. Compare tuition prices, admission requirements, and delivery methods carefully.

ARE ONLINE PROGRAMS BETTER THAN MAIL CORRESPONDENCE?
The first generation of distance-learning courses were called "correspondence courses." Instruction took place by mail correspondence. Students read their textbooks and completed written assignments. They then mailed these assignments back to the college for grading.

For many years, correspondence courses were considered a less favorable way to learn. This stigma was a result of colleges insisting that correspondence study was the equivalent of people educating themselves in isolation. Colleges argued that learning would be significantly enhanced by things such as live lectures, classroom discussions, and social interaction between students and faculty.

Many people do report that they enjoy online learning better than mail correspondence. This is because most online programs enable students and faculty to meet each other online and interact. It helps to have a learning structure and other people to bounce ideas off of. The learning structure and immediate feedback of an interactive online classroom helps many people stay motivated. Studying in isolation is more difficult for some people because of the lack of social suppport.

Isn't It Easy to Cheat?

If your professor never meets you, what keeps you from cheating? Actually it is *harder* to cheat in distance learning than it is to cheat in a classroom. As a distance learner you cannot peek over your shoulder at someone else's paper or exam. How do your professors know you are doing your homework and not someone else? They don't, but then the same is true of campus-based classes.

Most distance-learning programs use proctored exams to ensure academic honesty. A proctored exam is an exam that is supervised by a local official. Your homework will not usually be proctored, but your exams will be. Proctors might include people like librarians, human resource officals, and officials at a testing center operated by your neighborhood college.

Your distance-degree college will explain the qualifications of an acceptable proctor. You will probably be required to take all exams under the supervision of a proctor. He or she will receive the exam from the college and give it to you. You will have to show identification to the proctor to make sure you are who you say you are. Once you have completed the exam, the proctor will collect it from you and send it back to your college for grading.

Do I Have to Be a Computer Guru to Study Online?

No. Almost all internet-enabled distance-learning programs offer an introductory course online to teach you how to use their online educational system. The New York Institute of Technology (NYIT), for example, has offered degrees online for more than a decade. Everyone who enrolls with NYIT must take a special five-week course online. The course is called Introduction to Web-Based Computer Conferencing. The course teaches students everything they need to participate in online learning. If you can already operate a computer and get on the internet, chances are you can quickly learn how to use online message boards and instructional systems.

Aren't Most Distance Learning Schools Diploma Mills?

No. A diploma mill is any school that issues college diplomas based on your ability to pay the tuition rather than on your ability to complete rigorous coursework. Dozens of diploma mills do offer distance degrees. But at the same time hundreds of regionally accredited, bona fide colleges offer distance degrees and career credentials. We include complete information on college accreditation in chapter 3: College Accreditation and Degrees. This chapter will also alert you to distance-degree scams and fraudulent colleges.

If you attend a college that is accredited by a recognized agency you will be earning a valid degree. In most cases, in accredited colleges, distance courses are taught by the same faculty that teach on campus. The admission and degree requirements are also usually the same for distance students as they are for on-campus learners.

Can I Earn a Degree Based on My Life Experience?

Credit for career and life experience is a valid option at the majority of American colleges. We discuss these procedures and the limitations you may face in chapter 6: Earning Credit for Career and Life Experience.

Most colleges, even distance-learning colleges, are teaching colleges. As such they will require you to complete a certain number of courses directly under their tutelage in order to earn your degree, regardless of your transfer-credit standing or life experience.

Three special distance-learning colleges do not operate as teaching colleges. Instead, they operate as assessment colleges. Assessment colleges are special colleges designed to allow adults who have significant career experience to go through rigorous assessment procedures and have their career expertise documented and placed on a college degree transcript.

Thomas Edison State College of New Jersey, Regents College of New York, and Charter Oak State College of Connecticut, operate primarily as assessment colleges. It is theoretically possible to earn a degree from these regionally accredited colleges without taking a single formal college class. However, most students who attend these colleges do take some formal coursework to complete their degrees. Also, these colleges charge significant fees to assess life credit possibilities, as well as to cover the transfer of credits from other teaching colleges.

WILL GRADUATE SCHOOLS ACCEPT DISTANCE LEARNING DEGREES?

Yes, as long as you attend a regionally accredited college. Students from long-standing, regionally accredited distance degree colleges, such as Thomas Edison State College of New Jersey and Empire State College have been routinely admitted to all types of graduate schools, including Harvard, Princeton, and other Ivy League institutions.

In addition, many top-notch, regionally accredited graduate schools such as Duke University, Stanford University, Columbia University, and Colorado State University now offer complete degrees or career credentials via distance means. America's best distance-learning graduate schools are profiled in the book, *The Best Distance-Learning Graduate Schools: Earning Your Degree Without Leaving Home*, also from The Princeton Review.

IS DISTANCE LEARNING RIGHT FOR YOU?

While studies have proven that anyone can benefit from distance learning, certain types of people are more likely to succeed at and enjoy it. Our work with more than 7,000 online learners has shown that your chances of succeeding at distance learning will be enhanced if you meet most of the following ten criteria.

Ten Signs That Distance Learning May Work Well for You

You are:

1. Good at time management.
2. Comfortable with the technology used in course delivery.
3. Highly motivated to learn the subject at hand.
4. Not in need of a lot of emotional support or guidance to learn.
5. Able to study and take notes from videotapes and reading textbooks.
6. In possession of good reading and writing skills.
7. Comfortable not being part of a class or group.
8. Not prone to routine procrastination.
9. Able to enjoy working independently.
10. Able to learn best through written modes rather than through visual and oral means.

THINGS TO CHECK FOR IN A DISTANCE-LEARNING PROGRAM

CLEAR TUITION REFUND POLICIES

Before you register for a distance course, you should make sure you understand the course withdrawal and tuition refund policy. If you enroll in a course and decide that you do not like the course, or that you do not like distance learning, you should have from two to three weeks to withdraw and receive a refund. Educational institutions must provide fair refund policies.

COMPLETENESS OF THE CURRICULUM

Although the majority of colleges now offer courses through distance learning, fewer colleges offer all the courses needed for a degree or career credential through distance means. Check the curriculum to make sure that all the courses you will need for your credential can be completed through distance means. You can also combine distance courses with campus courses if you can commute to the campus from time to time. Combining distance courses with face-to-face courses in order to earn a degree is becoming a popular option at many publicly funded universities.

FACULTY RESPONSIVENESS

One of the most important aspects of the quality of any distance-learning program is how responsive faculty are to questions. In other words, if you send an assignment or question to your professor or an administrative officer via e-mail, surface mail, or the phone how long will it take your instructor or the college to respond?

The less responsive a college is, the more likely it is that you will grow frustrated and drop out of the program. Some distance-learning programs have dropout and course noncompletion rates as high as 50 percent. This means that as many as half the students who enroll do not complete a single course, let alone their degrees.

Your distance-learning program should have a policy of responding to student inquiries within 72 hours or, if the class meets online weekly, every week via message boards or other means.

AVAILABILITY OF STUDENT SUPPPORT SERVICES

Many colleges offer courses or single degrees through distance means, yet they do not have a system of student support available to distance learners. This can lead to extreme frustration. The best distance-learning programs offer access to the following services for all distance learners.

Orientation: Does the program offer a way for you to test drive the technology used to deliver instruction? For example, if the program is offered online, do they offer an orientation online so you can learn how to navigate their virtual campus? If you have technical problems, is technical support available by phone or e-mail?

Career and Academic Counseling: Can you access career and academic advisors in a reliable manner? For example, does your degree advisor have established telephone or online office hours for you to receive vital degree and career counseling?

Easy Library Access: The best distance-learning programs have online or phone access to their own library systems. If your college does not offer this option, you may have to obtain special permission from a college in your community to use their library. You may have to commute to a local library to do research.

Easy Administrative Access: Are there clear ways for you to communicate with vital support people in the college? For example, can you easily access and speak with financial aid advisors, order required textbooks, and speak with people in the registrar's or record keepers office when necessary?

Full Financial Aid Options: Does the distance-learning program offer the same kind of financial aid options as you'd be entitled to on campus? Some distance-learning programs do not administer government grants or loans. Other programs offer full aid. Check this option carefully before signing up to earn your degree.

5 SAVING TIME AND MONEY: MAXIMIZING YOUR TRANSFER CREDITS

You may not realize how easy it is to lose old college credits in the transfer process. Your old credits will have to "fit" into your new college's degree structure. Because no two colleges have identical degree requirements, the transfer process rarely results in a perfect fit. Credits that do not fit are commonly cast aside in the transfer process.

Does it matter if you lose college credits when transferring? Yes!

*L*osing credits is like losing your wallet.

Remember that it cost money to earn those credits! If you paid $100 per credit—a modest price—and you lose fifteen credits when you transfer into a new college, you have lost $1,500! Losing credits is also losing time. It probably took you five months of full-time study to earn those credits. Who wouldn't want to save $1,500 and five months of their time?

COUNTING TRANSFER CREDITS: A SMART FINANCIAL-AID OPTION FOR ADULTS

If you have college credits to transfer, it is important to take the time to understand the transfer credit policies of the college you are considering. In returning to college at midlife, you may be bringing along a dog-eared assortment of old transcripts taken at a hodgepodge of colleges and training institutes: credits earned at your local community college; courses taken at your local university's night school; training courses completed through work; military training transcripts; and professional continuing education courses.

If you are a typical adult learner, you may have taken quite a few courses over the years, a few here, and a few there. You may have had to leave college abruptly more than once due to corporate or military transfers, or real-life transitions, such as divorce.

> *O*ne of the main responsibilities of your academic advisor is to help you make sense of how your past education "fits" into your new college's degree requirements.

The issue of college transfer at midlife is far from academic. The ability to transfer as many old credits as possible toward a new degree can literally result in thousands of dollars in extra savings. While some colleges have policies that favor the liberal transfer of older existing credits, others have policies that may force you to start at educational square one regardless of your true transfer credit standing. This chapter explains the many factors that affect transfer credit standing and provides tips for getting the most credit from your prior academic efforts.

ARE MY OLD COLLEGE CREDITS STILL GOOD?

It's a good idea to start with the assumption that all your old college credits will be good for transfer at a new college. Start by gathering together the transcripts of all your old college and training courses. (We discuss how to do this in chapter 2: Preparing for College Admission at Midlife.) Many factors can influence whether or not a new college will accept your old credits in transfer. Let's begin by examining ten crucial issues that can affect your transfer credit standing.

1. ACCREDITATION COUNTS

The most important factor in transfer credits is the accreditation of the college where you took your courses. All colleges are not accredited, and among those that are, they are not all equal in their accreditation. (See chapter 3: College Accreditation and Degrees.)

If you've never done this before, now is the time to check on the accreditation status of your previous colleges. The vast majority of degree-granting colleges in the United States, especially those that award the four-year bachelor's degree, are regionally accredited by one of the six agencies mentioned in chapter 3. Your college transcript, if you have one, should state the accrediting agency that covers the college you attended. If you can't find an accrediting agency on your records, call the registrar at your old college and ask for the name of the accrediting agency.

The problem that many adults encounter in transferring old college credits is that they have taken courses at nonregionally accredited colleges, and they now want to complete a degree at a regionally accredited college. *This is a problem because the majority of regionally accredited colleges will not accept credits earned at nonregionally accredited colleges.*

If you have taken courses at nonregionally accredited colleges and wish to have them evaluated for transfer toward a regionally accredited degree, there are special programs that can help you. If your courses are rejected because of accreditation, ask your academic advisor to explain the options to you. Options will vary from college to college, but at most colleges your options will include some form of using special credit for experience programs. You might be able to take special challenge or test-out exams in certain courses. A passing score on such an exam would exempt you from having to retake a course that you have already completed, but at a nonaccredited college. (See chapter 6: Earning Credit for Career and Life Experience for details on using exams and assessment programs to earn college credit.) Or, you may be asked to develop a written academic portfolio to further document what you know. You may request that your new college grant you transfer credit for at least a portion of your nonregionally accredited college experience.

2. GRADE POINT AVERAGE (GPA) MATTERS

GPA is short for Grade Point Average. Colleges require a minimum GPA for admission and matriculate with a degree. The first step toward understanding your GPA is to understand that colleges take letter grades, such as a C, and assign a numerical value to them on a 4-point (4.0) scale. They then add up these points and average them to get the GPA.

Grade Point Scale

A = 4.0	C = 2.0
A− = 3.7	C− = 1.7
B+ = 3.3	D+ = 1.3
B = 3.0	D = 1.0
B− = 2.7	D− = .7
C+ = 2.3	F = 0.0

> *C*umulative GPA = All grade points added together divided by the number of courses you have taken.

Someone who has a 4.0 has a straight A average. Someone who has a 2.0 has a C GPA. Most colleges require a 2.0 transfer grade average for regular admission. A few may require a GPA in the range of 2.5 to 2.75 or a C+ to B– average. All accredited colleges require a minimum 2.0 GPA to earn a degree. They also require a 2.0 GPA in your major area of study to earn a degree.

When you transfer to a new college, they will add up all your old course grades and calculate what is called your "cumulative GPA." Your old transcripts may also each note a cumulative GPA. You can determine your cumulative GPA by adding together all your grade points and dividing this by the number of courses you have taken. For example, if you took two courses and earned an A and a C in those courses, your GPA would be calculated as follows: 4.0 (A) + 2.0 (C) = 6.0. To get your cumulative GPA, divide the 6.0 by the number of classes you took (6/2 = 3.0). Your cumulative GPA is a 3.0 or a B average.

You should be able to transfer courses that carry a grade of C or higher. Lower grades may not transfer. Colleges vary. Some will accept D grades. Some will reject C– grades. Some other colleges may accept D grades, unless they were earned in your major area, or in a required subject, such as freshman composition. A few colleges will accept D grades in transfer if your cumulative transfer GPA stands at 2.0 or higher, regardless of how many D or F grades you have previously earned.

If you have transfer courses with grades lower than a C, ask your advisor how these courses will be treated in transfer. Depending on your transfer GPA, and the policies of the college you decide to attend, you may be able to transfer all or none of your courses that carry grades below a C.

3. AGE OF CREDITS: DEMONSTRATING CURRENCY

Most colleges do not place limits on the age of general transfer credits. That said, many colleges do have special rules that apply to certain degree majors. These special rules may limit the transfer of credits taken ten or more years ago. These special rules are designed to make sure that knowledge in your major area of study is current. Predictably, these rules are called "demonstration of currency" rules.

> **S**tudents have successfully transferred courses that were completed fifty or more years ago toward a new degree.

Demonstration of currency rules affect students who major in areas where knowledge can quickly become outdated. Computer programming, for example, is a subject area where things have changed drastically in the last decade. Music theory and English literature, on the other hand, are examples of degree majors where the knowledge base has not changed much over time. Engineering is another area where rapid advances quickly make knowledge obsolete. Basically, any area where professional services are performed—for example nursing, molecular biology, or lab technology—may be subject to a demonstration of currency.

If any of your older courses are not accepted in transfer because of currency issues, ask your advisor to explain what options you have. In most cases, you can petition to have these courses accepted, but only if you can prove that your knowledge is still current.

> **Y**ou can prove that your knowledge is current and that your old courses should be accepted for degree credit.

One way to demonstrate your knowledge currency is to show that you have been continuously employed and practicing in the field that you intend to major in. For example, lab technicians in most states are required to attend a certain number of continuing education courses each year to keep their knowledge current. One client was able to demonstrate currency by presenting committee records from her employer that showed she had been working as a lab technician and attending continuing education courses every year since she completed her first college courses in lab technology. Many colleges either maintain or will convene special faculty committees to review academic currency issues. Speak with your degree advisor about your college's policy in this area.

Some colleges may ask their students to take special exams to prove currency in selected subject areas. I have had nursing student clients, for example, who were asked to prove that their knowledge was current by taking special exams in nursing. One such set of exams is called Regents College Examinations or RCEs. The New York Regents offers a set of exams in nursing, as well as exams in key business areas. By taking these exams, and achieving a passing score, older students can demonstrate that they possess current knowledge in many subject areas. We discuss several types of these exams, which are also called "challenge exams," in detail in chapter 6: Earning Credit for Career and Life Experience.

Depending on the policies of your chosen college, you may be able to take special exams or submit written documentation of ongoing training to demonstrate that your knowledge remains current.

4. Transferring From a Two-Year to a Four-Year College: Course Levels Count

College courses are designed on two levels. Courses that are introductory, designed to be taken in either the freshman (first) or sophomore (second) year of a degree program, are called lower-level courses. Courses that are commonly taken in either the junior (third) or senior (fourth) year, and which cover more advanced subjects, are called upper-level courses.

For example, if you wanted to earn a degree in psychology, the first year you would take a course called Introduction to Psychology or Survey of Psychology. This course would be a beginner's course. This beginner's course would cover the basics of what psychology is, and how it is applied. Introduction to Psychology is considered a lower-level course. If you liked Introduction to Psychology, you might decide to take another course in psychology. A second course, often taken in the second year of college, is Child Psychology. Child Psychology is a common sophomore-level course.

If you decided to major in psychology, you would go on to take more advanced courses in psychology. Common advanced or junior/senior courses include Abnormal Psychology and Experimental Psychology.

If you are earning an associate's degree, you do not need to worry about credit levels. An associate's degree is a two-year degree. Community colleges, or junior colleges as they are sometimes called, specialize in awarding associate's degrees. *Community colleges only teach lower level courses. You do not need to earn any upper level credits to earn an associate's degree.*

If you are earning a bachelor's degree, you will need to pay attention to how many lower-level courses you have taken versus how many upper-level courses you have taken. To earn a bachelor's degree, colleges will always require that you take a minimum number of upper-level or junior/senior courses. You will be required to take most of these upper-level courses in your major area.

Most colleges will require that from half (60 semester credits) to one-quarter (30 semester credits) of your bachelor's degree consists of upper-level courses. Harvard University's evening degree program for adult learners, for example, requires that at least 60 semester credits of any bachelor's degree be earned at the upper level. This is half the degree, or the last two years of full-time study.

If you do not pay attention to the need for upper-level credits, you can end up with a lot of lower level credits that will not be accepted in transfer toward a four-year bachelor's degree. (See the discussion in chapter 3: College Accreditation and Degrees for a discussion of all the issues to watch out for if you intend to transfer from a two-year to a four-year degree program.)

5. Residency Requirements Must Be Met

Regardless of how many credits you have already earned, almost all colleges require that a certain number of credits be earned from them, under their academic guidance, in order to earn a degree. This is called a "residency requirement."

The standard residency rule in earning a bachelor's degree is that you must take at least 30 semester credits from the college that is going to award your degree. This is one year of academic study. For example, to earn a bachelor's degree from Central Michigan University, a typical four-year public university, you must take at least 30 credits of formal coursework with them.

To earn an associate's degree, expect to take at least one semester or 12 to 15 credits from your degree-granting college. Cerro Coso Community College, a typical two-year college in Ridgecrest, California, requires associate's degree students to take at least four courses or to earn at least 12 credits in residence with them.

A few colleges have slightly higher residency requirements. You may encounter colleges that expect you to take up to half your degree with them. Other colleges may be willing to waive or bend their residency rule, but only if you take the initiative and petition them to allow you to transfer in a greater number of credits.

Meeting a college's residency requirement will be an issue for anyone who has earned enough credits for their degree, yet has earned these credits from many different sources. If you find yourself in this situation, compare colleges carefully to see which favor your transfer credit situation. Consider petitioning for a transfer of more of your credits if this will reduce the time and money it will take you to earn your degree. (We discuss the petition process at the end of this chapter.)

> You can take the initiative and petition colleges to bend their residency rule.

6. CREDIT FOR EXPERIENCE

If you've previously attended college, you may have earned credits by other means than formal courses. You may have taken challenge exams to earn college credit, such as those offered by the CLEP (College Level Exam Program). A challenge exam is any standardized exam taken in an effort to test out of selected college courses where you may already have knowledge or significant career experience. You may never have taken a challenge exam, but you may have documented your career expertise for college credit through a special academic portfolio process. (See chapter 6 for a full discussion on challenge exams and academic portfolios as nontraditional means of earning college degree credit.) Can you transfer these nontraditional credits to another college? This is a very tricky question.

Your new college will award transfer credits based on a review of all the transcripts provided to them by your old colleges. Study these transcripts. If you previously took a challenge exam, this should be stated on your old transcripts. Your old transcripts should list the title and type of exam taken, the score you earned on each exam, and the credits awarded.

While most colleges accept nontraditional ways of earning degree credit, it is also true that colleges have widely varying rules about the type and number of these credits they will accept in transfer. Harvard University's evening degree program will not accept any life experience or challenge exam credits in transfer, no matter how well they are documented. Harvard is unusual in this rule. (Remember that all colleges are free to determine their own standards!)

> You must shop around for the best college and kind of degree based on your unique transfer credit situation.

For example, Ohio University, a typical four-year, public university, does not accept General CLEP challenge exams for college credit. If you attended a community college, like Brevard Community College in Florida, and that college awarded you credits based on your performance on the General CLEP exams, can you expect Ohio to accept the CLEP credits that your old college, Brevard, awarded you? The answer, unfortunately, is no. Additionally, your new college may accept credits earned by exams, yet never accept credits earned through other nontraditional means, like the faculty assessment of an academic portfolio.

If you have already earned a significant number of credits through alternative means, compare colleges carefully on their policies for accepting these types of credits.

7. COURSE REPETITIONS WON'T COUNT

If you have attended several colleges, it's possible that you may have repeated courses. You may have purposefully retaken a course because you wanted to refresh your knowledge before taking more advanced courses. More commonly, you may have accidentally retaken courses at different colleges because different titles were used to describe what was essentially the same course.

For example, the courses English Composition I and Freshman Expression and Exposition are usually the same course. They may have different names, and they may use different textbooks, but they both cover the same academic area of introductory reading and writing. Similarly, the course Music 101 is likely to be the same music course as what is called Humanities: Musical Appreciation at another college. College Math 101 may be called Algebra Fundamentals at a college down the road.

Sometimes people retake the same course at different colleges because the first time they took the course they got a good grade, and they enjoyed it. If they then move to a new location and attend a new college, they may see a similar sounding course and take it again because they know they would enjoy it and get a good grade.

There are many people who have attended as many as fifteen different colleges over a forty-year period and in the process took the same course (with slightly different titles) at least a dozen times. Each college where they took the course gave them new credits. The problem came when they decided to attend one college and consolidate all their old credits into one degree. At that point, a comprehensive degree assessment revealed that they had taken the same course over and over again. In the end, they were only able to claim credit for that course one time.

If you are disallowed credits because a college determines that two courses taken at different colleges seem to be the same course, and you feel that this is not so, you can petition for a review of your records. You may be asked to obtain course descriptions and a course syllabus for the courses in question. These materials give details of what your old courses really covered.

It is worth mentioning that sometimes courses have very similar sounding titles, yet do not cover the same material. We have seen people disallowed transfer credits based on inaccurate assessments of their old transcripts. It pays to study your transfer records carefully.

8. Continuing Education Units (CEUs) Are Not Degree Credits

You may have taken short-study courses as part of your professional training. Real estate salespeople, insurance brokers, lawyers, beauticians, bankers, computer technicians, electricians, nurses, financial planners, engineers, teachers, counselors, and lab technicians are just a few of the professionals who must take professional courses to stay current on developments in their fields. These professional courses often award Continuing Education Credits, or CEUs.

CEUs are not the same thing as degree credits. If you took a course that awarded 3.0 CEUs, this is not the same as taking a course that awarded 3.0 degree credits. Courses taken for degree credit are much more academically intense than CEU courses. CEU courses also tend to not award grades nor to include any form of assessment other than a pass/fail mark.

CEU courses are typically brief and do not last nearly as long as academic degree courses. Degree courses require concentrated study every week for up to fifteen weeks. One CEU simply means that you completed ten contact hours of a learning activity, often at a one-day workshop.

CEU credits cannot be transferred toward a degree. However, you may be able to use CEUs to request degree credit through a credit-for-life-experience process, such as portfolio assessment. (See chapter 6.)

9. Quarter versus Semester Credits

Most colleges operate on a semester system. A semester lasts fifteen weeks, with courses meeting at least three hours a week. Typically, the fall semester runs from October through December. The spring semester runs from January through May. Many adult programs also run a summer session or semester. Colleges that run on semester systems award semester credits or units. (A credit is the same thing as a unit, by the way.) A typical course is worth three semester credits. Courses that require more work can award more than three semester credits, however.

While most colleges run on a semester system, a few run on a quarter system. The state university system in Georgia, for example, runs on a quarter system. A quarter is shorter than a semester. A typical quarter lasts only ten weeks, not fifteen.

> *M*any people mistakenly think that they cannot transfer quarter credits to a semester-based college and vice versa.

You will encounter no problem transferring quarter credits to semester-based colleges, and vice versa. However, because a quarter is shorter than a semester, a quarter credit is not worth as much as a semester credit. By the same token, a semester credit is worth more than a quarter credit.

It is easy to convert quarter credits to semester credits and vice versa. When you transfer, the registrar at your new college will convert all your credits into whatever system your new college uses. Use the chart below to determine how your credits will be converted in transfer.

Quarter Credits to Semester Credit Conversions

Quarter Credits =	Semester Credits
1	.67
2	1.33
3	2
4	2.67
5	3.33
6	4

Semester Credits to Quarter Credit Conversions

Semester Credits =	Quarter Credits
1	1.5
2	3
3	4.5
4	6
5	7.5
6	9

Note: Some colleges may "round off" credits in transfer. For example, you may end up with 3.3 semester credits rather than 3.33 for 5 quarter credits.

10. Credits That Don't Fit: Limited Allowance for Electives

Once you decide to earn a degree, your transfer credits will be evaluated for how they fit into that one degree. Every degree has a structure that includes required courses, recommended courses, and electives. You must take the required courses. You might want to take the recommended courses. The elective area of your degree consists of courses that you do not have to take, but "elect" or opt to take instead. This area is also often called "free electives."

Some degrees have little room for electives. This is especially true of professional degrees like engineering, nursing, accounting, legal assisting, architecture, and so on. If you know which degree you intend to earn, get a copy of the degree requirements and study them carefully. Compare what is required to the credits that you have already earned. Will most of your old credits "fit" into your new degree? If not, you may lose credits in transfer. Or, you may get to transfer all your credits, but few will actually be applied to meeting the requirements of your new degree. It is possible, for example, to successfully transfer eighty credits, yet when these credits are applied by the school to your new degree, only thirty of them actually fit. This is most likely to happen when you change majors or types of degrees.

DEALING WITH ACADEMIC EXCEPTIONS AND PETITIONS

What if you are accepted into a new college but you have been granted significantly less transfer credits than you expected? Your new college should issue you a transfer credit report shortly after you are accepted for degree study. Your academic advisor is the person who usually is available to review this transfer credit report with you. First, study your transfer credit report. Study it carefully. The college should give you a full report of what courses they have accepted in transfer with notes on how they have applied these credits to meet your new degree requirements. Make a note of courses not accepted in transfer. Try to determine why these courses were not accepted in transfer. What is the issue? Did you attend an unaccredited college? Is your transfer GPA too low to allow you to transfer courses that do not carry at least a C grade? Is currency the issue? Do you have too many lower level credits?

Next, make an appointment to speak to an admissions advisor or your academic advisor if you have been assigned one. Take your notes with you. Ask about each course that did not transfer. Once you have determined why your courses were not accepted, talk to your advisor about petitioning for more transfer credits. Do you agree with the reasons why you were denied credit or allowed a reduced transfer credit? If not, consider petitioning for more credits.

The majority of people who take the time to prepare an intelligent academic petition are successful at gaining additional transfer credits.

Your advisor can inform you about the petition process at your college and either give you the appropriate forms or refer you to the appropriate people for beginning an appeal process.

CHECKLIST FOR PETITIONING FOR TRANSFER CREDITS

1. Identify courses that did not transfer.
2. Note why you think each course did not transfer (e.g., accreditation, currency, CEUs, elective, course repetition, etc).
3. Meet with your advisor to discuss each course in question.
4. Determine with your advisor if you want to petition for more transfer credits.
5. If you decide to petition, ask your advisor for details on the petition process, and if available, samples of successful petitions made by other students in your academic situation.
6. Prepare your petition.
7. Ask your advisor to review your petition and make suggestions on any changes.
8. Submit your petition to the appropriate Dean or Academic Committee.

The policies on transfer credits should be detailed in the official college catalog. If you do not have a copy of your college's catalog, ask your admissions officer to provide one. Some colleges sell their catalogs through the campus bookstore. The catalog should also outline how to petition for exceptions to academic policies.

6 EARNING CREDIT FOR CAREER AND LIFE EXPERIENCE

Imagine going back to college as a successful executive who has built a multimillion dollar marketing firm. You completed three years of your bachelor's degree in business administration way back in 1967–1969. But then you started your own company, and, well, that turned out to be a lot more fun and lucrative than taking college courses. Now, here you are with kids of your own in college, and it's time, for reasons of self-satisfaction, to finish that college degree.

You go in prepared to complete the final semester of your senior year, only to be told by an academic advisor that your experience aside, you've got to start by taking Marketing 101 because while you may have taken it in 1967, you received an "incomplete."

There you are, back in college with thirty years of marketing experience, taking a course called Marketing 101—seems silly.

It is silly. This is why colleges have developed programs that adults can use to document their career and life experience for degree credit. This is why more than a dozen special college examination programs exist to let adult students "test out" of basic courses. If you have significant experience in marketing you may not have to take a course in Introductory Marketing. At most colleges, you can take a sixty-minute, multiple-choice exam in marketing principles. If you pass this exam you may be granted an exemption from having to take the formal course Marketing 101. Taking these special exams is a process called "testing out." As these exams let you challenge the assumption that you need to take a formal course, these exams are also commonly called "challenge exams."

Almost everyone over the age of 30 has acquired the equivalent knowledge of several entry-level college courses. The office manager who uses computers every day knows what's taught in COMP106 Computer Office Operations in her sleep. She'd be best advised to skip that academic course, or to take a challenge exam to test out of that course. Almost all colleges have special assessment programs for older learners who are returning to college. These special assessment programs can serve several purposes in your academic planning.

HOW CREDIT FOR EXPERIENCE OPTIONS HELP ADULT LEARNERS

SECURE PROPER COURSE PLACEMENT

English and math placement exams are often used to determine what level of course one should begin with in college. Those with higher knowledge levels may be placed in advanced courses while those with rusty skills can begin in refresher courses.

GAIN A COURSE WAIVER OR EXEMPTION

Most colleges have required courses that everyone must take to earn a degree. If you have already acquired this knowledge through work training, you can take a challenge exam to test out of an otherwise required course.

EARN ADVANCED DEGREE CREDIT

Using challenge exams and other credit for career experience programs to earn academic degree credit can significantly lower the cost of your degree and accelerate your academic process.

In this chapter we will explore all the processes and special programs that your college of choice may make available to you to help you advance or accelerate your degree process.

ARE CREDIT FOR EXPERIENCE OPTIONS ACADEMICALLY SOUND?

Universities exist to teach. Or do they? Universities were originally developed for kids who had little experience of the world. The first universities were institutions where very young men (most of them dreaming of the day they might shave!) came to learn the trade secrets and philosophies of their future professions.

When universities were first founded, information was not accessible. There were no printed books, magazines, videotapes, or public libraries. There were no printing presses to make books. And there were no copy machines.

As times have changed, so has the mission of the university. Information is so accessible nowadays that "information anxiety" infects us. We may feel we are falling behind because we do not have enough time to digest this wealth of information. These days, a savvy learner does not have to trek to a university in the Himalayas to discover the meaning of ancient philosophies. An hour online can literally yield as much information as people of yore were subjected to in a lifetime.

Colleges today grapple with how to best "educate" an information-rich population. Colleges have begun to ask what they should do with adults who have already learned some of what colleges were designed to teach them.

If colleges exist to teach, but adults have already learned some of what is taught at the college level, what then is the role of a college? The answer, at least partially, has become assessment.

If you already know what is being taught, the job of a college shifts from teaching you these subjects to assessing what you already know about these subjects. As an older student, how a college assesses what you already know may be as important as how well equipped they are to teach you new skills. Credit for experience options are academically sound because they provide standardized ways for faculty to award older learners credit for the college-level knowledge that they have already acquired through life and work experience.

What Kinds of Experiences Qualify for College Credit?
We learn all the time. Many of us have learned to use a computer in the last decade, and we probably acquired this knowledge without the help of a computer science professor. Today, most colleges require students to take a course in computer literacy. But if you are the 39-year-old manager of your company's information systems department, should you be required to take a beginner's course in computer literacy? Of course not!

Most adults have acquired some knowledge from work and leisure activities that corresponds to the knowledge taught on college campuses. Tens of thousands of subjects are taught on college campuses each year—everything from quilting to nuclear physics. Some of the more common skills that adults may have taught themselves include practical courses such as accounting, office management, introduction to management, microcomputer applications, salesmanship, total quality management—and the list goes on.

Hobbies, readings, and volunteer work are excellent sources of college-level learning.

If you have a hobby, or are an avid reader, you may already have college-level knowledge in courses like: personal finance, jazz music, computer programming, science fiction literature, poetry, gardening, Spanish, the history of the civil war, volunteer management, herbal medicine, and American history—to name a few!

As adults have returned to college in knowledge-savvy packs, colleges have been busy reengineering themselves. Most colleges now teach new knowledge and they assess those subjects that adults have mastered on their own. Once assessed, this knowledge may be placed on a college transcript. Credit is given where credit is due.

Colleges have developed numerous ways to evaluate what you already know, so if you are a middle-aged mother who has successfully raised three children and managed a retail store, you will probably not have to take courses in effective parenting or retail management. The self-taught journalist, whose work has been published scores of times, will not be asked to sit through beginning courses in news writing.

What options exist for documenting the knowledge you already have? Which options will work best for you—and your budget? Let's look at the options in detail, beginning with the most common option: challenge exams.

THE CHALLENGE EXAM OPTION

Challenge exams are standardized tests, administered at a college testing center. CLEP (College Level Exam Program) is the most popular exam program. Most challenge exams cover the equivalent of what is taught in one college course, such as business law or American history. Most challenge exams consist of a hundred or more multiple-choice questions. If you take one of these exams and achieve a passing score, you may either be granted college credit or be allowed to skip a required course in the same subject area. (Which option you choose will depend on the policies followed by your college of choice and your overall degree plan needs.) Fees are charged to take these exams. Fees vary with the type of exam taken.

*T*he following major challenge exams are accepted by most colleges:

College Level Exam Program (CLEP)

Defense Activity for Nontraditional Education Support (DANTES)

Thomas Edison State College Exam Program (TECEP)

Regents College Exams (RCE)

University of North Carolina Exams (UNCE)

Ohio University Exams (OUE)

Graduate Record Exams (GRE)

New York University Foreign Language Tests

In addition to these nationally standardized exams, colleges often develop their own tests. These tests are made available to those who want to test out of selected courses. Western Illinois University, for example, accepts all types of standardized challenge exams, such as the CLEP, but they also offer their own departmental exams in forty-three college subjects. Check with your college for their policy on departmental exams.

FREQUENTLY ASKED QUESTIONS ABOUT CHALLENGE EXAMS

Can I Earn a Letter Grade on a Challenge Exam?

Most exams are not graded. Most exams are scored. You pass the exam if you score at or above the average score earned by learners who completed a formal college class in the same subject. If you need letter grades, investigate the programs that award letter grades rather than scores. For example, Ohio University Exams result in letter grades on a regular college transcript, like normal campus classes. Ask your college if they offer their own departmental exams. Departmental exams, which are developed "in-house" by college faculty, sometimes carry letter grades.

Can I Earn Upper-Level (Bachelor's) Credits Using Exams?

Most challenge exams test introductory knowledge taught the first two years of junior college or at a community college. If you specifically need upper-level (junior/senior) credits for bachelor's degree completion, the challenge exam option may be less useful. A few exam programs, such as TECEP, offer upper-level exams in specialized subjects, such as business. Many of the RCEs award upper-level credit. Each college will have its own rules about acceptance of challenge exams and what level of credits they will award for any exam.

Never assume an exam will be accepted at the upper level or meet a specific degree requirement at your local college. Ask your college for a copy of their exam acceptance policies before taking any challenge exams. Also, ask your degree advisor to preapprove any exams you decide to take. By preapproval, we mean that you should ask your degree advisor to check your college's policies on the acceptance of challenge exams and to guarantee you in advance that if you pass a particular challenge exam, your college will accept this exam for degree credit or course exemption reasons.

Can I Arrange for Special Exams?

What if no exams exist in your knowledge areas? If you need exams in special areas' the following two programs may help you. You may also want to consider developing a written portfolio for college credit rather than take a challenge exam. (The written portfolio option is covered later in this chapter.)

Ohio University (CCE Program)

The Course Credit by Exam (CCE) program will attempt to arrange for challenge exams in any subject that Ohio University regularly teaches on campus, with the exception of lab courses. You may register to take these exams at a local college or public library. Contact Ohio University, Adult Learning Services, External Student Program, Tupper Hall 301, Athens, OH 45701-2979; Phone 800-444-2910; E-mail: independent.study@ohio.edu.

Regents College of the University of the State of New York (Special Assessments)

The Regents Office of Testing and Assessment will attempt to arrange Special Assessments in any single academic subject area (except nursing). These comprehensive oral exams must be taken before faculty panels in Albany, New York. At least two faculty members who are specialists in your area will conduct your assessment. Contact Regents College, Office of Testing and Assessment, 7 Columbia Circle, Albany, NY 12203-5159; Phone 518-464-8500.

Do I Have to Be a Genius to Pass a Challenge Exam?

Students from ages 18 to 80 tackle challenge exams with mixed results. Most do pass the exams. The smartest students take the time to systematically self-study textbooks and exam aids before tackling an exam. Remember that challenge exams are based *on the theory rather than the practice of the subjects they test.* Just because you ran a marketing company for twenty years does not mean that you know the latest academic research on marketing. Studying college textbooks will help you to master the theory of a subject area.

How Can I Get Books to Self-Study?

The companies that design exams usually provide free bibliographies of the best textbooks for self-study. Locating and studying at least one of these textbooks is a good idea. Try your local college bookstore. Also try your library for study books that cover test content areas.

Finally, anyone can order a college textbook. Most publishers have 800 numbers. Once you know the textbook you need, call 800 directory assistance for the publisher's number. Textbooks aren't cheap though! Your best buys will be used texts from secondhand bookstores in college towns. One excellent bookstore that stocks used textbooks and that routinely provides textbooks via mail to adult learners is Specialty Books, 5833 Industrial

Drive, Athens, OH 45701, via e-mail at: order@specialty-books.com. You may also visit them on the web at http://www.specialty-books.com.

Can I Earn an Entire Degree through Credit for Experience Options?

Most colleges limit the number and type of credits that can be earned through credit for experience options. The typical limit is 30 semester credits or one year of college. Some four-year colleges may allow up to two years or 60 semester credits. Central Michigan University, a typical publicly supported, four-year university, will accept up to 60 credits, or half your bachelor's degree, in experience credits.

Two distance-learning colleges in the United States, Thomas Edison State College of New Jersey and Regents College of the University of the State of New York, operate as assessment colleges, not teaching colleges. These two special colleges allow students to earn entire undergraduate degrees or certificates through credit for experience options. However, in reality, most students who attend these two colleges also complete some formal college courses to earn their degrees. (See the Appendix for information on these two special distance-learning assessment colleges.)

TYPES OF CHALLENGE EXAMS

COLLEGE LEVEL EXAM PROGRAM (CLEP)

The CLEP is the most widely accepted challenge exam program in the country. More than 2,800 accredited colleges accept CLEP for degree credit. The CLEP program features 29 single subject exams and 5 general exams. Single subject exams cover the same material that you would cover in a single course on a single subject. For example, the College Algebra CLEP covers the material that is commonly taught in one college course in algebra.

You can register for CLEP exams through the Educational Testing Service (ETS). Any of the 34 CLEP exams may be taken at your local college testing office or through military educational offices nationwide. Most CLEP exams consist of 100 multiple-choice questions. A few exams may require supplemental essays to receive full credit. ETS issues a score report for each exam. You should have these score reports sent to your degree-granting college. Your degree-granting college will then transcript your CLEP score, awarding college credits or course exemptions for what they deem to be passing scores. CLEP exams cost $43 each.

The American Council on Education (ACE) is the organization that determines what a passing score is on a CLEP exam. Most colleges accept ACE levels when deciding to award credit. Ask your degree-granting college which CLEP exams they accept, and what their minimum acceptable score is for awarding credit or course exemption on each exam.

Be aware that some colleges require higher scores than those recommended by ACE. Ohio University, for example, sometimes requires higher scores before they will award degree credit based on a CLEP exam. Ohio also does not accept all CLEP exams. It is up to your degree-granting college to decide whether or not to accept CLEP scores, and if so at what score level, and for how many credits.

Who Should Consider CLEP?

Most CLEP exams cover lower-level (freshman or sophomore) subjects. CLEP exams are good for earning credit toward an associate degree or for earning credits in the first two years of the four-year bachelor's degree. If you have already completed the introductory two years of college, or an associate's degree, CLEP exams will be less useful to you. Most single subject CLEP exams, like Introductory Psychology, award 3 semester credits. The General Exams, which cover more material, may be valid for up to 6 semester credits apiece.

The five General Exams cover freshman-level knowledge in broad subject areas such as art, literature, and cultural trends (humanities). If all five exams are passed, you may earn up to 30 credits—the equivalent of an entire freshman year of college.

If you are well read, and did well in high school, the General Exams are a good place to try out your test-taking aptitude. In addition to being used to award college credit, many colleges use the CLEP General Examinations to determine proper placement in college courses like English, mathematics, and science literacy.

General CLEP Examinations
English Composition
Humanities
College Mathematics
Natural Sciences
Social Sciences and History

Humanities
American Literature
Analysis and Interpreting Literature
Freshman College Composition
English Literature

Humanities—Foreign Languages
College French
College German
College Spanish

History and Social Sciences
American Government
American History I: Early Colonizations to 1877
American History II: 1865 to the Present
Human Growth and Development
Introduction to Educational Psychology
Introductory Macroeconomics
Introductory Microeconomics
Introductory Psychology
Introductory Sociology
Western Civilization I: Ancient Near East to 1648
Western Civilization II: 1648 to Present

Science and Math
Calculus with Elementary Functions
College Algebra
Trigonometry
College Algebra—Trigonometry
General Biology
General Chemistry

Business
Principles of Accounting
Information Systems and Computer Applications
Principles of Management
Introductory Business Law
Principles of Marketing

Further Information

Free informational pamphlets are available from the Educational Testing Service. The pamphlet "Information for Candidates and Registration Bulletin for the CLEP" explains the CLEP program, gives sample test questions, and contains test registration forms. The free pamphlet "CLEP Colleges" identifies colleges that accept CLEP for degree credit and provides a directory of colleges that maintain public test sites where you can take CLEP exams. Both pamphlets are available from Educational Testing Services, PO Box 6601, Princeton, NJ 08541-6600, 609-771-7865. E-mail: CLEP@ets.org. Or visit them on the World Wide Web at http://www.collegeboard.org.

The Official Study Guide for the CLEP Examinations, a detailed book, is available from The College Board, Publications and Orders, Department #W66, Box 886, New York, NY 10101-0886, 800-323-7155, or 212-713-8165 or on the web at http://www.collegeboard.org. The book costs $18 plus shipping and handling. The study guide explains the CLEP process, gives the content areas covered in each exam, provides sample exams, lists college test sites and colleges that accept CLEP scores, provides strategies for studying for CLEP, and recommends specific books for self-study prior to taking a CLEP in any one subject area. Another good resource is *Cracking the CLEP*, published by The Princeton Review. This book includes diagnostic exams that will predict your score on the CLEP, as well as test-taking strategies to help you score higher.

DEFENSE ACTIVITY FOR NONTRADITIONAL EDUCATION SUPPORT (DANTES)

DANTES exams were originally designed to test military students but are now available to the public. Individual exams are from 65 to 100 multiple-choice items. Some exams also require written essays. You may take DANTES at more than 600 college testing sites nationwide or, if you're on active duty, through your military education officer. Exams cost $23 each.

As with the CLEP, score reports are sent to your degree-granting college. Your degree-granting college decides whether or not to give credit on your college transcript. The number of credits awarded for each exam and the required passing score will vary by the degree-granting college, although most DANTES award 3 semester credits.

Credit awards and passing scores are based on the recommendations of the American Council on Education (ACE). Check with your degree-granting college for their policy on the acceptance of DANTES exams. Ohio University, for example, will not accept DANTES exams for degree credit, although they do accept most CLEP exams.

Who Should Consider DANTES?

Most DANTES test lower-level (freshman or sophomore) subjects. Some advanced exams in business and the social sciences/history, like the Rise and Fall of the Soviet Union, and Business Law II, have been reviewed by the American Council on Education for upper-level credits (senior or junior) for bachelor's degree candidates. The free DANTES bulletin, available from the address below, specifies passing ACE score levels and upper-level exams.

DANTE Examinations

Mathematics
Introductory College Algebra
Principles of Statistics

Social Science
Art of the Western World
Contemporary Western Europe: 1946–1990
An Introduction to the Modern Middle East
Human/Cultural Geography
A History of the Vietnam War
The Civil War and Reconstruction
Foundations of Education
Life Span Developmental Psychology
General Anthropology
Introduction to Law Enforcement
Criminal Justice
Fundamentals of Counseling
Drugs and Alcohol

Physical Science
Astronomy
Here's to Your Health
Environment and Humanity
Principles of Physical Science I
Physical Geology

Business
Principles of Finance
Principles of Financial Accounting
Personnel/Human Resources Management
Organizational Behavior
Principles of Supervision
Business Law II
Introduction to Computers with Programming in Basic
Introduction to Business
Money and Banking
Business Mathematics

Humanities
Ethics in America
Introduction to World Religions
Principles of Public Speaking

Applied Technology—Free Electives
Technical Writing

Further Information

Contact the DANTES Program Office, The Chauncey Group International, 664 Rosedale Road, Princeton, New Jersey 08540, 609-720-6740, or e-mail: DANTES@Chauncey.com, for the free DANTES Candidate Information Bulletin. The bulletin explains the DANTES program and contains a registration form. The free "DANTES Institutions Booklet" provides a directory of colleges that will proctor DANTES exams and/or accept DANTES for degree credit. You may also request a free fact sheet/study guide on any exam that interests you. The fact sheets outline the content of each exam, give sample questions, and list recommended textbooks for each DANTES.

Thomas Edison College Exam Program (TECEP)

The faculty of Thomas Edison State College of New Jersey has developed a series of challenge exams called TECEPs. The students who take these exams are working toward a campus-free, distance degree with Edison, but other colleges also accept these exams. TECEPs are not as widely accepted as CLEP and DANTES, however.

TECEPs are registered for through Edison and may be taken at local college testing sites or through Military Educational Offices. The exams are offered monthly. The fee is $60 per exam for degree-seeking students who are registered with Thomas Edison State College, $100 for others.

Passing scores for TECEP exams are set by Thomas Edison State College at 60–70 percent.

Unlike CLEP and DANTES, where the Educational Testing Services scores the exam and issues a score report to a college, TECEP scores are transcripted for college credit and kept on file at Thomas Edison State College.

Who Should Consider TECEP?

While TECEPs were designed for people earning distance degrees through Thomas Edison State College, they can sometimes be used to earn degree credit at other regionally accredited colleges. Thomas Edison State has recommended several TECEPs, like Shakespeare and business exams, for upper-level credit, but you should approach your degree-granting college for their policies on TECEP acceptance. Most exams are designed to award 3 semester credits. A few carry 6 credit awards.

TECEP Exams

Humanities
TEART101 Art History and Appreciation I
TEART102 Art History and Appreciation II
TELIT300 Introduction to Shakespeare
TEPHO160 Introduction to the History of Film
TETHA101 Introduction to the Art of Theater
TEJOU110 Introduction to News Reporting
TECOM210 Public Relations Thought and Practice
TEENG101 Written Expression I
TEENG102 Written Expression II
TEENG102 Technical Writing

Social Sciences
TESOS301 Alcohol Abuse
TEANT101 Cultures of the World
TEPSY360 Industrial Psychology
TEPOS101 Introduction to Political Science
TEPSY370 Introduction to Social Psychology
TEPSY203 Introduction to Transactional Analysis
TEPSY352 Psychology of Personality
TESOS302 Substance Abuse: Fundamental Facts

Science and Mathematics
TEBIO330 Anatomy and Physiology
TECOS210 BASIC Programming
TECHE111 General Chemistry
TEPHY111 General Physics I
TEPHY112 General Physics II
TEMAT340 Introduction to Statistics

Business—General
TEACC302 Managerial Accounting II
TEACC421 Tax Accounting
TEBUS311 Business in Society
TEBUS421 Business Policy

Business—Finance
TEFIN331 Financial Institutions and Markets
TEFIN332 International Finance and Trade
TEFIN301 Principles of Finance
TEFIN321 Security Analysis and Portfolio Management

Business—Human Resources
TEMAN322 Advanced Labor Relations and Collective Bargaining
TEMAN321 Labor Relations and Collective Bargaining
TEMAN301 Principles of Management
TEMAN411 Organizational Theory and Organizational Analysis
TEMAN311 Organizational Behavior

Business—Marketing
TEMAR323 Advertising
TEMAR331 Channels of Distribution
TEMAR321 Marketing Communications
TEMAR441/2 Marketing Management Strategy I and II
TEMAR411 Marketing Research
TEMAR322 Sales Management

Business—Management of Information Systems
TEMIS311 Database Management
Business—Operations Management
TEDAP101 Introduction to Data Processing
TEOPM301 Introduction to Operations Management
TEOPM441 Quantitative Managerial Decision Making

Professional Areas—Free Electives
TECOU321 Behavior Modification Techniques in Counseling
TEHEA301 Community Health
TECOU322 Counselor Training: Short-Term Client Systems
TEMIS311 Database Management
TEHUS101 Introduction to Human Services
TEPUA101 Public Administration I
TECOU341 Women in Treatment

Further Information

Contact Thomas Edison State College, Office of Testing and Assessment, 101 West State Street, Trenton, NJ 08608-1176, or 609-633-2844, for a free TECEP brochure and registration form. *TECEP Examination Program: Test Descriptions*, is a book published annually by Thomas Edison State College. This book explains TECEP exams, outlines exam areas, provides sample exams, and recommends preparation books for each exam. DANTES exams are also covered in this book. A special appendix gives 800 numbers for popular textbook publishers. The book costs $10 plus handling. Contact Thomas Edison State College, Office of the Bursar, 101 West State Street, Trenton, NJ 08608-1176; Phone 609-984-4099.

REGENTS COLLEGE EXAMS

Regents College Exams (RCEs) were developed by the faculty of Regents College of the University of the State of New York. Some exams require essays, but most are multiple choice. The faculty of Regents College scores the essays. The exams are offered nationwide at college test sites in October, November, February, March, May, and June. You may also take these exams anytime in computer-based form at Sylvan Educational Technology Centers nationwide and abroad. Fees range from $45 to $140 for these exams.

As with other standardized exams, passing scores and credit awards come from recommendations made by the American Council on Education (ACE). These exams can yield from 3 to 8 credits. Nursing exams yield higher credit awards at the upper levels.

Who Should Consider Regents Exams?

While many who take RCEs are working on a distance degree from Regents College, other college programs, especially in New York State, accept these exams. The nursing sequence is commonly taken by practicing nurses who have acquired advanced skills on the job and now want this knowledge documented as part of a college degree at both the associate's and bachelor's levels. Some business exams cover upper-level areas also.

Regents Exams
Humanities
English Composition
Ethics: Theory and Practice
Religions of the World

Social Sciences
Abnormal Psychology
American Dream (Part 1)
Foundations of Gerontology
History of Nazi Germany
Life Span Developmental Psychology
Psychology of Adulthood and Aging
Research Methods in Psychology
War in Vietnam
World Population

Sciences
Anatomy and Physiology
Microbiology
Pathophysiology

Business
Production/Operations Management
Business Policy and Strategy
Human Resource Management
Labor Relations
Organizational Behavior

Education
Reading Instruction in the Elementary School

Nursing—Associate Level
Fundamentals of Nursing
Maternal and Child Nursing
Maternity Nursing
Commonalities in Nursing Care: Area A
Commonalities in Nursing Care: Area B
Differences in Nursing Care: Area A
Differences in Nursing Care: Area B
Differences in Nursing Care: Area C
Occupational Strategies in Nursing

Nursing—Bachelor Level
Adult Nursing
Maternal and Child Nursing
Psychiatric/Mental Health Nursing
Professional Strategies in Nursing
Health Support: Area I
Health Support: Area II
Health Restoration: Area I

Further Information

Free study guides for each exam, and a test registration bulletin are available from Regents College Exams, Test Administration Office, Regents College, 7 Columbia Circle, Albany, NY 12203-5159; Phone: 800-RCE-EXAM or 518-464-8500. You may also request materials via e-mail at testeadmn@regents.edu or visit Regents College online at http://www.regents.edu to download free study guides for any exam and a registration bulletin.

University of North Carolina Exams (UNCE)

The University of North Carolina offers challenge exams through their independent study division. You may petition the independent study division for the right to earn credit by exam for any of the courses they teach via independent study. The exams offered vary with course offerings, but the program routinely offers courses in business, foreign languages, humanities, social sciences, mathematics, and the natural sciences with several upper-level offerings in each topic area.

University of North Carolina faculty grades all exams. Most exams are recorded as pass/fail rather than with letter grades. The University of North Carolina issues a college transcript once an exam is passed. The exam fee is $80. Fees include a study guide with a recommended bibliography for each exam. Textbooks can be ordered directly from the University of North Carolina.

Who Should Consider UNC Exams?

UNC exams are good to explore if you seek upper-level credits in subject areas not covered by other testing programs. For example, the program offers exams in courses like Managerial Accounting and Teaching Stress Management. When you register for an exam, you get a course syllabus and textbook to help you self-study for the exam. This structure will make it easier for you to enroll and prepare for an exam all in one quick step. The exam you take will cover the course material as it is presented in the one textbook that you are given to study.

Further Information

Contact the University of North Carolina, Independent Studies, CB#1020 The Friday Center, Chapel Hill, NC 27599-1020; Phone: 919-962-1134 or 800-862-5669. Ask for their catalog of independent study courses and special instructions on their credit by examination option.

OHIO UNIVERSITY EXAMS (OUE)

The faculty of Ohio University has developed exams that are widely accepted by other degree programs. Upon registration for an exam, you will receive a syllabus that gives details on the exam and how to study for it. Exams cost $34 per quarter credit for regularly offered course exams as listed below. Most exams award 4 to 5 quarter credits. Exam availability will vary.

Contact Ohio University for a current list. Expect colleges to accept the level indicated by the Ohio course numbers given below. Courses numbered in the 100s are freshman level. Those numbered in the 200s are sophomore level. Courses numbered 300 and 400 are junior and senior (upper level) for bachelor study.

Who Should Consider Ohio Exams?

While many who take Ohio exams are seeking a degree from Ohio via their distance-degree program, the exam program is open to the public, and is often used by students attending other degree colleges. Unlike most exam programs, letter grades are awarded. All exam grades, including Fs, are recorded on an Ohio University academic transcript.

Ohio University will attempt to arrange for a challenge exam in any subject that their faculty teaches, with the exception of facility-dependent courses, such as clinical nursing or lab courses. This is a very good program for people who need upper-level (bachelor's) credits or who need special exams that may not be offered by other programs.

Ohio Exams

Accounting
201 Financial Accounting
201 Managerial Accounting

Afro-American Studies
101 Afro-American History I, 1526–1865
225 History of the Black Worker

Aviation
110 Private Pilot Ground Instruction
240 Private Pilot Flight Course
310 Advanced Aeronautics for Commercial Pilot Ground Instruction
340 Commercial Flight Course I
343 Commercial Flight Course II
350 Instrument Ground Instruction and Air Traffic Control

400 Commercial Flight Course III
420 Commercial Flight Course IV
425 Commercial Flight Course IV (Multiengine)
435 Flight Engineer
440 Flight Instructor Ground Instruction
445 Flight Instructor Course
450 Instrument Instructor Ground Instruction
455 Instrument Instructor Flight Course
460 ATP Ground Instruction
465 Flight Instructor Operations (Multiengine)

Biological Sciences
103 Human Biology
345 Human Physiology
384 Bioethical Problems in Biology and Medicine
390H Biology and the Future of Man

Business Administration
101 Business and Its Environment
101 Marketing: Consumer Survival in the Marketplace
201 Introduction to Business Statistics
301 Marketing Principles
310 Operations: Principles of Operations
325 Managerial Finance
420 Human Resources Management

Business Law
255 Law and Society
356 Law of the Management Process
357 Law of Commercial Transactions

Communication
342 Communication and Persuasion

Economics
301 Introduction to Economic Analysis
302 Introduction to Economic Analysis
304 Macroeconomics

Electronics Technology
112 Solid-State Devices and Industrial Electronics
120 Digital Electronics
134 Direct Current Circuit Analysis
135 Alternating Current Circuit Analysis
220 Electrical Motors, Control Circuits, and Computers
236A Microprocessor and Computer Basics
236B Microprocessor and Computer Basics
289 Electronic Troubleshooting and Repair

Engineering
Engineering Drawing I
Humanities—English Language and Literature
201 Critical Approaches to Fiction
203 Critical Approaches to Drama
301 Shakespeare, the Histories
302 Shakespeare, the Comedies
303 Shakespeare, the Tragedies
312 English Literature: 1500–1660
313 English Literature: 1660–1800
321 American Literature to the Civil War
322 American Literature Since the Civil War
341 American Literature

Humanities–Literature
107 Humanities–Great Books
108 Humanities–Great Books
109 Humanities–Great Books
307 Humanities–Great Books
308 Humanities–Great Books
309 Humanities–Great Books

Humanities—Foreign Language & Literature
111 Elementary French
112 Elementary French
113 Elementary French
211 Intermediate French
212 Intermediate French
213 Intermediate French
355 Introduction to French Literature
356 Introduction to French Literature
111 Elementary German
112 Elementary German
113 Elementary German
211 Intermediate German
212 Intermediate German
213 Intermediate German
111 Elementary Spanish
112 Elementary Spanish
113 Elementary Spanish
211 Intermediate Spanish
212 Intermediate Spanish
213 Intermediate Spanish

Geography
101 Elements of Physical Geography
121 Human Geography

Health and Sports Sciences
202 Health Science and Lifestyle Choices
227 First Aid
406 Organization and Administration of Physical Education

Hearing and Speech Sciences
213 Anatomy and Neurology of Speech
250 Speech and Hearing Science

History
101 Western Civilization in Modern Times
102 Western Civilization in Modern Times
103 Western Civilization in Modern Times
211 American History to 1828
212 History of the United States, 1828–1900
213 History of the United States, Since 1900
317A Ohio History Before 1851
317B Ohio History Since 1851
329A Ancient Egypt and Mesopotamia
329B Ancient Greece
329C Ancient Rome

Journalism
105 Introduction to Mass Communication
311 History of American Journalism
411 Newspaper and Communications Law

Mathematics
101 Basic Mathematics
113 Algebra
120 Elementary Topics in Mathematics
121 Elementary Topics in Mathematics
122 Elementary Topics in Mathematics
130 Plane Analytical Geometry
163A Introduction to Calculus
211 Elementary Linear Algebra
263A Analytical Geometry and Calculus
263B Analytical Geometry and Calculus
263C Analytical Geometry and Calculus
263D Analytical Geometry and Calculus
340 Differential Equations
410 Matrix Theory

Music
160 Music Fundamentals

Office Administration Technology
121 Introductory Typing
122 Intermediate Typing
123 Advanced Typing
231 Machine Computation
262 Report and Letter Writing

Office Management Technology
111 Beginning Shorthand
112 Intermediate Shorthand
121 Keyboarding
122 Keyboarding II/Formatting
131 Office Communications
231 Machine Computation

Philosophy
120 Principles of Reasoning
130 Introduction to Ethics
301 Introduction to Philosophy

Physical Science
100 Survey of Astronomy
101 Physical World
121 Physical World

Physics
201 Introduction to Physics
202 Introduction to Physics
203 Introduction to Physics
251 General Physics
252 General Physics
253 General Physics

Political Science
304 State Politics

Psychology
101 General Psychology
121 Elementary Statistics for Behavioral Sciences
273 Child and Adolescent Psychology
275 Educational Psychology
310 Motivation
315 Behavior Genetics and Individual Differences
332 Abnormal Psychology
335 Environmental Psychology
337 Social Psychology of Justice

Sociology
101 Introduction to Sociology
220 Introduction to the Family

Further Information

Contact Ohio University, Adult Learning Services, 301 Tupper Hall, Athens, Ohio, 45701-2979; Phone: 800-444-2420 or 614-593-2150. Request a brochure on the External Student Program and the Credit by Exam program. You can also e-mail at independent.study@ohio.edu or visit the program on the internet at http://www.ohiou.edu/~indstul.

Graduate Record Exams (GRE)

The Graduate Record Exam advanced Subject Tests are taken each year by students who have completed a bachelor's degree and wish to attend graduate school. The exams, which last 2 hours and 50 minutes, may be registered for through Educational Testing Services (ETS). They may be taken at a local college or at a computerized testing center in your community.

Unlike most other single subject exams, such as the CLEP, the sixteen GRE Subject Tests do not test what is taught in one college course. The GREs test the equivalent of what is taught in ten or twelve college courses, all in one subject area, such as psychology.

The Psychology GRE, for example, covers the knowledge that you would normally have gleaned from completing a traditional college major in psychology. The content covered in the Psychology GRE is equivalent to what is typically covered in the following psychology courses: General Psychology, Child Psychology, Abnormal Psychology, Tests and Measurements, Social Science Statistics, History of Psychology, Psychology of Cognition, Psychology of Learning, Psychology of Personality, Experimental Psychology, and Social Psychology.

Each GRE costs $96. You may register to take either a paper-based or computer-based version at colleges or testing centers worldwide. The computer-based test is scored automatically. Your score report is issued as soon as you complete the exam. Exam scores are considered valid for five years and are only kept on file for that period of time.

Who Should Consider GRE Subject Exams?

The GREs are harder to study for than a single-subject exam, like the CLEP. They are also much less commonly accepted for undergraduate degree credit. Before taking a GRE in hopes of earning degree credit, check with your degree-granting college to see if they will accept the GRE. (Many do not!)

> The GRE Subject Exams are good exams for earning a large number of credits in one subject area.

For example, if you already work as a lab technician in a molecular biology lab, and have significant training in molecular biology but do not have a college degree, taking the GRE in Cell and Molecular Biology can lead to a large credit-award.

Passing scores usually result in a credit award of 24 to 36 semester credits. Lower- and upper-level credit awards can vary widely depending on the scores, as well as the subscores on these tests. If 30 credits are earned, you could expect up to half these credits (15) to be awarded at the upper level. Each college individually assesses how much credit they will award for each GRE.

GRE Subject Exams
Biochemistry, Cell and Molecular Biology
Biology
Chemistry
Computer Science
Economics
Education
Engineering
Geology
History
Literature in English
Mathematics
Music
Physics
Political Science
Psychology
Sociology

Further Information
Contact the Graduate Record Exam, Educational Testing Service, PO Box 6000, Princeton, NJ 08541-6000; Phone 609-771-7670. Ask for a free GRE Information and Registration Bulletin and a free subject test booklet in any subject that interests you. You can access information on the GRE on the web at http://www.gre.org or via e-mail at gre-info@ets.org.

Study-books for each subject test, for example, *Practicing to Take the GRE in Engineering*, are available from Educational Testing Services, for a cost of $11 to $16, plus shipping. Books can be ordered from Educational Testing Services, PO Box 6014, Princeton, NJ 98541-6014, 800-537-3160, or 609-771-7243. The Princeton Review also has GRE test-preparation guides for Biology, Literature, Psychology, Math, and Chemistry.

NEW YORK UNIVERSITY FOREIGN LANGUAGE TESTS
New York University faculty has developed language tests that include written and oral proficiency assessments. Students register through New York

University to take these exams at local college test-sites. Fees are $150 for the 12-credit exam and $225 for the 16-credit exam. The faculty at New York University who scores the exams determines passing scores.

Who Should Consider NYU Exams?

Anyone who has acquired considerable foreign language speaking or writing skills from noncollegiate training programs, residency abroad, or from being raised bilingual, may take these exams. The NYU program offers exams in forty-one languages as diverse as Albanian, Yiddish, Japanese, and Tagalog.

The amount and level of credit awarded will depend on the level of the exam and the final scores. You can take one of two versions of any exam. One version covers beginning and intermediate language skills for 12 credits (lower level). The 16-credit version usually covers advanced language abilities (12 lower-level credits, plus 4 upper-level credits). Levels awarded will vary with the degree-granting college.

Further Information

Contact New York University School of Continuing Education, Foreign Language Program, 48 Cooper Square, Room 107, New York, NY 10003, 212-998-7030. Ask for an information and registration packet on their Foreign Language Proficiency Testing program.

THE PORTFOLIO ASSESSMENT OPTION

Many people use challenge exams to earn credit or receive course waivers. For others, the exam process is not always the best option. People who do well on challenge exams are usually comfortable taking theory-oriented, multiple-choice exams. People who excel at challenge exams often have good test-taking skills. Timed tests do not make them anxious. They are comfortable studying textbooks and self-help books on their own. Other people are not good test takers. Some people express themselves better in written form, via papers and essays. For these people, it may be wiser to consider earning college credits for career and life experience by putting together a special written academic portfolio rather than by taking multiple-choice exams.

Some people are simply not good at taking tests. Some express themselves better in written form, via papers and essays.

When we tell adult students that they should document their life and work experience for college credit through an academic portfolio process, we often get a reluctant, "Well…maybe," in response. The word "portfolio" seems to throw people. It is a word usually associated with artists, or those who put their work into collection form for exhibit. An academic learning portfolio is a similar concept to an art portfolio; it is a concrete way to showcase your knowledge and achievements. But you don't have to be Van Gogh to showcase yourself for academic credit! If you have significant life or career learning experience that cannot be adequately assessed through challenge exams you should consider using a written portfolio process to document your learning for college credit. Following are the five general areas of informal learning adults most commonly think about for documentation through a portfolio process:

- Work Training
- Volunteer or Unpaid Home Experience
- Hobbies
- Travel
- Reading on Selected Subjects

For example, your personal hobby may be reading science-fiction literature. You know a lot about science-fiction literature from your own reading on the subject. If no challenge exam is available in this subject, you can put together written documentation of your knowledge in this area instead. College faculty can then read and review your documentation to determine if you know enough about your subject from your independent reading and learning activities to be awarded college credit. Written documentation may include things like a bibliography of science fiction books that you have read, or copies of essays you have written that compare and contrast science fiction books you have read. Other types of written documentation might include copies of short science-fiction stories that you have written.

Who Should Consider Portfolio Assessment?

When should you take challenge exams and when should you consider earning credits through a written portfolio process? If you answer "true" to most of the statements below, you are probably a good candidate for earning credits through the portfolio process:

1. Challenge exams are not offered in your areas of expertise.

2. You are not a good test taker.

3. You express yourself better when writing papers than you do when taking multiple-choice or objective tests where there is only one right answer.

4. You feel more comfortable designing a showcase of your actual achievements for evaluation by faculty than you do taking an exam on the theory of a subject area.

5. What you know is applied knowledge, rather than textbook theory.

6. You have concrete products, such as artwork, certificates, papers, articles, software, videos, or written reviews, that attest to your competency in some subject area.

Challenge exams and the written portfolio process are not mutually exclusive. Many colleges offer both options. Many adult learners use both challenge exams and a portfolio process to earn degree credit. For example, a client of mine had read all her daughter's college psychology and sociology textbooks (her daughter was a psychology major). She would read the textbooks along with her daughter, then discuss the books with her. In essence, the mother went to college without attending the actual classes. As the daughter completed a psychology course, the mother took the equivalent challenge exam for each course.

On the other hand, this woman did not use challenge exams for all her experience credits. She used a portfolio to document some of her independent studies. She chose a portfolio for activities where she could provide written documentation, and where her knowledge had been gained not by studying the theory of something but by completing projects that could serve as evidence that college-level learning had occurred.

For example, she was very active in community theater. She had played major roles in six Shakespearean dramas with a semiprofessional group. To perform in these dramas she had to read, memorize, and understand these plays. Therefore, she chose to document the equivalent of a college course in the plays of Shakespeare using a portfolio process, not by taking a challenge exam. Her portfolio documentation included a videotape of her performances, notebooks she kept on character motivation during the rehearsals, and an eight-page paper that expressed her ideas on the representation of women as mothers, wives, and warriors in Shakespearean times.

How Do I Put Together a Portfolio?

You will be asked to follow formal procedures when putting together a learning portfolio for faculty review. If you choose to use a portfolio process, the college you enroll with will provide guidance. Most colleges that accept portfolios for review require adult learners to enroll in a course to learn how to put together a portfolio.

Students at Ohio University, for example, must complete the course Life and Career Experiences Analysis to learn how to compile a portfolio. Similarly, learners at Indiana University must complete the course Development of the Self-Acquired Competency Portfolio. The homework for these courses involves working with an advisor to identify and document your college-level knowledge for degree credit.

Some colleges, like Thomas Edison State College in New Jersey, have Portfolio Assessment Handbooks. Students follow the steps in these written handbooks to put together a portfolio on their own. The portfolio process will vary by college, but a portfolio generally contains several written sections. A common design would include three main sections:

- Your Learning Autobiography (10–20 pages)
- A List of College Course Titles You Seek Credit For (1 page)
- Documentation for Each Course You Seek Credit For (3–7 pages)

If you think you'd like to compose a portfolio, excellent research, writing, and organizational skills are required. Most colleges will not allow you to begin a portfolio process until you have completed college courses in writing or English composition.

How Do I Select Documentation for My Portfolio?

What types of documentation do colleges require for the portfolio process? Usually, for each course you attempt through portfolio, you must provide some documentation—other than the fact that you say that such learning occurred! Documentation can take many forms. Common forms include:

- Course Transcripts from Nonregionally Accredited Colleges
- Certificates of Award
- CEU Transcripts
- Resumes

- Bibliographies
- Brochures Produced
- Letters from Supervisors
- Letters from Experts
- Articles Written
- Essays Written
- Artwork
- Photographs
- Audio Tapes
- Videotapes
- Slides

Note that transcripts of courses completed through nonregionally accredited colleges, such as vocational training academies, are often included in portfolios. The portfolio process allows learners with nonregionally accredited coursework the chance to further document this learning and request that some of it be applied toward a regionally accredited college plan. If you have professional certificates that list CEUs for training programs, you can also use these certificates to document your learning and request that some of this learning be recognized as college level for your degree plan.

THE AMERICAN COUNCIL ON EDUCATION: PROGRAMS ON NONCOLLEGIATE SPONSORED INSTRUCTION (ACE/PONSI)

Colleges are not the major providers of adult education. Surprised? Private corporations spend more time, money, and teaching effort on adults than all the formal colleges in America combined. Many large corporations have their own "corporate universities" that teach employees everything from time management to UNIX programming. Did you know that the McDonald's Corporation runs one of the best food service management universities in the world? Hamburger University. Hamburger University is the alma mater of the cream of the crop in fast-food sales and service. It provides excellent training to McDonald's managers. Yet Hamburger U. is not an accredited university.

CORPORATE TRAINING PROGRAMS

The educational fervor among corporations is good news for adult learners. As we've already discussed, noncollegiate training programs can often be converted to college credits through a portfolio process. However, some larger corporations, such as McDonald's, have submitted their courses to a special review process sponsored by the American Council on Education's Program on Non-Collegiate Sponsored Instruction (ACE/PONSI). This program is also known as the College Credit Recommendation Service.

ACE/PONSI is a program that allows noncollege educators, such as McDonald's Corporation, AT&T, and the United States government, to have their in-house training courses reviewed by college assessors. These faculty assessors review course content, textbooks, and classroom procedures. If they find that individual courses are "college level," they recommend that a certain number of college credits be routinely awarded for successful course completion.

Credits earned in ACE/PONSI courses can, in theory, be transferred to regionally accredited colleges. This equivalency exists in theory only, however. ACE/PONSI only "recommends" that regionally accredited colleges accept ACE/PONSI courses as "the equivalent of regionally accredited college coursework." Regionally accredited colleges remain free to decide if they will accept ACE/PONSI credit recommendations—and if so how many and what kinds of credits they will actually award.

About half of all regionally accredited colleges accept ACE/PONSI recommendations. The other half may not accept them, or may severely restrict the number and kinds of ACE credits they will accept in transfer. If you have ACE/PONSI credits; make sure you understand your college's policy on ACE/PONSI credits. If you have a wealth of ACE credits, talk with a degree advisor about ACE/PONSI credit use. Try to attend a college that will let you maximize use of these credits toward your final educational goal. To find out which corporations participate in ACE/PONSI, consult the American Council on Education's book, *The National Guide to Educational Credit for Training Programs*.

ACE/PONSI is a great way to earn free college credits on the job. Ask your training department if they participate in ACE/PONSI or the College Credit Recommendation Service. If you have already completed ACE/PONSI courses, ask your human resources department for a transcript of your ACE/PONSI work. If you have completed ACE/PONSI courses, a record of your credits may be on file with the American Council on Education, Registry of Credit

Recommendations, 1 Dupont Circle, Washington, D.C. 20036-1193, 202-939-9434.

NONREGIONALLY ACCREDITED COLLEGE PROGRAMS

Credits earned at nonregionally accredited universities are not widely accepted in transfer by regionally accredited colleges. To help learners use these credits in transfer, some nonregionally accredited colleges have had some of their courses reviewed through ACE/PONSI. For example, the largest and oldest Distance Education and Training Council (DETC) accredited school, International Correspondence Schools, or the ICS Center for Degree Studies, has had some of their degree courses approved by ACE/PONSI. ICS credits can be transferred toward a regionally accredited college degree (provided that the regionally accredited college you attend accepts ACE credits).

If you have attended a nonregionally accredited school, check with the registrar to confirm if any of your old courses had ACE/PONSI approval at the time you completed them. Check with individual regionally accredited colleges about their policies for accepting credits from nonregionally accredited schools. Remember that ACE courses only carry "credit recommendations." No regionally accredited college is obligated to accept these recommendations.

PROFESSIONAL LICENSES AND CREDENTIALS

The American Council on Education (ACE) has also reviewed several professional certifications or career credentials offered by noncollegiate agencies and made credit award recommendations in their official *National Guide to Educational Credit for Training Programs*. We highlight a few of these professional credentials and licenses below:

- Automotive Excellence Service Exams
- Certified Public Accountant
- Certified Payroll Professional
- Cardiovascular Credentialing International
- Certified Computer Programmer
- Certified Novell Administrator
- Certified Novell Engineer
- Certified Novell Instructor

- Certified Professional Secretary
- Certified Purchasing Manager
- Chartered Financial Consultant
- FAA Pilot, Engineer, Mechanic Licenses
- Registered Professional (Court) Reporter
- Respiratory Therapy Technician

In addition to these ACE/PONSI approved professional designations, individual colleges often accept nationally recognized or state licenses. Aviation licenses, real estate licenses, and professional health certifications, such as nursing diploma training, are all commonly accepted for college credits. If you hold any professional license or certification, ask each college if they will accept these for direct credit. Remember that professional certifications and licenses may also be "converted" to college credits through a portfolio process. But, if your license or credential is already recognized by ACE/PONSI, you can save time and money by not going the portfolio route.

MILITARY TRAINING PROGRAMS

The military is a huge provider of specialized training and education. If you have served in the military since Vietnam, you may have received the equivalent of an associate's degree in military training without ever knowing it. ACE publishes an annual, whopping four-volume set on how military training and occupational specialties translate into college degree credits through the ACE review process.

> *If* you've been in the military in the last decade, you probably have ACE military credits. Boot Camp or Basic Training alone is usually worth several free elective credits in first aid, personal hygiene, physical education, and marksmanship.

What credits might you be entitled to for your military training? The process of determining military credits is fairly easy, but never quick! Like many tasks related to earning your degree, a lengthy paper chase may be required. Active duty personnel begin the process by completing "DD Form 295: Application for the Evaluation of Educational/Learning Experiences During Military Service." If you're in the Army, you may also submit an "AARTS: Army/American Council on Education Registry Transcripts System" form. See your base educational services officer to have these forms completed. These forms will identify any ACE credit awards that lurk in your military training and occupational specialty records.

Veterans must have on hand "DD Form 214: Armed Services of the United States Report of Transfer or Discharge." Veterans should also request official transcripts of all in-service training schools attended. Veterans may submit requests for the "DD 214" and related educational transcripts to: General Services Administration, National Personnel Records Center, Military Personnel Records, 9700 Page Boulevard, St. Louis, MO 63132. Additional forms may be required, depending on your service orientation.

Begin your ACE credit search with the above documents. Additional military records may be required depending on your branch of service, term of duty, and type of training you received. For example, if you served in the Air Force after 1972 and attended training sponsored by the Community College of the Air Force, you may be asked to secure transcripts directly from that institution. Check with your degree-granting college for any additional records they may require. Remember that ACE only makes "credit recommendations." Colleges are free to limit the number and types of ACE military credits they will accept in transfer.

CAUTIONS ON CREDIT FOR EXPERIENCE OPTIONS

CAUTION: WATCH FOR LIMITS ON CREDIT FOR EXPERIENCE

Is it possible to earn a college degree based solely on what you already know or through a combination of credit for experience programs? The cautious answer is yes, sometimes, but rarely. It may be possible for you to earn an entire degree or college credential without taking any college courses simply by using combinations of the alternative credit means we have discussed in this chapter. A few people I've worked with have successfully earned certificates, associate's degrees, and bachelor's degrees, or met graduate school prerequisites, solely through judicial use of alternative means. These people are college graduates who have literally never been to college.

In order to earn a degree solely through alternative means, you would have to attend a college that operates as an assessment college, not as a teaching college. The most famous assessment colleges are two special distance-learning colleges: Thomas Edison State College of New Jersey, and Regents College of the University of the State of New York. No campus visits and no formal coursework is required for degrees from either of these colleges. However, most students who attend these two colleges do take some formal college courses to earn their degrees, especially at the bachelor's level. (For more information on Thomas Edison State College and Regents College see chapter 4 on distance-learning colleges.)

Colleges that have residency requirements, or teaching colleges, commonly accept only a limited number of credits in transfer from other colleges or from any combination of alternative means. For example, most colleges limit the number of challenge exam credits they will accept to 30 credits or one year of college, likewise for portfolio or ACE credits. Typically, the last 30 semester credits (the senior year) of any regionally accredited bachelor's degree must commonly be taken directly from your degree-granting college in formal coursework. These last 30 credits usually cannot be substituted with challenge exam, portfolio, or ACE credits.

CAUTION: CREDIT FOR EXPERIENCE IS NOT USUALLY FREE

Many older learners are enticed by the idea of earning a college degree based on their experience, or at long last being able to turn a dozen patchwork transcripts into one solid degree. Assessment programs attract these kinds of students. If you work with an assessment program be prepared that they may charge you hefty fees. Even if you use a teaching college, you will commonly be subject to "assessment fees" to have your challenge exams or portfolio credits evaluated and placed on your degree transcript.

What is an assessment fee? An assessment fee is what is charged for the services associated with reviewing and approving transfer and alternative-degree credits. Teaching colleges make their money primarily from course tuition—teaching—not from assessment. Learners enroll in a course and pay the tuition for that one course. Instead of charging course tuition, assessment colleges charge assessment fees to learners who want to have their credits transferred, reviewed, transcripted, and "consolidated" into a single academic credential.

If you are considering several colleges, compare them carefully for the fees they charge to use any alternative means of earning credit. Very few colleges charge no fees for these services. A few colleges charge as much per credit to use these services as they charge to take a regular course. It is possible that 30 credits earned through exam and portfolio could cost you nothing, $300 dollars, or more than $3,000. The final cost of earning credits through alternative means will depend on how much your college of choice charges you to use these assessment methods.

Caution: Transferring Alternative Credits Can Be Tricky

Transferring credits earned via portfolio or challenge exams can be tricky. Transferring credits earned through alternative means is always trickier than transferring credits earned through attending formal classes. For example, Regents College of the University of the State of New York, one of the most lenient assessment colleges, routinely accepts portfolio credits documented through Ohio University or Thomas Edison State College. But Regents only sometimes accepts portfolio credits documented through Indiana University.

A few colleges use the "block" method of awarding portfolio credits. In the block method you are not awarded credits for individual courses. Instead, a faculty review panel may recommend that a block of credits, say 15 credits, be awarded for your total experience of starting and running a small business for twenty years. The college gives you 15 business credits on your transcript. If you have block credits from previous portfolio assessments, ask your new college if they accept block credits in transfer. Block awards will be the most difficult to transfer. Many colleges that otherwise accept portfolio credits in transfer will exclude block awards from consideration.

7

BACK IN COLLEGE: REAL LIFE STRATEGIES FOR SUCCESS

Getting admitted and registered for your first class takes a lot of planning and effort. Unfortunately, you can't sit on your educational laurels for long. The bell rings—or beeps like a sick alarm clock, because it's all electronic these days—and class begins.

*Y*our first lesson: How to be a student again.

What's it like being a student in today's more open and nontraditional college classroom? Why is everyone sitting in a circle, not in a neat row? What happened to the chalkboard, and why is there no card catalog in the library? In fact, why do there seem to be no books in the college library, only blinking, blue computer terminals that demand not your library card but your student access code?

Much has changed about the classroom, the campus, and the role of the student in the last decade. This chapter is designed to help you learn how to deal with the new collegiate classroom and with innovations like the bookless electronic library.

FEEL FREE TO ASK STUPID QUESTIONS

Every crackerjack college kid should know the following: There are no stupid questions. You are back in college, and college is literally a foreign country to you. It doesn't matter that you have chosen to attend a college located only a mile from your home. Colleges are miniature villages or learning communities. Like all villages, colleges have rules and a local language all their own.

Your advisor may rattle off terms that mean little to you: prerequisite, proctor, and academic progress. You may find yourself secretly searching in the dictionary or the back of your college catalog for the definitions of these strange terms. The librarian may point you to computer terminals and tell you that everything you need to know is now online. That's fine, provided you know how to get online, but what if you don't?

Arriving back on campus after years of living in the real world can be a tremendous shock. The best way to cope with "campus shock" is to understand that it is normal. Perfectly normal. Tourists who travel to foreign countries frequently experience culture shock. Culture shock is what happens to people when they are taken out of their familiar, everyday environment and placed in an environment where everyday things are done differently. Being on campus means adjusting to a new vocabulary and a new role—that of a student.

> Campus shock is what happens to normal adults when they are taken out of their comfortable everyday roles as parents, bosses, truck drivers, and nurses, and placed into a structured academic environment.

HOW TO BE A CLASS ACT IN CLASS

One of the most frequent back to school questions I hear from older learners is "How should I act in the classroom?" The answer: "Like a decent human being." The truth is that your professor will appreciate good manners, as will your fellow students. In fact, one of the things that I enjoy about teaching older students is that they generally have better manners and social skills than younger students. Good manners—things like holding up your hand to ask questions, arriving on time, paying attention when others are talking, and not talking during lectures—are essential ingredients in a good learning environment. If the classroom is chaotic, no one will learn.

STUDY THE SYLLABUS

The first session of every class should include an introduction to the material that will be covered, as well as an introduction to how your class will be administered. You should receive a syllabus or course outline at the first session of every class. A syllabus is an important item. The syllabus will lay out your weekly reading assignments, your homework assignments, and information on how you will be graded in the class. It will tell you when papers are due, and when exams will occur. Keep the syllabus close at hand. Use it to plan your weekly study sessions for each class.

UNDERSTAND THE GRADING CRITERIA

Study the syllabus to make sure you understand what criteria will be used to judge your progress and to award your final grade. All professors do not use the same criteria to award grades. A few professors may make your grade dependent on the results of only two exams, a midterm, and a final. Others may not use exams at all. In place of exams you may be asked to write papers or make classroom presentations.

It is helpful to note that not at all professors use the same criteria in grading a student's performance. If you feel that you learn better through using certain methods, such as written papers, rather than others, such as exams, you should compare different professors on the criteria they are using in different sections of the same class. For example, it is highly likely that the Psychology 101 class has several sections. Each section probably meets at a different time, and with a different professor. If you attend the first session of any class and feel that you do not like either the professor or the grading criteria, remember that you can usually switch class sessions. You may discover that Professor Arner who teaches Psychology 101 at 6 p.m. on Wednesday is a better match for you than Professor Wingnut who teaches the same class at 6 p.m. on Thursdays.

Can the professor or the grading criteria used in a class make much difference? Absolutely! Some professors are much better at making learning interesting and fun. The more interesting and fun a course is, the more likely it is that you will attend and be motivated to learn. One of the most important things to look for in an instructor is a sense of humor. Studies have shown that professors who have a sense of humor make it easier to learn material of all types.

Also, everyone does not learn in the same way. Some people learn best when they are required to use their memories. People who have good memories are usually good test-takers because they can retain a lot of facts. But memory is only one small component of intelligence. Other people learn best and can display it best by writing papers. People who do well at writing papers usually love to research and organize information in written form. Still others may excel at showing what they know through oral forms like classroom presentations and debates.

Because people learn in different ways and have different strengths, it is important that you understand and respect this in yourself as a student. It makes sense that you seek out classes where the grading criteria are based on the type of learning presentations that you enjoy the most.

COME PREPARED

A common mistake that many students make is waiting to study or do any work in a class until the last minute. Many students do not read the syllabus, let alone the textbook, until the week before the first exam. This is a mistake. The most effective way to learn is step by step. Learn a little every week, and it will amount up to a much better learning experience for you. In addition, learning a little every week will mean that you arrive at crucial points in the class prepared for quizzes or exams without going through exam panic.

Most classes meet every week. Make sure then that you prepare for your classes every week. Check the syllabus and complete all assigned reading before class starts. If you arrive at each class with your reading completed you will find that class makes more sense to you. What you hear in the class, whether through lecture or discussion, will help reinforce the material that you have read on your own. The best students in every class are those that prepare every week and come to class ready to ask questions and participate. (We cover how to establish a weekly study schedule in chapter 8: The Personal Juggling Act.)

PARTICIPATE IN CLASS

Not everyone likes to talk in class. In fact, only a few vocal students commandeer most classroom discussions. Most students sit quietly making little comment. We strongly recommend that you try to comment at least once in every class session.

Why? Because asking questions or making comments on someone else's questions is another way of reinforcing what you have already learned by reading on your own. Asking questions or making comments is like studying out loud. It gives you a chance to understand better what your textbook and other reading materials have presented to you in written form. If you suffer from dyslexia or other reading disorders, classroom discussions and questions may be an invaluable way to understand material that makes less sense to you in written form.

If you feel too shy to talk in class, make a point of asking your professor or classmates about things before or after class. Most professors arrive a little early and leave a little late for their classes because they understand that some students prefer to ask questions in private. Also, if your class has a break halfway through, feel free to use this time to approach your instructor and ask for help. Most professors are happy to answer questions whenever you feel like asking them.

MASTER THE ART OF NOTE-TAKING

If your class is mostly lecture or lab work you will want to take notes. As with speaking up in class, note-taking will also help reinforce what you have read and what the professor is saying. Taking down spoken ideas on paper is a very helpful way of studying. In general, the more ways you can review and rehearse class information the better your retention will be for exams and quizzes.

*M*any students do not know how to take notes.

This is another skill your college can help you master. Lessons in note-taking are generally offered for incoming students as part of the free orientation sessions that cover things such as how to use the library. If your note-taking skills have never been Grade A, make sure you brush up on this skill as part of your return to college.

Many colleges now require that incoming students who want to earn degrees take a first semester course in reading comprehension and basic essay writing. These courses, called English 101 or Basic Freshman Composition, often cover note-taking, how to outline material so you can study it better, and how to write and reference basic college papers.

ASK FOR ASSISTANCE

If your class requires written papers, it may be helpful to look at sample papers from previous classes. Most professors keep a file of papers from past classes. If you have not written a paper in a while, ask if your college has a learning center or tutors that give tips and assistance in researching and writing papers. If this is your first paper in a long while, ask the professor if you can submit an outline or draft of your paper a few weeks before the final paper is due. The professor can then read your outline or draft and give you crucial feedback on how to improve your paper while it is still in development.

When it comes to writing papers many students mistakenly feel that they should be able to write a complete paper during one sitting. But even professional writers write their papers in drafts, and they often make an outline first. They may do some research and draft a few paragraphs about the points in their outlines, and then wait a few days and draft some more. It can take several days or weeks to write a good paper. Do not be afraid to write in drafts. Writing this way will pay off in the long run.

If, at any point in a class, you feel that you are falling behind or that you need special assistance, take immediate action. Every class exists to help you learn something. If you do not learn that something, then the class itself is not succeeding. The best thing you can do is to give yourself every possible advantage in doing well now that you are back in college.

FAILING OR TAKING AN INCOMPLETE

If you find yourself failing a course or feel that you are in over your head, talk to your instructor. In most cases, if you are too far behind to catch up, you can withdraw from a class with no penalty on your academic records. We mention this option because colleges used to always note if a student withdrew from a class at a time when she or he was failing or not doing well. College registrars used to note "Withdrawal/Failing" on transcripts so that such withdrawals were permanently and embarrassingly recorded on public grade transcripts. A few colleges still use this embarrassing designation, but most are more concerned with helping you address whatever is keeping you from succeeding than they are with embarrassing you.

In some cases, if you have completed most of the work for your class, but you cannot complete a final paper or exam on time, you should be eligible to file for a temporary "Incomplete." Your instructor can explain the "Incomplete" option to you. In most cases you must file a form with your instructor that specifies exactly when you will complete all the requirements for the class. For example, maybe you were almost done with your final paper when your kids caught the flu or your boss required overtime work for a week. In most cases, you can usually arrange to submit a final paper or take an exam two or three weeks later than the rest of the class.

LEARN TO USE THE LIBRARY

If you are serious about succeeding as a college student you will need to know where the library is and how to use it. You must know this or you will not be able to research and write the kind of papers that a college education requires. One of the things that adult students fear most about going back to school is that someone will discover that they do not know how to use a library.

The truth: Only about one in ten adults actually know how to use a library.

The sooner you learn how to use a library the sooner you will begin to excel in your college studies. How do you learn to use a library? There are so many people that do not know how to use a library that all colleges offer library orientation sessions or courses for new students. New York University, one of our nation's largest providers of continuing education for older learners, offers an adult transition seminar at the beginning of each semester. One of the skills covered in this seminar is learning how to use the NYU library. Similarly, the Community College of Vermont offers a free workshop called Library Skills and Resources. If you want to learn how to use your local college library, simply call your librarian and ask her or him when the next orientation session begins.

TEST-TAKING: LEARN ANTI-ANXIETY STRATEGIES

*A*lmost everyone is afraid of tests, even students that do well.

Why all the fear? Anytime we are being tested we are being judged. In the case of a college test, if you do not pass the test, you may not pass the course. If you do not pass a test, you may feel that you are stupid. Doing poorly on any test can bring up issues of insecurity and feelings of failure. We all fear tests because they involve judgment, and we all want to avoid failure.

How can you deal with test anxiety? First, realize that everyone feels test anxiety. Test anxiety is normal. Second, sign up for a test anxiety workshop at your college so you can learn productive ways to to reduce test anxiety. The Community College of Vermont, for example, offers free one-day workshops that teach enrolled students how to take tests of all types. We have never seen a college that does not offer some sort of test-taking help. Usually tutors or professors offer this service through campus student services or library services. If your college does not offer any help with test anxiety, refer to our self-help steps below.

What will you learn in a test-taking workshop? The Vermont workshop teaches students how to read, analyze, and respond to open-book, objective, essay, and other types of exams. One of the most important skills you can learn is how to take different types of tests. It is worth mentioning that people who do poorly on tests are often people who never learned how to take tests. Test-taking is a skill. It is a skill that can be learned just as you learn how to write better papers.

For example, different skills are required to do well on multiple-choice tests than on essay tests. Multiple-choice tests will present you with four or five possible answers and ask you to select the correct one. Multiple-choice tests actually test your recall—that is your ability to recall a correct answer when you see it presented on paper. Recall is a simple form of long-term memory. If you know that you are going to be taking a multiple-choice test you will naturally want to focus on memorizing a lot of factual information. Essay exams, on the other hand, do not give you answers to select from. Instead, essay exams ask you to blindly write answers to complex questions. If you know that you are going to be taking an essay exam, you will want to study the connections and relationships among different issues that you have studied. If you need to memorize facts—the required stuff of multiple-choice tests—you will not study in the same way that you would if you knew you were going to be called on to point out connections and relationships or write summaries—the stuff of essay exams. To help reduce test-taking anxiety, you should always make sure that you know exactly what kind of exam you will be taking. This will enable you to study in a way that will help you retain the kind of information that the exam will be testing.

We summarize below other skills that you can master, either on your own or as a part of a class on test taking. These five self-help steps will reduce your test anxiety and improve your exam scores.

1. Review Sample Exams

Ask your professor if you can review sample exams. In some cases, professors place old exams or sample versions on file in the college library or student services office. Reading through old exams can help you understand and prepare psychologically for the real thing.

2. Use Practice Quizzes

Most textbooks have end-of-chapter quizzes and self-tests. It is easy to skip these sample exams. We'd advise you to always take these self-tests. Moreover, you should take these end-of-chapter tests every week until you achieve a passing score on each of them.

Taking a self-test or quiz each week will help reinforce your memory. In addition, many midterm and final exams are not written by college professors themselves. Most exams are put together these days by your professor from a bank of test questions and sample exams that are written by your textbook author. The chances that your real test will include questions identical to or similar to your end-of-chapter quizzes are very high. By practicing the end-of-chapter exams, you may be practicing the real exam more closely than you realize.

3. Use Self-Study Guides

Most textbooks come with paperback study guides. These study guides generally contain chapter outlines, definitions of key terms introduced in your textbook, and additional sample quizzes or tests. Many professors require students to purchase these study guides and use them as weekly workbooks to help reinforce their studying. The study guide can be an excellent tutor and study buddy. By working through the study guide each week you will greatly improve your understanding and memory of what you have read in the textbook. If your professor does not require you to purchase and use the study guide ask the bookstore to order it for you anyway. There is no better or cheaper tutor than a programmed study guide. The practice quizzes and exams they contain are often worth their weight in gold.

4. Join a Study Group

Some people have poor study habits and test-taking skills while others have excellent ones. One of the best ways to get help with your studies and reduce test-taking anxiety is to join with a study buddy or a study group. Ask others in your class if they want to join a study group with you. The advantage to belonging to your own study group is that members of the group can quiz each other on class material weekly and construct and give each other sample exams or quizzes. In some cases, if a member of the group is especially good at taking tests, he or she can help other members of the group master better test-taking habits.

5. Ask for Assistance

Many people do not realize that they can ask for help while an exam is in progress. If you encounter questions that do not make sense to you, remember that you can raise your hand and ask for assistance. If you are not sure if a question means one thing or another, ask the instructor for clarification before answering.

If you get your test back and you disagree with the grading, make an appointment to speak with your instructor. Instructors can make mistakes in their grading. Moreover, sometimes test questions are ambiguous, and you can genuinely argue that your chosen answer is as correct as any.

FACE UP TO YOUR ENGLISH AND MATH PHOBIAS

Most college students are terrified of either math or English. Some are terrified of both. This terror is real. It is real enough that we've seen very talented people drop out of college without even attempting a math or English course. And we've encountered not a few brilliant people who flunked their basic math or English courses decades ago and still have nightmares about it.

We were all *made* to take math and English several times in our schooling. People have different aptitudes and types of intelligence. Some people are very good at manipulating numbers, and so they excel at math. Some people are very good at manipulating words, and so they excel at English. Few people excel equally at both types of skills. Chances are you found yourself less than perfect in either math or English at some time in your grade school or high school career, perhaps many times. Those of us who were not fortunate enough to have good teachers who took the time to teach us at our own pace ended up afraid of math or English.

Most people who fear one of these subjects can trace their feelings of failure as far back as grade school. The very idea of taking math, to some, brings up childlike feelings of being back in the third grade failing at math up at the blackboard while the entire class watched. The same with English. Most who fear English assignments can trace these feelings back to grade school. "I'm just not good at English or math!" they cry, even though they have not taken an English or math class for thirty years.

WHY DEAL WITH YOUR PHOBIAS?

First, it is essential if you want to succeed at college. Almost every college class requires some writing, and how well you express yourself in writing is highly correlated with grade point average.

Second, almost every degree will include a requirement in math or quantitative analysis. You will have to take less math to earn a degree than you will English, but you will almost always be required to take one or two courses in math to earn any kind of degree.

HOW TO DEAL WITH YOUR PHOBIAS

Even though the idea of approaching a multiplication table or an essay may make you feel ill, it is indeed possible for you to learn to deal with such phobias in a straightforward manner. College can teach you this.

First, check with your college to see if they have math and English tutoring or remedial classes. Most do. Rio Salado Community College, in Tempe, Arizona, for example, offers their students a Learning Assistance Center. The Center provides free tutoring for students enrolled in English, math, reading, accounting, biology, and foreign language courses.

In addition to taking preparatory remedial courses, Rio Salado students can obtain tutoring in groups, individually, or on the phone as they study at home using an innovative Beep-A-Tutor program. Like many colleges these days, especially community and two-year colleges, Rio Salado assumes that many students will need some type of special assistance to rectify old self-defeating fears and succeed in college.

DON'T LET THE WORD *REMEDIAL* SCARE YOU

Taking a remedial course is often the only way that you are going to get the invaluable chance to master the basics again. The worst thing you can do is try to ignore your fear and register for a class that you may not be ready for. If you do, you will end up reinforcing the idea that you cannot do the task at hand.

Most colleges require incoming students to take placement exams to honestly assess their skill levels in math and English. The results of these exams are used to place incoming students in the appropriate level of course. Do not be disheartened if you are told that you need to take a remedial or refresher course. Welcome it as an opportunity to build the kind of academic understanding that you will need to excel in college.

BE BRAVE AND BUILD A SOLID FOUNDATION

Do not be afraid to start with the basics and work your way up. Most people who fear math and English do so because they missed the basics. Because they do not understand the basic rules they cannot perform higher level functions. Trying to do college-level math or English without laying a solid foundation is like trying to build a skyscraper on top of a pile of quicksand. It will eventually fall apart, and so will your academic career.

TREAT ENGLISH AND MATH AS FOREIGN LANGUAGES

People think that either you understand math or English or you don't. This is not a productive way to think. While it is true that some people are naturally better at math or English than others, it is also true that anyone can learn math or English if they take the time and care to master the basic rules of both disciplines.

The best advice we have ever heard about how to approach math or English is to approach both as foreign languages. Go ahead. Open a math book and say, "This all looks like another language to me." This is how most people feel: that math and English make no sense to them; that they might as well be reading Greek.

The truth is that math is a foreign language. If you do not know the basic vocabulary of how to multiply, divide, and treat equations you will not be able to solve a word problem. You must learn and practice the basic rules of math the same way you would learn the vocabulary and rules of a new language.

We are all much more comfortable with the English we speak than with the English we write.

The same advice can be applied to English. Pick up an English grammar book and say, "This is a foreign language to me." The truth is, formal, written English is a foreign language. You do not need to know where to put a semicolon when you speak. You just talk, pausing where it seems appropriate. But when you write down your ideas, you must learn the complex rules that come with writing as opposed to speaking. We all know how to speak English. Writing it requires that we literally learn the complex rules of a foreign language.

It's okay if math and English feel like foreign languages to you. Approach them as you would any foreign language. Give yourself permission to learn them as you would any foreign language, one word at a time.

UNDERSTAND YOUR DEGREE REQUIREMENTS

Colleges have their own rules and regulations. They also speak their own language when it comes to things like prerequisites, general education options, and academic units or credits. It is never too early to make an appointment with an academic advisor and review your standing in relation to the requirements for any degree that you have chosen or may choose down the road.

Many people do not choose a formal major or area of degree specialty until their second or third year of college. In thinking of a major, consult your college catalog. The catalog will contain a listing of all the courses that are required to earn any particular type of degree. Review these listings soon after you enroll so you know what will be required of you. If any of the degree requirements mentioned in your catalog do not make sense to you, make an appointment to discuss them with an advisor.

It is important to realize that failure to understand or follow degree requirements can mean that you waste both time and money taking courses that may not help you toward your final goal of earning a degree or professional certificate. To prevent this, understand the requirements of your chosen program as early as possible in your academic career.

CONSIDER DESIGNING YOUR OWN DEGREE

You find yourself enrolled in college and doing well, but then you discover that the college you are attending does not offer a specialty in an area that intrigues you. You may still be able to stay at the college of your choice and complete an individualized major.

For example, one woman decided, halfway through her traditional English literature degree, that she wanted to study the publishing industry. Her goal was to open her own small publishing firm to publish children's books and learning products. Although her local college did not offer a formal major or area of specialty in publishing or children's literature, she was able to design several independent studies to teach herself about publishing. With the help of her advisor, some of the faculty in the English department, and by looking at the course offerings and requirements of several colleges offering formal degrees in publishing; she then designed independent studies that closely mirrored these formal degrees.

Many colleges support individualized independent study programs within their regular curriculum and offerings. New York University, for example, supports a special division called the Gallatin School of Individualized

Study. Faculty mentors at Gallatin help students use independent study and readings, work internships, and courses offered across different departments and universities to custom-design degrees that meet unusual career and life needs.

Hofstra University, in Hempstead, New York, also offers a special program for people who want to design their own degrees. The program is called New College. Hofstra's New College is modeled after the first New College of Oxford University in England. Under the New College system, students, generally older adults, design unique degrees around main subject areas. New College students work with faculty to design learning contracts. Learning contracts are like course syllabi. They define exactly what is to be studied, for example the history of American publishing. They then outline the learning activities that the student will complete in lieu of formal weekly classes. Such learning activities may include independent readings of classic books or journals in the subject area, attendance at special seminars or events, interviews with working professionals, maybe even a semester-long work internship in the study area.

Even if your college does not operate a formal New College, it probably has some provision for letting students design custom courses or degree majors. Never assume that the majors listed in your college's catalog are the only majors that you can study at your chosen school.

You should always look for ways to individualize your program of study to better meet your unique needs.

One word of caution. Some majors are regulated by professional licensing agencies. State or national institutions, rather than colleges themselves, regulate such licensing agencies. For example, pharmacists, nurses, radiologists, teachers, social workers, psychologists, architects, and engineers are a few of the professions that may require learners to earn specially regulated degrees that are offered only by specially accredited college departments. Speak with your advisor or career counselor to see if you can design an individualized degree that will meet state or national licensing requirements in your intended career area.

8 THE PERSONAL JUGGLING ACT: TIME AND LIFE MANAGEMENT TIPS

If you are a single parent, a member of the single largest back-to-school group in the nation, you may need to juggle child care along with your collegiate concerns. Both women and men face fears about how to do it all and stay sane as they assume higher profile roles as single parents and as sole family breadwinners.

Unlike the traditional 18-year-old college kid, as the older adult you will probably have to negotiate your return to college with a significant other, a boss, children, perhaps even parents. Sharp study skills and native intelligence are great to have as collegiate companions, but native smarts alone won't earn you a degree. To return to college and stay sane you will need to develop almost superhuman time- and life-management skills.

This chapter is designed to help you learn how to negotiate for the time and support you will need from your children, significant others, parents, and employers as you begin your journey back to college.

TIME MANAGEMENT 101: YOUR TICKET TO SUCCESS

One of the most common complaints in modern life is the shortage of time. While I can't wave a magic wand and increase your waking hours, I can show you proven steps that can help you stretch your time and use it more wisely.

STEP 1: DETERMINE HOW MUCH TIME YOU HAVE

When working adults, especially parents, think about going back to school, many see no way to squeeze college into their hectic daily routines. They feel they have no time to explore schools, fill out financial aid paperwork, or commute to a class, let alone study for exams! Feeling they have no time, many adults throw in the towel and give up on their dream of college. The truth is that, technically, the average working American has about 30 hours of free time per week. That's right: 30 hours. The key is learning how to manage your time as tightly as many manage their money.

Keep a Time Log

Start saving your time the same way you would start saving your money. Keep track of your time for two weeks or fourteen days. Get a small note-book and write down what you do each day, hour by hour, from the time you wake up until your head hits the pillow. Keeping track of time during your work hours should be easy. There is little free time inside most workdays, unless you are self-employed.

Pay special attention to what you do with your time before and after work, and on weekends. You may not arrive home from work until 7 p.m., but what do you do after that? You may do the housework every Saturday morning from 9 a.m. to 11 a.m., but what do you do after that?

Isolate Chunks of Free Time

Once you have a log of your time, go through it with a red pen. Circle potential free time, times when you could have done something other than what you were doing. You may be surprised to discover how many red time circles exist in your life.

> The most common culprit of free time is TV. Most adults spend about 20 hours per week of their free time watching TV.

We are not suggesting that you never watch TV; We are suggesting that you give up watching the TV programs that do not really interest you. Keep watching your favorite TV shows. Reducing your TV time can result in as much as 10 free hours of time per week that you can then devote to your education. Ten hours of free time is enough to launch any educational plan.

Start Out Part-Time

Remind yourself that you do not have to attend school full-time. Almost all adult students attend college part-time while continuing to work full-time. Full-time study is defined as taking four or more courses each quarter or semester. Part-time study is defined as taking two or fewer courses per semester or quarter.

Many adults take only one course their first semester back in college. "One course!" you cry. "What good will one course do me? I need a whole degree!" Yes, it is true that you will probably need more than one course. You will need about thirty courses to earn an associate's degree and about sixty courses to earn a bachelor's degree.

What good will one course do you? A world of good. That one course, that first course, will determine whether or not you ultimately earn the degree or career credential of your dreams. As the old Chinese proverb goes, "A journey of a thousand miles begins with a single step." Look at your first course as the first stepping stone toward your degree.

How do you know how many courses you can take at a time and remain sane? The best way is to figure that each course will require about 5 hours of study time per week. Some courses, especially courses where you may need tutoring, can require up to 7 hours of study time per week. If you plan to enroll in two courses, be prepared to put aside a total of from 10 to 14 hours of study time per week.

STEP 2: PUT YOUR DREAMS AND GOALS IN WRITING

Earning a degree or career credential will not be easy. You will encounter a lot of obstacles. Though it may sound silly now, we strongly encourage you to write down why you want to return to college. Write down all your reasons and put them where you will see them often, like the refrigerator or the bathroom mirror.

Below are some of the reasons our clients have pasted to their bathroom mirrors. Note that there are no good or bad reasons. College is your dream. Feel free to list as many reasons as possible for why a college education is important to you.

*C*ollege Is Important to Me Because I Want . . .

To prove to myself that I am as intelligent as I feel

To get a better job

To qualify for a raise

To change my career

To make my children proud of me

To understand the world better

To learn how to paint in oil colors

To qualify to take the public accountancy exam

To learn how to speak French and tour France next summer

To learn how to write a novel

To enhance my knowledge of literature

Learn to Do the 1-2-3

Next, learn to do what we call the 1-2-3. List the first three steps that you must complete this week in your journey toward a better education. These steps will vary based on where you are in your educational process. If you have not yet investigated colleges, your first step might be to call the admission offices at colleges A, B, and C and ask for admission packets and catalogs, and so on, as illustrated below.

1. Call colleges A, B, and C and ask for admission packets.

2. Call the financial aid offices of colleges A, B, and C and ask for financial aid packets.

3. Friday night, March 13, from 7 to 9 p.m., read all college catalogs and make a new 1-2-3 list.

Notice that every 1-2-3 list should end with the mandate that once you've completed your existing 1-2-3s you must make a new 1-2-3 list. Why do the 1-2-3? Because doing your 1-2-3s on a weekly basis will give you a sane step-by-step plan to keep you moving toward your long-term goal. Think of each 1-2-3 list as a single stepping stone down a very long path. At the end of that path is your degree or career credential.

STEP 3: CREATE A PRIVATE LEARNING ENVIRONMENT

Many adults return to college only to drop out three weeks into their studies. Why? One of the most common reasons is that they were not prepared to take their studies seriously. By this we mean that they came home with some books and a course syllabus, and then they sat these on the dresser for a week. When it was time to go to class again they picked their books up off the dresser and lugged them to class. They never found the time to sit down and read their first or second week's assignments. After three weeks of lugging their textbooks around, but not reading them, or doing any homework, they found themselves too far behind to catch up. They panicked and dropped out of college.

Claim a Study Space

How can you guard against premature dropping out? The first step is to look around your house and find a place that you can claim as your own. It is crucial that you find and claim a private, quiet study place. Many people find their study space in the family garage, in the basement, in the attic, or in the laundry room. One woman converted her grown children's backyard tree house into a study den. Single parents often love to set up a study station close to the washer and dryer so they can do the laundry and study on the same night.

After you've claimed your study space, make sure that everyone in the family understands it is your sacred space. Set up a desk with a lamp and some notebooks and several good pens. Organize everything in and around the desk the same way you organized your desk when you were in grade school. This means you should make it a personal and comfortable study space. Now, when you come home from school, drop your books and study materials at your study station. This way you will always be prepared to study when the time comes.

STEP 4: MAKE A STUDY PLAN AND STICK TO IT

Now that you have a study place it is time to make a study schedule. In fact, your first task at your study space should be to make a time schedule. Remember, if you have registered to take one class per week, you will need to establish a home-study schedule of about five hours per week.

Go back and check your time log. Decide what two times each week will make for the best study times. Pick two times that are at least two hours long each, for example, Wednesday nights 7–9 p.m. and Sunday night 6–8 p.m.

We advise you to pick two days for regular study time because it is best to read new chapters and materials and take notes the first time you study, then go back a few days later and review your reading and work on any written homework or materials.

Now that you have identified your regular study times, make sure you tell everyone in the family. Post a notice on the refrigerator that you will be studying at predetermined times each week. Ask family members to respect this time. Make sure everyone understands that you are not to be disturbed during your study time.

Even if you are not yet registered for college, now is a good time to claim your study space. Set up your study station. Begin using your scheduled study times to do the research necessary to complete your back-to-school plans. Make your first 1-2-3 list and continue from there to hatch a complete back-to-school plan.

STEP 5: COMBAT PROCRASTINATION AND PERFECTIONISM

Once you've made the decision to return to school, you may find that you are getting cold feet. Maybe you've enrolled in your first class, but it's not a class you really like; instead it is a dreaded required class. You may be tempted to skip your study times or put off reading your textbook. Don't. Never skip a study time. Make it a rule to always sit down at your study station at study time. Do this even if you don't have pressing homework to complete. Keeping a tight schedule will help prevent procrastination.

If you find yourself sitting at your desk and staring at your books but not actually reading, remind yourself that you only have to study for X amount of time. Set a timer. At the end of that time close the book and give yourself a break.

If you feel yourself growing frustrated or afraid that you'll not be able to master everything all at once, step back and give yourself a break. Remind yourself to take it one chapter at a time. Don't look at all the pages you still have to read. Focus only on the pages that you have to read within your given study time.

If procrastination and perfectionism begin to immobilize you, seek help. Your college probably runs workshops as well as counseling sessions to help students learn how to relax, overcome procrastination, and study more effectively. Never be afraid to seek out help. Better study habits and time management are two great things that you can learn at college that will help you in your daily life.

STEP 6: PLAN FOR CHILD AND ELDER CARE ISSUES

If you have children, you'll need to plan for their care when you go back to college. For most working adults the option of paid, professional child care is an expensive one. Moreover, most professional daycare centers are not open weekends or late at night, times when most adults enroll in classes. Scout around for ideas when considering your child-care options. Below is a list of options to consider.

Check for a College Day-Care Center: Your college may operate a care center for children. Your college may operate this center free, or at minimal cost for students and faculty.

Check with Older Neighbors: Many retired people are looking for extra odd jobs that can be done from their own homes.

Check with Family Members: Perhaps your sister will baby-sit for you if you then agree to take her kids for a weekend or two—you can suggest that she and her husband have a romantic weekend free of children and interruptions.

Form a Parent Pool with Fellow Students: Chances are you will be attending class with other people who are parents. Ask people in your class if they want to start a parent pool. You may be able to watch your classmate's kids on Wednesday nights when she has calculus in exchange for her watching your kids on Monday night when you have computer programming.

STEP 7: SEEK THE SUPPORT OF SIGNIFICANT OTHERS

It is usually a huge decision to return to college at midlife. People attend college for many reasons, and most people who return to college as adults do so with a fierce determination to succeed. What many are not prepared for is the opposition that the idea sometimes stirs up—in their spouses, in their children, and even in their own parents.

Why would someone oppose someone else's earning a college degree? There are many reasons. Husbands, for example, may fear that they will look dumber once their wives earn a degree. Wives may worry that their husbands will get too chummy with their younger study buddies. Your parents may feel that college is for kids and that you are too old to cut the academic mustard. I have seen the parents of 45-year-old college students literally insist that any extra family income go toward educating the grandchildren instead. Children are very often threatened and take great offense to mom or dad turning over chores such as making dinner in an effort to steal back more study time.

People have all sorts of ideas about what is appropriate behavior and what is not. Chances are someone in your family will simply not be in favor of your determined midlife march toward a college degree or career credential. It may be very difficult for you to disappoint those that you love. What we recommend is that you stand firm. Remind your loved ones that contrary to how they feel, your return to college is not meant to take anything from them; it is meant only to give more to you. Point out that they too will share in your eventual rewards, such as your increased income and heightened self-esteem.

STEP 8: SEEK THE SUPPORT OF YOUR EMPLOYER

All people do not handle going back to school in the same way. Some people are very excited about being a college kid, so they tell the world about their new classes. Other people are embarrassed by the fact that they do not have a formal education. These people tend to keep quiet because they do not want to draw attention to the fact that they have not yet earned a college degree.

You alone must decide how to handle public announcements that you are about to buy a book bag and become a college kid. Keeping quiet about your college plans may make it difficult for you to get the support you need at work. For example, you may need to leave work fifteen minutes early on Wednesdays to make your nursing class. If so, you may need to tell your immediate supervisor that you are enrolled in a college class.

Is it always smart to tell your boss and coworkers that you are back in college? This is a decision that you will need to make based on how well you know your boss and your working situation. In my experience, most employers are extremely supportive of employees returning to college. Most bosses will gladly arrange for slight alterations in work schedules to help you out. Furthermore, as we discuss in chapter 9, many employers will subsidize at least part of their employee's tuition and training bills.

STEP 9: EXPLORE YOUR COLLEGE'S SUPPORT RESOURCES

Returning to college is a time of great stress as well as great joy. It can often be an emotional time because college students face a lot of stress. It is hard to be back in school doing algebra homework at the same time as your own children. It is hard being back in college looking at new career options and wondering how you will ever make that big career change. It is hard doing all the paperwork and budgeting that college requires. It can also be scary to take out educational loans, even small ones.

One of the nicest things about college campuses is that they often offer a lot of free or low-cost support services. For example, many colleges offer day care, support groups for older students, mental health counseling, medical and dental plans, career counseling, tutoring for English as a second language, access to adaptive technologies for the learning impaired, career internship programs, family counseling, and even free access to the campus health center, gym, and pool.

If you find yourself depressed or stressed out during your first semester, explore the counseling services that your college offers. Most colleges offer free support groups where single parents can get together to blow off steam and get support for how hard it is to be single and a college kid at the same time. Most colleges also offer free or low-cost family or couples counseling if the stress of returning to school proves too much for you and your significant other.

Exercise is one of the best stress busters. A free campus gym pass could literally keep you up and running. Also, if you have children, it may be possible for you to spend Saturday morning in the campus library cracking the books while your kids go swimming.

9 Money Matters: Financing Your College Education

First, the bad news: The cost of higher education has skyrocketed in the last decade. According to annual surveys by *U.S. News & World Report,* tuition at regionally accredited colleges rose about 33 percent from 1986 to 1996, while the median family income rose less than .3 percent in that same ten-year period.

The average family income in 1998 was $35,000, while the average cost of one year of tuition and room and board at a private college in the United States was about $20,000. Ouch! While costs have risen drastically, the amount of student aid available through government sources has declined over the years. The system of government aid available to students of any age is far from perfect.

The average college graduate leaves campus burdened with a debt of $13,500. And that is the average student. Those who attend private colleges often have loans in excess of this by the time they put on their mortarboards and march up the aisle. Yes, you can earn a college degree. But the challenge does not end after you've been admitted to the school of your dreams. Before you take a seat in the classroom, you must do your homework to determine the best way to pay for your college education.

Now, the good news. There are multiple steps you can take to both reduce the cost of your degree and increase your eligibility for aid. In this chapter, we help you understand what financial aid is and how your eligibility for aid will be determined. We draw your attention to steps that you can take to lower the overall cost of your degree. We explain about sources of free money—grants and scholarships—and where to search for these. We explain about loans, both private and government-sponsored student loans, and how to comparison shop for the best loan deals. Finally, we look at real-life creative sources, like corporate tuition assistance, that you can tap to help reduce the high cost of college.

STEP 1: CONSIDER THE TYPE OF COLLEGE: PUBLIC VERSUS PRIVATE

You've probably heard it said that public colleges cost less than private colleges. This is generally true. One year of tuition and room and board went for about $8,000 at a public four-year college in 1998. Compare that to $20,000 a year in 1998 at a private college.

> Generally speaking, a private college charges about twice that of a public one for access to the same course of study.

Why do private schools cost more? Many people mistakenly think that private colleges cost more because they provide a better education. This is not necessarily true. The reason that private colleges cost more is that they do not receive significant government tax-dollar support. Public colleges, on the other hand, are heavily subsidized by tax-dollars, and, as a result, may generally charge significantly less in tuition and fees.

However, you cannot always assume that public colleges cost less than private colleges. In rare cases, the tuition charged by a public college may be as high or higher than the tuition charged by a private college. This can happen if you live in a state or county that allots little tax money to education. The less your state or county contributes to higher education, the more you must pay in tuition dollars to attend your public university system.

Put another way, it can cost a lot more to earn your degree from a publicly funded college in one state than in another. For example, California invests a lot of tax dollars in a statewide system of higher education. Residents of California can earn a two-year associate's degree from a publicly funded college like City College of San Francisco for about $1,000. This is one of the bargain college deals in the United States. Vermont also supports a publicly funded system of colleges. Yet because Vermont puts little of its tax money into higher education, it costs about $6,000 to earn a two-year degree from the Community College of Vermont. The $5,000 difference in sticker price for a two-year publicly supported degree in Vermont versus the same degree in California is due to differences in state tax support for higher education.

STEP 2: CONSIDER RESIDENCY REGULATIONS: IN-STATE VERSUS OUT-OF-STATE

Publicly funded colleges generally charge lower tuition for state residents than they do for out-of-state students. Why? Because state tax dollars help support publicly funded universities. State residents have, in theory, already contributed to publicly funded colleges via their tax payments. Out-of-state students are asked to pay more to help make up this difference. Private colleges charge the same tuition regardless of your state of residency because they are not tied to government tax funding.

If you apply to a public college you will be asked about your state of residency. Most colleges will not consider you a state resident until you have lived in the state for at least one full calendar year for reasons other than attending college.

If you live near the border of two or more states, check to see if your state has a reduced tuition agreement with neighboring states. Minnesota, for example, has special agreements that allow residents of Wisconsin and Canada to attend some publicly funded Minnesota colleges for a lower tuition rate. Many geographic regions, notably the South and New England, have special pacts that allow students from one state to attend college at a lower tuition rate in a neighboring state.

STEP 3: SCRUTINIZE PROPRIETARY COLLEGES AND TRAINING INSTITUTES

A proprietary college is a for-profit college. It is a business that exists to turn a profit on teaching activities. Most proprietary colleges specialize in teaching vocational skills. Many beauty schools and computer training institutes, for example, are for-profit career colleges.

In the last few years it has become increasingly common for career schools that specialize in business, computers, and information and engineering technology to operate as proprietary schools. Some of the more popular degree-granting proprietary colleges in the United States include the DeVry Institute of Technology, ITT Technical Institute, and the University of Phoenix. These colleges operate chain campuses or franchises in urban areas throughout the United States.

The primary difference between proprietary schools and nonprofit colleges is that proprietary schools exist to make a profit on educating you. The courses proprietary schools teach are often more career oriented than what is taught at a traditional nonprofit liberal arts college. Though traditionally founded to offer career certificates and vocational two-year degrees, more and more proprietary schools are offering four-year bachelor's degrees, as well as graduate and professional training.

Proprietary schools can be either more or less expensive than nonprofit colleges. You will want to compare costs carefully. One thing to watch out for is that some proprietary schools may ask you to sign a retail contract that obligates you to pay for a full semester, or even a full year, of college tuition up front. Before you sign any long-term tuition agreement, make sure you understand how and when you can drop out of school and still get your money back. If you have not been in school for a while and are uncertain that you will like college, it is unwise to sign an agreement that promises that you will pay for a full year of college up front.

Additionally, some proprietary schools charge hefty interest rates to help you finance your education. Check interest rates carefully.

Never sign an agreement to purchase educational services until you have read and understood all the financial documents that you have been asked to sign.

STEP 4: MAKE FRIENDS WITH YOUR FINANCIAL AID OFFICER

Each college you apply to will have a financial aid office that will be staffed with financial aid advisors. Your financial aid advisor is the person who is charged with helping you to apply for any aid that the college has to offer. We advise you to take the time to connect with a financial aid advisor at each college you might attend.

To begin, a good financial aid advisor can make applying for college aid much less stressful. A good aid counselor can also help you locate special aid that might be available only to older students or to students who fit special categories, such as single mothers or women who intend to major in nontraditional areas. Most financial aid offices also have libraries that are chock-full of invaluable information on how to locate, apply for, and obtain college aid.

Finally, your financial aid counselor will help you go over award options—scholarships, grants, and loans—and help you to understand how and where you might apply for additional aid—aid that the college may not have awarded you the first time an assessment was made. Your financial aid advisor is the person who can help you in this process.

Like most things in life, financial aid is often negotiable.

STEP 5: UNDERSTAND AND APPLY FOR GOVERNMENT AID

FEDERAL GOVERNMENT AID

The majority of students who attend college to earn a degree or a certificate use government-sponsored financial aid, primarily student loans. If you're new to government financial aid programs, your first reaction will probably be confusion; your second reaction may be disappointment.

Like colleges themselves, government-aid programs were never designed to be used by independent adults who work full-time and study part-time. While the cost of a college education has skyrocketed, the amount available through government sources has not risen. The average four-year college graduate leaves campus with a debt of $13,500: Keep this in mind as you consider what might be a reasonable amount to borrow to finance your own degree.

The federal government sponsors both loans and free grants to help students finance their education. Government-aid programs have many requirements attached to them. Some programs are the most beneficial to full-time students. Full-time students are those who take and complete at least four courses each semester. Most adult students work full-time and study part-time, taking one, sometimes two courses, each semester. In addition, most government-aid programs are only available to students who are taking courses as part of a degree or a certificate program at a college that is accredited by an agency that is recognized by the U.S. Department of Education. (See chapter 3: College Accreditation and Degrees for a full discussion on accreditation.)

What Kind of Aid Does the Government Award?

The federal government offers both student loans, which must be paid back, and student grants, which are free money. How do you know what specific kinds of (loans or grants) the government has available each year? Consult *The Student Guide to Financial Aid*, a free publication available each year from the United States Department of Education. The guide explains government loans and grant programs. It is available from the U.S. Department of Education at 800-4-FED-AID or from the financial aid office at your local college. If you have internet access, you can download a copy of the guide from the Office of Postsecondary Education online at http://www.ed.gov/offices/OPE/Students/student.html.

Submit Your FAFSA: How do you apply for federal aid?

"The Free Application for Federal Student Aid" (FAFSA) is a form that you must file each year so colleges can determine the amount of your "aid eligibility" or "financial need" using standard mathematical formulas. For a free copy of the FAFSA and information on student aid and loans from the government call 800-433-3243, or visit the comprehensive federal government student-aid resource center online at http://easi.ed.gov.

> *M*any students mistakenly assume they make too much money to qualify for aid, so they fail to apply.

We strongly encourage all adult students to complete the FAFSA. Qualifying for financial aid is a complex process. It is a process that is affected not just by how much money you make but also how many dependents you have, whether or not you have children in college, the value of your business and life assets, and your overall indebtedness.

The only way you can reliably determine what kind of aid you might qualify for is to apply each year and let the government and the colleges you wish to attend calculate your official level of need. The FAFSA must be completed and submitted to the government after January 1 each year that you attend college.

Study Your Student Aid Report (SAR)

About three weeks after you submit your FAFSA, you will receive a document called a Student Aid Report (SAR). The college you are going to attend will also receive a copy of your SAR. The SAR will reveal your "Expected Family Contribution" (EFC), or how much money you will be expected to contribute to your college bill based on the complex financial data that you provided in your FAFSA.

The financial aid counselor at each college you have applied to will use the SAR to make your aid award. It is important to note that every college will use your Expected Family Contribution number to determine how much aid you are eligible to receive. For example, if your EFC is $5,000, and it will cost you $8,000 to attend the college of your choice, you can expect the college to come up with an aid package that will give you access to $3,000—the gap between your EFC and the real cost of attending the college that you have chosen. What kind of aid you are offered—loans or grants or a combination of the two—is what we consider next.

FEDERAL GOVERNMENT STUDENT LOANS

The largest financial aid program operated by the government is the student loan program. In addition, the government oversees more than one kind of student loan. Student loans vary in interest rates and repayment terms. Some loan programs, such as the Perkins, which carries the most favorable interest rate of 5 percent, are open only to those with exceptional financial need. (Note: Unfortunately exceptional need is not determined by how much you feel you need but by the official results of your annual SAR (Student Aid Report).

Perkins Loans are awarded directly by your college and will only be awarded if your official Student Aid Report (SAR) reveals exceptional financial need. The Perkins allows undergraduate students to borrow up to $3,000 per year for a total of $15,000.

If you are enrolled at least half-time in a degree or certificate program, you may be eligible for two types of student loans: a Federal Direct Loan or a Federal Family Educational (FFEL) or Stafford Loan. The differences between these loan programs are minor. For example, in the Direct Loan program your loan amounts are sent to you directly by the government rather than a private bank. Minor administrative differences may be reflected in payment schedules as well. Undergraduate students are allowed to borrow from $6,625 to $10,500 per year under these loan programs. You will need to consult with your local financial aid advisor to determine your loan amount limits each year.

Government student loans may be subsidized or unsubsidized. The subsidized form of a student loan is available to students with financial need. The government pays the interest on these student loans—subsidizes the interest payments—while you remain enrolled in college. Subsidized loans are better financial deals than unsubsidized ones because they give you a break on interest payments. Unsubsidized loans are available to students who have less financial need. Interest rates on student loans are adjusted each year in July. The interest on student loans will vary but never exceeds 8.25 percent.

Regular government-backed student loans are available at around 8 percent variable interest for the majority of students. The average middle-class student is most likely to qualify for one of the 8.25 percent government student loan programs.

If you have children in college and have taken out student loans on their behalf, be sure to discuss this with your financial aid counselor. In some cases you may be able to consolidate different types of student loans to make repayment easier over time.

FEDERAL GOVERNMENT GRANTS

The federal government also sponsors two grant programs for undergraduate students who demonstrate exceptional financial need. The Federal Pell Grant program entitles needy students to a maximum award of $2,700 per year. The Pell Grant is free money. It is awarded based on exceptional need. It need not be repaid.

The Federal Supplemental Educational Opportunity Program (FSEOG) is the second free-money program offered by the government. The FSEOG is awarded directly by colleges to their neediest students. FSEOG awards ranged from $100 to $4,000 per year in the 1998–1999 academic year.

What is exceptional financial need? Level of need, as determined by the government, is a complicated matter. The level of your need will be officially calculated each year using the data that you provide on the FAFSA form. Your college will use the SAR based on your FAFSA data to determine if you have enough need to qualify for a Pell or a FSEOG Grant.

STATE FINANCIAL AID

In addition to federal government aid, each state operates its own financial aid program. Each state also awards grants or free money for the needy through a partnership program with the federal government. This program is called the State Student Incentive Grant (SSIG). Other supplemental loan or grant programs may be available for residents of certain states, especially if you plan on attending college in-state. Some states are educationally rich in their aid programs—Minnesota and Wisconsin for example—while other states provide little or no economic incentive for adult students.

Adult students in New York State enjoy some of the best state-benefit programs. New York State administers several programs for adult students: Tuition Assistance Program (TAP), Aid for Part-Time Study (APTS), the Vietnam Veteran's Tuition Awards (VVTA), and the Empire State Scholarships of Excellence. These are only some of the awards that residents of New York can qualify for through their state financial aid programs.

How do you find out about state aid programs? All colleges will send state financial aid information and application forms if you request them. Every state maintains a state office of financial aid that acts as a clearing-house for state loan, grant, and scholarship programs. If you can't locate your state's financial aid office, call your local college's financial aid office and ask for a referral. The Federal Government Student Aid Center also maintains links to state departments of education within their online center at http://www.ed.gov/offices/OPE/agencies.html. If you lack internet access, you can call the Federal Aid Center at 1-800-4-AID or write them at PO Box 84, Washington, D.C. 20044-0084, and ask for a referral to your State Student Aid Center.

MILITARY AID

If you are in the military, either on active duty or recently discharged, be aware that all branches of the armed services offer tuition assistance programs. Military aid programs are as complicated as any form of government aid. Many rules apply when qualifying for military aid. Options range from free tuition at military schools like the Community College of the Air Force to partial but hefty scholarships offered through college ROTC (Reserve Officer Training Programs).

ACTIVE DUTY

If you are on active duty, meet with your educational benefits advisor. Get a complete orientation to your benefits package. Benefits vary widely with branch of service, rank, dates of enlistment, and terms of active duty. Your educational benefits advisor can assist you in interpreting your benefits package in regard to any college degree or training program.

Your military educational advisor can also guide you to Service members Opportunities Colleges (SOCs). SOCs work with military students to maximize transfer credits already earned through specialized military training. You will want your advisor to provide you with a directory of all college programs that are preapproved for military benefits under the SOCs program.

The Department of Defense DANTES program also maintains a central web site for enlisted personnel. If you are on active duty check the DANTES web site at http://voled.doded.mil, for information on special college programs for active-duty personnel.

If you are in the military and think you can't attend college because you are stationed in a remote area, ask your educational advisor for information on distance-learning programs. Distance-learning programs, where courses are delivered over the internet or via satellite or cable or videotape, are widely used by the military. In addition to the publicly accessible distance-degree programs that we profile in chapter 4, the military sponsors many distance-learning programs that are delivered only to military personnel by special arrangement.

The Department of Defense DANTES contains a special directory of distance-learning college programs that serve active duty military personnel worldwide.

VETERANS

If you are a veteran, your post-service educational entitlements probably expire at a preset date. If you are a recent veteran contemplating a college education, start by contacting your local Department of Veteran's Affairs (DVA) and speaking with the Educational Benefits Officer (EBO). If you don't know where your closest DVA is, ask your local librarian for help, or check the local yellow pages for a phone listing under "Government—Federal." Only your DVA can check your service record and determine your eligibility for college aid.

If you have already decided on a college, speak with a financial aid counselor at that college. Most colleges have at least one person on staff who specializes in processing military aid. Ask to speak with your college's military aid advisor for the most helpful assistance.

Again, if you're no longer enlisted, only the DVA can report on how much and what kinds of aid you might be eligible for. Individual colleges can help you understand military aid as it may apply to your tuition and fees if you study with them, but individual colleges can't tell you if you are "eligible" for veteran's educational aid and for how much.

The good news is that the DVA is liberal in funding education and training. The frustrating news is that determining your eligibility and arranging for reimbursement is probably not going to be your favorite part of your great educational adventure.

STEP 6: SEARCH FOR FREE MONEY: PRIVATE GRANTS AND SCHOLARSHIPS

In addition to aid that is offered by the government, you will want to investigate scholarships or grant monies offered by private organizations. While the majority of private scholarship programs are restricted to recent high school graduates, a growing number of private agencies are earmarking scholarship funds for older or nontraditional students.

For example, if you live in Vermont and you are a single parent with a child younger than twelve, you might qualify for the Bernice Murray Scholarship. This special scholarship awards up to $2,000 to qualified Vermonters who need assistance paying for child care while they work toward their college degree. Similarly, the Burlington, Vermont Business and Professional Women's Organization offers college scholarships of $100 to $1,000 to Vermonters who are single parents with financial need. This information and information on scores of other special awards is made available free to Vermonters through the Vermont Student Assistance Corporation (VSAC). You can visit them on the web at http://www.vsac.org. VSAC is the financial aid clearinghouse for the State of Vermont.

Your local library will house several scholarship directories that you can search through for free. There are very good and comprehensive scholarship guides for undergraduate students: *Scholarship Book 2000*, by Daniel Cassidy, from Prentice Hall; *Free Money for College*, by Laurie Blum, from Facts on File; and *The Scholarship Advisor* and *Paying for College Without Going Broke*, both from The Princeton Review. Your state financial aid clearinghouse may also have listings of scholarship programs available only to state residents. To determine the phone number of your state's financial aid clearinghouse, either contact the financial aid office of your local college or phone the federal government's Federal Aid Center at 800-4-AID. You may also write the Federal Aid Center at PO Box 84, Washington, D.C. 20044-0084, and ask for a referral to your state financial aid clearinghouse or resource center.

The financial aid office of the college you plan to attend may also have special scholarship directories that are restricted to students who attend their degree programs. Check all these resources for any private scholarship aid that might be available to you.

One note: In searching for private scholarships, study the qualifying rules carefully. Most private scholarship competitions are restricted to individuals who meet very specific criteria, such as being members of a specific ethnic or disadvantaged group. In addition, most private scholarships are further restricted to those who demonstrate the greatest financial need according to their Student Aid Report (SAR).

INTERNET SEARCH SITES AND SCAMS

There are great, free scholarship-search databases on the World Wide Web, and a slew of sleazy scholarship scams. Be careful when searching for free money for college online or elsewhere: Keep one hand on your purse and keep your common sense close at hand.

How do you spot a scholarship scam? Most scams operate by asking you to send in a sizable amount of money, say $175, to receive a "private list" or "computer diskette" stuffed full of scholarship sources that the scam company promises will "award you millions in otherwise unclaimed aid." The truth is these "private lists" are generally not even as comprehensive as the scholarship books that you could reference for free at your local library.

Additionally, most of these "private lists" contain a majority of scholarships that are only open to high school juniors or seniors who have earned a certain score on standardized exams like the SAT or ACT—exams that older adults rarely have taken. It is much harder to find private scholarships that are open to older, nontraditional learners. For these reasons we never recommend that older learners pay to use any type of scholarship search service.

We also never recommend that students pay a fee to apply for any type of scholarship. If a scholarship program charges an "application" or "processing fee," generally $25 to $100, you can almost bet that the program is a scam that works by collecting application fees from thousands of applicants while never awarding any money at all in scholarships.

If you have internet access you can check on scholarship scams at the web site of the Federal Trade Commission at http://www.ftc.gov. The Federal Trade Commission is the government agency that investigates and prosecutes scams of all types. They have, over the years, identified and prosecuted several scholarship scam companies through their special Project $cholar $cam. If you suspect a company of scholarship fraud, you can also phone the National Fraud Information Center at 800-876-7060 for a list of scholarship scam operations and free consumer advice on how to spot financial-aid scams.

FREE SCHOLARSHIP SEARCH SERVICES ON THE INTERNET

The following web sites maintain free college scholarship search systems that are worth visiting.

- CollegeNET Mach25
  http://www.collegenet.com.mach25

- Financial Aid Information Page
  http://www.finaid.org

- FastWEB
  http://www.fastweb.com

- Free Scholarship Searches
  http://www.freschinfo.com

- Sallie Mae/College Aid Sources for Higher Education
  (CASH) Scholarship Search
  http://scholarships.salliemae.com

- Plato's Scholarship Resource Network
  http://www.plato.org

STEP 7: EXAMINE TAX WRITE-OFFS AND DEDUCTIONS

If you pay your own college tuition, can you take a tax deduction? Probably. Under new tax laws at least some of your tuition and fees should be deductible. At the end of each calendar year your college should send you a tax form called a 1098-T. This form will itemize your tuition payments. You may be eligible to take all or some of your tuition and fees payments in either Hope or Lifelong Learning tax deductions when you file your tax return. In 1998, students were allowed a maximum deduction of $1,500 for the Hope Tax Credit and $1,000 for the Lifelong Learning Credit.

THE HOPE CREDIT

Who can take the Hope Tax Credit? The Hope Tax Credit applies only to students who are in the first two years of college. You can take a full tax credit for the first $1,000 you spend on education, and up to 50 percent of the second $1,000 you spend in an academic year. The credit is phased out for taxpayers in higher income brackets, however, so check with your accountant before assuming that you qualify.

THE LIFELONG LEARNING CREDIT

The Lifelong Learning Tax Credit is a new program designed especially for adult students who want to return to college for retraining in their careers or skills. You do not have to be seeking a degree or certificate to take this credit. This credit applies to juniors, seniors, or graduate students, including those who only take one or two courses. A single family is allowed to deduct up to 20 percent of the first $5,000 they spend on tuition through the year 2002. After that, up to $10,000 may be used toward the deduction.

SELF-EMPLOYED BUSINESS DEDUCTIONS

If you are self-employed, your education may be deductible as a business expense, just like your office supplies. The deduction is taken on "Schedule C: Profit or Loss from Business." Not all educational expenses are "allowable" business deductions for the self-employed. Uncle Sam has shifting rules about the kinds of education or training that are allowable deductions.

Allowable deductions must relate to your business. For example, a bookkeeper would have no problem deducting classes in tax law or real estate finance. But that same bookkeeper would be hard-pressed to justify a deduction for a class in novel writing. If you are self-employed, call the IRS helpline at 800-TAX-FORM and request: "Publication 508: Educational Expenses," or "Publication 334: Tax Guide for the Small Business," for more on educational deductions.

STUDENT LOAN WRITE-OFFS

You can claim income tax write-offs for the interest paidthey pay on any bona fide student loan. If you have begun repaying student loans, your lender should send you form 1098-F by February 15 each year. Form 1098-F states how much of your annual student loan payments went toward paying off the interest rather than the principal. Up to $1,000 of student-loan interest was eligible for deduction on 1998 tax returns. In 1999, up to $1,500 may be deductible. In 2000, the deduction goes to $2,000, with the deduction capping at $2,500 thereafter.

Check the booklet that comes with your tax forms each year or check with your accountant for new regulations on student loan deductions, the Hope credit, and the Lifetime Learning Credit. Tax laws can change from year to year.

STEP 8: CONSIDER CREATIVE ALTERNATIVES TO GOVERNMENT AID

COMPANY TUITION BENEFITS

*Y*our first stop should be your boss's office. Less than 5 percent of the corporate money earmarked for employee education is used each year.

Find out if your company has a tuition benefits program, then find out if you are eligible. Eight out of ten of my clients had educational benefits where they worked, but almost as many did not know they had such benefits when they first considered returning to college. Most were surprised to find out how much their companies would pay them to go back to college.

Some companies will pay 100 percent of an employee's college tuition provided it is work related. Many companies will pay a maximum amount each calendar year, often up to $2,000. A few companies will even foot the tuition bill for your children or your spouse through special company-run charitable foundations. Even small companies will often pay a part of the tuition bill if approached with the notion that an investment in your knowledge base will be an investment in the knowledge base of the company as a whole.

Never assume that your company won't pay at least some of your tuition bill. Negotiate for such benefits if they don't already exist. One of my clients in a small firm in Atlanta negotiated a tuition deal with her boss after he clearly told her that the company had absolutely no interest in footing her tuition for a Bachelor of Business Administration in the Management of Information Systems.

The client thought over her strategy and tried again three days later. In her new presentation, she asked the boss to cover the tuition only for four specific courses. These four courses were all related to her plan to develop a new marketing database that would save the company ten times her course tuition in one year. She had a company tuition check in hand when she left work that evening.

Private Student Loans

Realizing that government-backed student loans are not always the best deals or the most accessible credit lines for working adults, more colleges are instituting their own nongovernmental programs by contracting with outside firms to provide private educational loans for working adults.

A new generation of low-interest student loans is being made available through private, nonprofit lenders to credit-worthy adults regardless of their official need for such aid. Your college financial aid-advisor can explain these private student loan options to you. Leaders in the field include The Education Resources Institute (TERI) and PLATO.

TERI Loans

TERI was founded in 1985 to help middle-income adults gain increased access to loans for education regardless of their income and asset levels. To qualify, you must have a good credit history and you must attend a college that participates in or is approved for the TERI program.

TERI educational loans are available in amounts beginning at $500, at prime or prime plus rates. (The prime rate as we write is 8.5 percent.) TERI programs for adults include the TERI Alternative Loan, available to undergraduates enrolled at least half-time in a TERI-approved school and the TERI Continuing Education Loan for up to $15,000 a year with no school approval required at rates of Prime plus 1.5 percent.

To find out more about TERI private student loans, contact your student-aid advisor or TERI at 800-255-8374. You may also visit TERI online at http://www.teri.org.

PLATO Loans

PLATO loans are available from Educap, Inc., another nonprofit, private educational loan company. PLATO low-interest student loans are available to students who have an income of at least $15,000 per year and a good credit history. Loan amounts range from $1,000 to $25,000 per year with a lifetime cap at $100,000. Loan interest rates are tied to your credit worthiness and run from 7.75 percent to 8.81 percent. Rates vary with the prime rate each year. Borrowers who stay in good stead for three years may qualify for interest rate reductions as well.

Information on PLATO loans is available at 800-263-3527 or online at http://www.plato.org. Applicants may also write to PLATO at 205 Van Buren Street, Suite 200, Herndon, Virginia 20170.

Sallie Mae to the Rescue

If you are confused about student loans and uncertain about how much you should borrow, or from whom, we highly recommend a call to Sallie Mae. Sallie Mae is a company that buys and manages student loans from many sources. Sallie Mae maintains a free phone hotline for the confused borrower. The Sallie Mae College Answer Service is staffed from 8 a.m. to 11 p.m. EST at 800-891-4599. Counselors will gladly answer your questions about student aid. They will also assist you in completing financial aid forms and in understanding scholarships, grants, and other aid sources.

If you have internet access, the Sallie Mae web site at http://www.salliemae.com, houses several free interactive aids to help you understand financial options. Financial Aid 101 is an interactive program that will walk you through financial aid terms and options. The site also has several interactive programs that will help you understand how your financial need will be calculated by colleges, how much you should borrow, and how to set up the best repayment plans based on your current income and indebtedness.

FAMILY LOANS

Several clients have said no to formal student loans and gone on to forge unbeatable loan deals with their parents or other relatives. In 1999, 6 percent was considered a good return on a safe bank CD. If the bank will pay your mother 6 percent for use of her money for 3 years, why don't you up the ante and offer her 7.5 percent for the same privilege?

One word of advice: Treat a loan from a relative just as you would one from the bank. Agree in writing to the terms: amount loaned ($3,000); interest (7 percent); repayment schedule (begin January 1, 1995 and end January 1, 1998 for a total of 36 monthly payments of $92.97).

> *F*inance not your best talent? No problem. Anyone can figure loan repaments. Your public library or local bank should have an Amortization Handbook. This handbook will instantly reveal what your monthly payments would be for any amount you borrowed for any length of time at any interest rate.

While a family loan can be a good option, remember that interest on a student loan is only tax deductible if you borrow from a bona fide public student loan fund. You may not be able to deduct the interest paid on a family loan.

HOME EQUITY LOANS

Home sweet home is the greatest piece of equity owned by most working adults. Home equity loans usually carry a lower interest rate than other lines of commercial credit, and they can be very easy to qualify for.

Call several banks in your neighborhood and ask to speak with their home equity loan officer. Banks will vary in what they offer, but usually a bank will loan up to 80 percent of your paid equity at rates at or below those offered by Uncle Sam on a bona fide student loan.

One good thing about home equity loans is that the interest on them is generally tax deductible. Still, you will want to consult with your accountant or financial planner to determine if taking out a home equity loan to assist in your education would be a wise financial move given your overall tax situation.

PENSION PLAN BORROWING

One woman was sure that she could not afford a Bachelor of Science in Nursing. Her house was double mortgaged. She had a bad credit history, so no use going to the bank. She was shocked when it was suggested that she use her sizable pension plan or 401-K from work to finance her nursing degree. Use her retirement nest egg? Withdraw that money and get socked with extra taxes for early withdrawal? No way she wanted to do that!

The woman did not realize that she was allowed to borrow against her own pension at a low rate of only 6 percent. Of course, she'd have to pay that money back over time. It was still a loan. But it was a very reasonable loan that would allow her to return to school under a low interest repayment plan of her own making.

Similarly, many adult students are able to borrow against their life insurance or other investments that they thought were untouchable. Take a good look at your whole financial situation when considering how to finance your continuing education. You may have more borrowing capacity than you imagined. Most adults do.

TUITION FREEZES, SALES, AND DISCOUNTS

Tuition "sales" or "discounts" are being offered today by bona fide colleges to entice adults back into the Ivy Halls. Liberty University, a private college in Virginia, for example, offers a "spouse discount." Liberty University lowers tuition considerably if both a husband and wife enroll in the same course. While not quite a two-for-one sale, it is a price break in an area that a decade ago was never subjected to such markdown tactics. A few colleges also now offer "family discounts" if parents and children attend simultaneously. Family tuition discounts are not yet offered by most schools, but they are offered by enough private schools these days that you should inquire about them if more than one member of your family will be enrolled in the same college at the same time.

In addition, many colleges are now offering guaranteed tuition rates or tuition freezes. Under these programs a college guarantees that they will not raise tuition rates on you for as long as you are enrolled and working toward a degree. Since colleges tend to raise tuition rates from 3 to 5 percent each year, a four-year freeze could save you up to 20 percent on your overall college bill.

Senior Discounts

The graying of America has resulted in senior discounts on practically everything—but a senior discount on your college degree? That's right! At least twenty-three states have enacted legislation that mandates publicly supported state colleges to offer discounted tuition to senior residents.

*S*ome state colleges routinely offer half off of tuition for residents over the age of sixty, while others charge no tuition at all to seniors.

Pennsylvania State University, for example, has a program called "The Go 60 Program" that allows Pennsylvania residents 60 years old or older to enroll in many degree programs for half of the regular tuition. Illinois state universities such as Western Illinois University allows Illinois residents 65 or older who have annual incomes under $12,000 to attend college tuition-free. South Carolina law requires that all state-supported colleges offer courses tuition-free to residents of the state who are at least 60 years old and not gainfully employed.

The age that one is considered a senior for educational discounts can range from sixty to seventy-five. Also, some senior discount programs apply only to certain programs while others will apply to all types of study. In some cases seniors can study for free, provided they are taking courses only for their personal fun and enrichment and not as a part of a formal degree program. Check with your local publicly funded college for specific information on their tuition discount programs for seniors.

APPENDIX

DIRECTORY OF REGIONALLY ACCREDITED DISTANCE DEGREES

In this section we profile regionally accredited distance degree or career credential programs that can be completed largely or entirely from the comfort of your own home. Some programs require brief campus visits to plan degrees or meet with faculty tutors. Check the Campus Visits section of each profile for details on any brief residency requirements. The majors offered by each program are detailed in the Areas of Study section.

Key: (C) = Certificate or Diploma; (A) = Associate's degree; (B) = Bachelor's degree

Andrews University ────────────────────────────

Home Study International Office
Nethery Hall
Berrien Springs, MI 49104-0070
616-471-6200
800-471-6210
E-mail: zork@andrews.edu (Susan Zork)
URL: n/a

Campus Visits: None.

Areas of Study: General Studies (B), Personal Ministries (A), Religion (B).

Admissions: High school GPA of 2.75 and high school diploma or GED with test scores of 60 or higher. The majortiy of students adhere to the Seventh Day Adventist religion but no particular religious affiliation is required for admission.

Program Features: Andrews University is a private Seventh Day Adventist University, founded in 1874.

Tuition/Fees: $165 per credit; 50 percent discount for seniors 60 or older.

Arapahoe Community College

Colorado Electronic Community College
9075 East Lowry Boulevard
Denver, CO 80220
800-801-5040
E-mail: n/a
URL: http://www.cecc.cccoes.edu/main.htm

Campus Visits: None.

Areas of Study: Liberal Arts/General Studies (A).

Admissions: The degree is open to any person 16 or older who has a VCR and a computer/modem for course access.

Program Features: Arapahoe is one of the community colleges of the state of Colorado. Arapahoe offers a complete degree online via the Colorado Electronic Community College (CECC) network.

Tuition/Fees: $120 per credit.

Atlantic Community College

Distance Learning
Mary Walls, Ph.D. Director
Associate Dean of Business, CIS, English and Social Science
5100 Black Horse Pike
Mays Landing, NJ 08330
609-343-4987
E-mail: wall@atlantic.edu (Mary Wall)
URL: http://www.atlantic.edu

Campus Visits: None.

Areas of Study: General Studies (A).

Admissions: Open.

Program Features: Atlantic Community College, founded in 1966, is one of the two-year community colleges of the state of New Jersey. Courses are offered online and via mailed videotapes as well as on cable TV for local residents.

Tuition/Fees: $55.80 per credit.

Atlantic Union College

Adult Degree Program
338 Main Street
PO Box 1000
South Lancaster, MA 01561-1000
978-368-2300
800-282-2030
E-mail: adp@atlanticuc.edu
URL: http://atlanticuc.edu/academics/adp

Campus Visits: Two seminars (9-day and 11-day) are required in January and July.

Areas of Study: Art (B), Behavioral Science (B), Business Administration (B), Communications (B), Computer Science (B), Early Childhood Education (B), Elementary Education (B), English (B), Environmental Studies (B), General Science (B), General Studies (B), History (B), Humanities (B), Interior Design (B), Modern Languages (Foreign Languages) (B), Office Management (B), Personal Ministries (B), Philosophy (B), Physical Education (B), Psychology (B), Religion (B), Social Science (B), Theology (B), Theology-Bilingual Ministries (B), Women's Studies (B).

Admissions: Limited to those 25 or older with a high school diploma or GED.

Program Features: Atlantic Union is a private Seventh Day Adventist, Pentecostal college founded in 1882. Massachusetts teaching certification is available for Education majors.

Tuition/Fees: $3,500 per semester.

Baker College
Online Program
1050 West Bristol Road
Flint, MI 48507
810-766-4370
800-469-4062
E-mail: online@baker.edu
URL: http://www.baker.edu

Campus Visits: None.

Areas of Study: Business Administration (A/B), Computer Information Systems (C), Leadership (C), Financial Planning (C), Health Care Management (C), Human Resources Management (C), Industrial Management (C), Integrated Health Care (C), International Business (C), Marketing (C), Microsoft Professional Certification (C).

Admissions: Applicants need a computer, modem, and internet access. Courses are delivered in an online format only.

Program Features: Baker is a private, comprehensive college founded in 1888. Courses are offered online in an accelerated 6-week format. The Financial Planning Certificate may meet the educational requirements to sit for the national Certified Financial Planner (CFP) exam. The Microsoft Professional Certificate meets educational requirements for the Microsoft Certified Systems Engineer (MCSE).

Tuition/Fees: $140 per quarter credit.

Ball State University
School of Continuing Education
Carmichael Hall, Room 200
Muncie, IN 47306
317-285-1581
800-872-0369
E-mail: distance@wp.bsu.edu
URL: http://www.bsu.edu/distance

Campus Visits: None.

Areas of Study: General Studies (Liberal Arts) (A).

Admissions: Open.

Special Features: Ball State is a comprehensive, government-supported university. The distance program was launched in the 1980s. Courses are offered via surface mail, videotape, and online. Indiana residents may also attend broadcast courses at reception sites throughout the state.

Tuition/Fees: $110 per semester credit; Tuition discount for those 60 years or older (senior discount).

Bellevue Community College

Distance Education
Room D-261
3000 Landerholm Circle S.E.
Bellevue, WA   98007-6484
425-641-2438
E-mail: n/a
URL: http://distance-ed.bcc.ctc.edu

Campus Visits: None unless labs are required.

Areas of Study: Liberal Arts (A); Web Authoring (C).

Admissions: Open.

Program Features: Bellevue Community College is part of the publicly funded two-year college system of Washington State. Courses are delivered via videotape and online. Local students may also receive courses on cable TV.

Tuition/Fees: $258 per 5-quarter credit course; $309.60 per 6-quarter credit course.

Bellevue University

Online Admissions
1000 Galvin Road South
Bellevue, NE 68005-3098
E-mail: bellevue_u@scholars.bellevue.edu
URL: http://bruins.bellevue.edu

Campus Visits: None.

Areas of Study: Criminal Justice (B), International Business Management (B), Management (B), Management of Information Systems (B).

Admissions: Open. Most applicants have 60 semester credits or the equivalent of an associate's degree in college credits or life experience when entering.

Program Features: Bellevue is a private comprehensive university founded in 1965. Courses are delivered online.

Tuition/Fees: $250 per semester credit.

Bemidji State University

Center for Extended Learning
Deputy Hall
Bemidji, MN 56601-2699
218-755-3924
800-475-2001, ext. 2738
E-mail: cel@vax1.bemidji.msus.edu
URL: http://cel.bemidji.msus.edu/cel

Campus Visits: None.

Areas of Study: Criminal Justice (A/B), History (B), Liberal Studies (A), Social Studies (B).

Admissions: Open.

Program Features: Bemidji State University, founded in 1919, is part of the government-supported university system in Minnesota. The distance-learning option began in 1973. Courses are delivered via mail, videotape, fax, and e-mail.

Tuition/Fees: $62.22 per quarter credit (Minnesota residents); $128.97 per quarter credit (others).

Bethel College

Verda Deckert, MSN, RN, CNA
RN Outreach Director
300 East 27th Street
North Newton, KS 67117-0531
316-283-2500
800-522-1887
E-mail: vdeckert@bethelks.edu
URL: http://www.bethelks.edu

Campus Visits: Students attend three, two- to four-week residencies on campus.

Areas of Study: Nursing (B)

Admissions: The Bachelor of Science in Nursing (BSN) is open to RNs who hold associate degrees or nursing diplomas who also have malpractice insurance, CPR certification, and a 2.5 GPA.

Program Features: Bethel College, founded in 1887, is a private college affiliated with the Mennonite Church. The Bethel BSN is accredited by the National League for Nursing and the Kansas State Board of Nursing. Courses are delivered online, via fax, mail, and videotape.

Tuition/Fees: $285–$380 per credit.

Brevard Community College

Online Campus
1519 Clearlake Road
Cocoa, FL 32922
407-632-1111, ext. 63470
E-mail: bcconline@a1.brevard.cc.fl.us
URL: http://www.brevard.cc.fl.us/distlrn

Campus Visits: None.

Areas of Study: Computer-Aided Drafting and Design Technology (A), Criminal Justice (A), Electronic Engineering Technology (A), Environmental Science Technology (Hazardous Materials) (A), Fire Science (A), Hospitality Management (A), International Business Management (A), Legal Assisting (A), Liberal Arts (General Education) (A), Logistic Systems Technology (A), Marketing Management (A), Radio and TV Production (A), Solar Energy Technology (A).

Admissions: Open to anyone equipped with a computer and modem and access to the internet.

Program Features: Brevard Community College is part of the government-supported community college system of the state of Florida. Courses have been offered via distance learning since 1974. Coursework is offered online via computer-mediated electronic message boards and e-mail, in videotape form, and through other distance methods.

Tuition/Fees: $44 per credit (Florida residents); $140 per credit (others).

Brigham Young University

Bachelor of General Studies
PO Box 21515305 Harman Building
Provo, UT 84602-1515
801-378-4351
888-298-3137
E-mail: bgs@byu.edu
URL: http://coned.byu.edu/bgs

Campus Visits: Bachelor's degree candidates may be required to attend up to four, two-week seminars on campus. Inquire directly about campus visits as these regulations may be revised.

Areas of Study: Family History/Genealogy (C), Organ Playing (C), General Studies (B) with an emphasis in one of eight areas: General Studies/American Studies (B), General Studies/English and American Literature (B), General Studies/Family History (Genealogy) (B), General Studies/History (B), General Studies/Management (B), General Studies/Psychology (B), General Studies/Writing (B).

Admissions: For the bachelor's, applicants must be at least 23 years old and complete a Church of the Latter-Day Saint's Confidential Bishop's Report pertaining to personal values. Transfer students must be in good standing at the last college attended, with a 2.0 grade average.

Program Features: Brigham Young University was founded in 1875 by the Church of the Later Days Saints. Degrees by independent study began operating in 1971.

Tuition/Fees: $84 per credit.

Bucks County Community College

Distance Learning Admissions
Swamp Road
Newtown, PA 18940
215-968-8101
E-mail: learning@bucks.edu
URL: http://www.bucks.edu/distance/index/html

Campus Visits: None unless speech or lab courses are required.

Areas of Study: Entrepreneurship (C), Advanced Entrepreneurship (C), Liberal Arts (A), Psychology (A), Social Science (A), Management/Marketing (A), Business Administration (A).

Admissions: Open.

Program Features: Bucks County Community College is a publicly supported two-year college system. Distance courses are delivered online, via print, audio and other means.

Tuition/Fees: $66 per credit (county residents); $132 per credit (state residents); $198 (others).

Burlington College
Independent Degree Program
95 North Avenue
Burlington, VT 05401
802-862-9616
800-862-9616
E-mail: admissions@burlcol.edu
URL: http://www.burlcol.edu

Campus Visits: Learners attend two weekend seminars each year.

Areas of Study: Cinema Studies (B), Fine Arts (B), Individualized (B), Psychology (B), Transpersonal Psychology (B), Writing/Literature (B).

Admissions: Open to those with 60 semester credits, an associate's degree, or the equivalent. Applicants should have at least a 2.5 transfer GPA. Strong writing and independent research skills are required.

Program Features: Burlington is a private, liberal arts college, founded in 1972, dedicated to educational pursuits that embrace meaningful livelihood, responsible social action, and a global/multicultural perspective. The learning contract method is used, allowing learners to design projects related to their life goals. Some coursework occurs through online methods.

Tuition/Fees: $3,400 per full-time semester.

Caldwell College
Corporate and Adult Admissions
9 Ryerson Avenue
Caldwell, NJ 07006-6195
973-228-4424
800-831-9178
E-mail: caldadmit@aol.com
URL: http://www.caldwell.edu

Campus Visits: A weekend visit is required at the beginning of each semester of study.

Areas of Study: Accounting (C), Art (B), Business Administration (C/B), Computer Information Systems (C/B), Communication (B), Criminal Justice (C), English (B), History (B), International Business (B), Management (C), Marketing (C), Political Science (B), Psychology (B), Religious Studies (C/B), Social Studies (B), Sociology (B).

Admissions: Programs are open to those 23 or older who have earned at least 12 college credits.

Program Features: Caldwell is a private, Catholic college, founded in 1939 by the Sisters of Saint Dominic. The college has offered distance learning since 1979. Courses are offered via mail, fax, videotape, e-mail and computer electronic conferencing.

Tuition/Fees: $298 per credit. Reduced tuition for law enforcement officials and Catholic school employees.

California State University at Dominguez Hills

C/O Jones College Connection
9697 East Mineral Avenue
PO Box 6612
Englewood, CO 80155-6612
303-792-3111
800-777-MIND
E-mail: info@jec.edu
URL: http://www.jec.edu

Campus Visits: None.

Areas of Study: Nursing (B).

Admissions: Limited to Registered Nurses (RNs) with current licenses or interim permits who have completed at least 56 credits in transfer work with a minimum 2.0 GPA. A VCR and internet access are required.

Program Features: California State University at Dominguez Hills is part of the publicly funded California State University system. The Nursing degree is delivered online and via videotape through the JEC College Connection, a nonprofit cable TV and internet broadcast company. The degree is accredited by the National League for Nursing.

Tuition/Fees: $210 per credit.

Central Community College

Distance Learning Admissions
PO Box 4093
Grand Island, NE 68802-4903
303-389-6387
E-mail: scunningham@cccneb.edu (Sarah Cunningham)
URL: http://www.cccned.edu

Campus Visits: None.

Areas of Study: Accounting (A), Business Administration (A), General Education/Liberal Arts (A), (Computer) Information Technology (A), Office Technology (A).

Admissions: Requires high school diploma or GED.

Program Features: Central Community College is a two-year, publicly supported colllege founded in 1976. Courses are delived via the web, e-mail, print, videotape, and local satellite broadcasts.

Tuition/Fees: $38.60 per credit (Nebraska residents); $57.90 per credit (nonresidents).

Central Maine Technical College

Library Services and Distance Learning
1260 Turner Street
Auburn, ME 04210-6498
207-784-2385
E-mail: dwarner@cmtc.net (Debi Warner, Chair)
URL: http://www.cmtc.net/distlrn.html

Campus Visits: A one-week residency may be required for labs. Labs may also be transferred in or replaced by internship or portfolio assessment.

Areas of Study: Occupational Health and Safety (C/A).

Admissions: Open to qualified candidates with internet access. Courses are taught online.

Program Features: Central Maine Technical College is a government-supported, comprehensive two-year technical institution. The distance-learning option was launched in 1998.

Tuition/Fees: $68 per credit (Maine resident); $102 per credit (New England residents); $149 per credit (nonresidents of Maine and New England).

Central Michigan University

Independent Learning and Distance Delivery
127 Rowe Hall
CSB 105
Mt. Pleasant, MI 48858-9970
800-688-4268
517-774-3865
E-mail: celinfo@cmich.edu
URL: http://www.cel.cmich.edu

Campus Visits: None.

Areas of Study: Administration/Management (B), Health Sciences (B), Organizational Administration (B), Public Administration (B).

Admissions: Applicants should have a 2.0 transfer GPA.

Program Features: Central Michigan is a comprehensive public university founded in 1892. Courses are offered online, via surface mail, and mailed videotapes.

Tuition/Fees: $158 per credit.

Central Texas College

Distance Education and Educational Technology
PO Box 1800
Killeen, TX 76540
254-526-7160
E-mail: disted@ctcd.cc.tx.us
URL: http://www.ctcd.cc.tx.us

Campus Visits: None.

Areas of Study: Electronics Technology (C); Liberal Arts (A).

Admissions: Open to qualified candidates who have internet access.

Program Features: Central Texas is a two-year, government-supported college founded in 1967. Distance-learning courses are delivered online, and via CD-ROM, videotape, and printed materials.

Tuition/Fees: $60 per credit (Texas residents); $250 per credit (others).

Cerro Coso Community College

Online Program
Matthew Hightower, Coordinator
Eastern Cerro College Center
PO Box 1865
Mammoth Lakes, CA 93546
760-934-2875
888-537-6932
E-mail: mhightow@cc.cc.ca.us (Matt Hightower, Coordinator)
URL: http://www.cc.cc.ca.us/cconline/dised.htm

Campus Visits: None.

Areas of Study: Computer Information Systems (A), Business Administration (A), Liberal Arts/General Studies (A).

Admissions: Degree-seeking students should hold a high school diploma, GED or the California High School Proficiency Exam (CHSPE), or be at least 18 years old and show evidence of being able to benefit from college-level instruction. Access to a computer, modem, and the internet is required.

Program Features: Cerro Coso, established in 1973, is part of the community college system of the state of California. It is a two-year college serving the eastern Sierra Nevada and Eastern Kern County area of California. Cerro Coso launched an online learning program in 1997–1998.

Tuition/Fees: $12 per credit (California residents); $118 per credit (others).

Champlain College

Online Program
Skiff Hall—Continuing Education Division
163 South Willard Street
Burlington, VT 05402-0670
802-860-2777
888-545-3459
E-mail: online@champlain.edu
URL: http://www.champlain.edu/OLDE

Campus Visits: None.

Areas of Study: Accounting (C/A), Administrative Office Management (B), Business (C/A/B), Computer Network and PC Support (C/A/B), Computer Programming (PC Track) (C/A/B), Computer Programming (Mini Track) (B), Engineering Technology (B), Hotel/Restaurant Management (C/A/B), Legal Administrative Assistant (B), Liberal Studies (B), Management (C/A), Marketing (B), Medical Administrative Assistant (B), Paralegal/Legal Assistant (B), Public Relations/Communications (B), Radiography (B), Respiratory Therapy (B), Retailing (B), Sport Management (B), Telecommunications (C/A/B), Travel/Tourism (A).

Admissions: Open to applicants with a computer, modem, and internet access who hold a high school diploma or GED. Applicants to bachelor's study in most fields must hold a career-oriented associate's degree or its equivalent in their major area. Applicants should have a transfer GPA of 2.75.

Program Features: Champlain is a private, comprehensive liberal arts college founded in 1878. Electronic mail and online conferencing is used for all coursework and administrative communications.

Tuition/Fees: $305 per credit.

Charter Oak State College
66 Cedar Street
Newington, CT 06111-2646
860-666-4595
E-mail: info@cosc.edu
URL: http://www.cosc.edu

Campus Visits: None.

Areas of Study: Arts and Sciences (General Studies) (A/B) with 36-credits (B). Concentrations in: Anthropology (B), Applied Arts (B), Art History (B), Biology (B), Business (B), Chemistry (B), Child Study (B), Communication (B), Computer Science (B), Economics (B), Engineering Studies (B), Fire Science Technology (B), French (B), Geography (B), Geology (B), German (B), History (B), Human Services (B), Individualized Studies (B), Liberal Studies (B), Literature (B), Mathematics (B), Music History or Theory (B), Optical Business Management (B), Philosophy (B), Physics (B), Political Science (B), Psychology (B), Religious Studies (B), Sociology (B), Spanish (B), Technology Studies (B), Theater History (B).

Admissions: Open to anyone who has earned at least 9 college credits including those without a high school diploma or GED. Successful candidates tend to already have a great deal of college-level learning and be goal-oriented.

Program Features: Charter Oak was founded in 1973, and is the external degree college of the state of Connecticut. It operates primarily as an assessment institution, not a teaching college. Charter Oak serves 3,000 learners per year and maintains regional centers in Connecticut (New Haven, Bridgeport, Norwalk, and Waterbury) to advise learners. Students build degrees by transferring in credits, taking challenge exams, using portfolio assessment, and applying professional licenses toward degrees.

Tuition/Fees: $65–$95 per credit (Connecticut resident); $98–$130 per credit (nonresidents). Significant assessment fees are charged as follows for Connecticut residents and then for non-residents: enrollment fee $430–$628, annual fee (after first year) $298–$433; bachelor fee $245; graduation fee $130. Final degree costs will vary widely depending on options individual learners use to complete degrees.

Chemeketa Community College
Distance Education Degree Program
4000 Lancaster Drive, NE
PO Box 14007
Salem, OR 97309-7070
503-399-5191

800-330-5191
E-mail: donnac@chemek.cc.or.us (Donna Carver)
URL: http://www.lbcc.cc.or.us/occdec/chemeket.html

Campus Visits: None.

Admissions: Open.

Programs: Fire Protection (A), General Studies (A), Liberal Arts (A).

Program Features: Chemeketa, founded in 1955, is part of the community college system of Oregon. Courses are available online, via videotape, surface mail, and local cable TV.

Tuition/Fees: $36 per quarter credit plus fees.

Christopher Newport University

Online Program
Admissions
Newport News, VA 23606-2998
804-594-7015
800-333-4CNU
E-mail: online@cnu.edu
URL: http://cnuonline.cnu.edu

Campus Visits: None.

Admissions: Open to those who have a computer and internet access.

Areas of Study: Governmental Administration/Criminal Justice Administration (B), Governmental Administration/International Administration (B), Governmental Administration/Legal Studies (Pre-Law/Paralegal) (B), Governmental Administration/Public Management (B), Philosophy and Religious Studies (B), Political Science/International Relations (B), Political Science/Teacher Education (B).

Program Features: Christopher Newport University, chartered in 1961, is part of the government-supported college system of the state of Virginia. Courses are delivered online. The Legal Studies concentration is approved by the American Bar Association (ABA) and is intended to prepare learners to become certified legal assistants or to prepare them for law school admission. The Political Science curriculum has been state-approved for grades 9–12 teacher endorsement.

Tuition/Fees: $143 per credit (Virginia residents); $338 per credit (nonresidents).

City University

Undergraduate Admissions
919 Southwest Grady Way
Renton, WA 98055
425-637-1010
800-422-4898
E-mail: info@cityu.edu
URL: http://www.cityu.edu

Campus Visits: None.

Areas of Study: Accounting (C/B), Business Administration (B), Commerce/Marketing (B), Commerce/Management (B), Computer Systems/Applied Business (C/B), Computer Systems/Telecommunications Management (C/B), Computer Systems/C++ Programming (C/B), Cultural Diversity in Business (C), General Studies (A/B), Humanities/Mass Communications and Journalism (B), Humanities/Philosophy (B), Internetworking (C), Management (A/B), Marketing (B), Medical Office/Laboratory Technology (A), Paralegal Studies (C), Quantitative Studies/Multi-Science (B), Social Science/International Studies (B), Social Science/Psychology (B), Social Science/Sociology (B), Social Science/Political Science (B).

Admissions: A high school diploma or its equivalent is required. The Medical Laboratory Technology Associate is open only to established practitioners.

Program Features: City is a private university founded in 1973 with the goal of providing quality distance education to adult learners. All learners are required to have access to a personal computer. Some courses require communication via computer and modem with electronic classes held in an instructional center on the World Wide Web.

Tuition/Fees: $150 per quarter credit.

Clarkson College

Distance Education
101 South 42nd Street
Omaha, NE 68131-2739
402-552-2551
800-647-5500
E-mail: ajrami@clrkcol.crhsnet.edu (Heidi Ajrami)
URL: http://www.clarksoncollege.edu

Campus Visits: Clinical/nursing students will visit the campus 3 weeks in the summer for clinical trials. Business students may complete studies without campus visits.

Areas of Study: Nursing (B), Business Administration (B), Radiology/Medical Imaging (B).

Admissions: Health programs are advanced placement career programs open only to registered health professionals who are employed in their career areas (RNs or Radiography Technicians). A computer and modem are required to access online systems. Applicants should live at least 100 miles from the campus.

Program Features: Clarkson College is a private institution, specializing in teaching nurses and health services professionals. The college dates its founding back to 1869 with the opening of the Good Samaritan Hospital in Omaha. The distance program began in 1990 and offers courses in print, videotape, and online formats. The nursing program is approved by the Nebraska State Board of Nursing and accredited by the National League for Nursing.

Tuition/Fees: $272 per credit, plus distance learning fees.

College of West Virginia

School of Academic Enrichment and Lifelong Learning (SAELL)
PO Box AG
Beckley, WV 25802-2830
304-253-7351, ext. 366
800-766-6067
E-mail: saell@cwv.edu
URL: http://www.cwv.edu/saell/index.html

Campus Visits: None.

Areas of Study: Business Administration (C/A/B), Business Administration/Accounting (C/A/B), Environmental Studies (A), General Studies (A), Secretarial Science (Administrative) (A), Secretarial Science/Legal (A), Secretarial Science/Medical (A), Travel and Tourism (C/A), Nursing (B), Office Technology (C/A), Travel (C/A).

Admissions: Applicants with high school diplomas or GEDs who are at least 25 years of age are eligible for admission. The Bachelor of Science in Nursing (BSN) is open only to RNs (registered nurses). The ACT is not required for admission but is used for placement and assessment in English and math courses.

Program Features: The College of West Virginia is a private, career-oriented college founded in 1933. Distance-learning programs were launched in 1992. Distance courses are delivered using computer conferencing, mail, and audio and video tapes.

Tuition/Fees: $150 per credit; $200 prior learning assessment fee.

Columbia Union College
7600 Flower Avenue
Takoma Park, MD 20912-7796
301-891-4080
800-782-4769
E-mail: n/a
URL: n/a

Campus Visits: None except for the Bachelor in Respiratory Care, which requires 2 weeks on campus each summer.

Areas of Study: Business Administration (B), Computer Information Systems (B),General Studies (A/B), Psychology (B), Religion (B), Respiratory Therapy (B), Theology (B).

Admissions: High school diploma with a 2.5 GPA and college prep studies or GED. Applicants with GEDs should have composite scores of at least 50. Transfer students must have at least a 2.0 GPA. The Respiratory Care bachelor's degree is open only to those who are eligible to register with the National Board for Respiratory Care.

Program Features: Columbia Union is a private Seventh Day Adventist college. It was founded in 1904 and received regional accreditation in 1942. The independent study program began in 1969. The program is open to all religious denominations.

Tuition/Fees: $165 per credit; 50 percent discount for seniors 60 or older.

Concorida University
Human Services and Professional Development
275 Syndicate Street North
St. Paul, MN 55104
800-211-3370
651-641-8897
E-mail: gradstudies@luther.csp.edu
URL: http://www.csp.edu/hspd

Campus Visits: A five-day orientation is required on campus.

Areas of Study: Management of Human Services (B), Human Services/School Age Care (B), Human Services/Youth Development (B).

Admissions: Applicants should have relevant work experience and 60 credits or an associate's degree with a 2.0 GPA. A computer, modem, and internet access is required.

Program Features: Concordia University is a private institution, founded in 1893, and affiliated with the Lutheran Church. The distance program offers courses online.

Tuition/Fees: $160 per credit, plus computer lease fee.

Eastern Oregon University

Division of Extended Programs
1410 L Avenue
La Grande, OR 97850-2899
541-962-3378
800-544-2195
E-mail: dep@eou.edu
URL: http://www.eou.edu/dep

Campus Visits: Orientation and planning sessions must be attended online for some programs.

Areas of Study: General Studies/Liberal Arts (A/B), Office Administration (A), Business Economics (B), Individualized (B), Philosophy/Politics/Economics (B), Physical Education/Health (B).

Admissions: Varies by program. Writing proficiency exam required. A computer, modem, and internet access are required for most programs.

Program Features: Eastern Oregon University is a member of the publicly supported Oregon University System. The distance program offers courses online, via videotape, surface mail, e-mail, and computer conferencing. Oregon residents may also attend interactive TV courses and weekend courses at selected sites around the state.

Tuition/Fees: $85 per credit, plus computer technology and conferencing fees.

Eckerd College

Program for Experienced Learners
4200 54th Avenue South
St. Petersburg, FL 33711
813-864-8226
800-234-4735
E-mail: eckerdpelds@eckerd.edu
URL: http://www.eckerd.edu/pel

Campus Visits: A weekend workshop is required to begin the program. A 10-day comprehensive seminar may be required.

Areas of Study: American Studies/History (B), Business Management (B), Human Development (B), Organizational Studies (B).

Admissions: Admission is limited to those 25 years or older who have earned at least 30 credits at a regionally accredited college with a minimum 2.0 GPA. A proctored writing test is required of applicants.

Program Features: Eckerd is a private liberal arts college founded in 1958, affiliated with the Presbyterian Church. The Program for Experienced Learners (PEL) began in 1978. Over 2,000 students have earned bachelor's degrees through PEL.

Tuition/Fees: $615 per each 3.5 credit semester course.

Elizabethtown Community College

Continuing Education
EXCEL External Degree
1 Alpha Drive
Elizabethtown, PA 17022-2298
717-361-1411
800-877-2694
E-mail: n/a
URL: n/a

Campus Visits: Four Saturday seminars are required for degree seekers.

Areas of Study: Business Administration (B), Communications (B), Criminal Justice (B), Early Childhood Education (B), Human Services (B), Liberal Studies (B), Medical Technology (B), Public Administration (B).

Admissions: Admission is limited to those who reside within a 400 mile radius of campus. Applicants must have 7 years of work experience in their major. Applicants must have completed at least 50 college transfer credits with a 2.0 GPA.

Program Features: Elizabethtown is a private, comprehensive college founded in 1899 by the Church of the Brethern. Over 400 adults have earned their degrees through EXCEL since the program began in 1972. Learners arrange tutorials with faculty, but crucial work is also done through intensive campus-based Saturday Seminars.

Tuition/Fees: Minimum fees for bachelor's degree completion, including the four required on-campus seminars, is $3,300.

Embry-Riddle Aeronautical University

Center for Distance Learning
600 S. Clyde Morris Boulevard
Daytona Beach, Florida 32114-3900
904-226-6397
800-359-3728
E-mail: ecinfo@ec.db.erau.edu
URL: http://www.ec.db.erau.edu

Campus Visits: None.

Areas of Study: Professional Aeronautics (A/B), Aviation Business Management (A), Management of Technical Operations (B).

Admissions: Open to qualified aviation professionals in military and private sectors who can show evidence of college or college-level competency and hold a GED or high school diploma. Programs are open to pilots, aeronautical technicians, flight instructors, air traffic control personnel, aviation mechanics, managers of aviation enterprises, and other aviation professionals.

Program Features: Embry-Riddle is a private college which has long specialized in aviation degrees and training. Embry-Riddle also offers on-campus aviation programs in Prescott, Arizona, and Wiesbaden, Germany. Additional campus-based specialties include Aviation Computer Science and Engineering. Some independent study courses are available via the internet and e-mail, and some use videotapes. Special credit is given for most military and civilian aviation licenses and proficiencies.

Tuition/Fees: $134 per credit

Empire State College SUNY

Center for Distance Learning
Three Union Avenue
Saratoga Springs, NY 12866-4391
800-847-3000
518-587-2100
E-mail: cdl@sescva.esc.edu
URL: http://www.esc.edu

Campus Visits: None.

Areas of Study: Arts (A/B), Business, Management and Economics (A/B), Business, Management, and Economics/Accounting (A/B), Community and Human Services (A/B), Community and Human Services/Justice (A/B), Community and Human Services/Management of Health Services (A/B), Cultural Studies (A/B), Educational Studies (A/B), Historical Studies (A/B), Human Development (A/B), Science, Mathematics and Technology (A/B), Social Theory, Social Structure, and Change (A/B), Interdisciplinary Studies (A/B), Labor Studies (A/B).

Admissions: Open to those with a high school diploma, its equivalent, or the ability to benefit from a college education. Students wishing to access the college online and take courses via computer conferencing will need a computer, modem, and internet access.

Program Features: Empire State College is the adult learner's division of the State University of New York (SUNY). The Center for Distance Learning (CDL) was established in 1979. Some courses utilize computer conferencing.

Tuition/Fees Average $116 per credit for degree seekers; $140 per credit for others; $300 degree assessment fee. Additional fees apply to courses taken via computer conferencing.

Emporia State University

Office of Continuing Education
Office of Lifelong Learning
1200 Commercial Street
Emporia, KS 66801-5087
316-341-5385
E-mail: achleits@emporia.edu
URL: http://www.emporia.edu/lifelong/home.htm

Campus Visits: None.

Areas of Study: General Studies (B).

Admissions: Open to those with an associate's degree or two years of prior college who have internet access to complete courses online.

Program Features: Emporia State University is a comprehensive, government-supported university founded in 1963.

Tuition/Fees: $76 per credit.

Florence-Darlington Technical College

Admissions
PO Box 100548
Florence, SC 29501-0548
843-661-8133
E-mail: whitea@flo.tec.sc.us (Angela White)
URL: http://www.flo.tec.sc.us

Campus Visits: None.

Areas of Study: Liberal Arts (A).

Admissions: Applicants should be 18 with a high school diploma or GED.

Program Features: Florence-Darlington is a two-year, publicly funded technical college founded in 1963. Courses are delivered via videotape, interactive television (ITV), and the internet.

Tuition/Fees: $54.50 per credit (county residents); $60.50 (other state residents); $128 (out of state); $209 (international).

Goddard College

Off-Campus Programs
Plainfield, VT 05667
802-454-8311
800-468-4888
E-mail: admissions@earth.goddard.edu
URL: http://www.goddard.edu

Campus Visits: A 1-week residency is required at the beginning of each semester.

Areas of Study: Individualized Studies (B).

Admissions: Open.

Program Features: Goddard is a private college founded as a progressive experiment in higher education. The Adult Degree Program began in 1969. Learners design their own degrees. Much of the work is done through field experience, and individually designed learning contracts, rather than through prepackaged study courses. Every three weeks students exchange homework packets with campus faculty.

Tuition/Fees: $3,820 per semester, plus $295 residency fee each semester.

Graceland College

Outreach Programs
Division of Nursing
700 College Avenue
Lamoni, IA 50140

800-537-6276
E-mail: n/a
URL: http://Outreach.Graceland.edu

Campus Visits: Applicants complete two-week residencies on campus.

Areas of Study: Liberal Studies/Health Care Administration (B), Liberal Studies/Health Care Psychology (B), Nursing (B).

Admissions: Open to registered nurses (RNs).

Program Features: Graceland is a private college founded in 1895 by the Reorganized Church of Christ of Latter Day Saints (Mormons). Courses are delivered via online chat and conferencing, phone conferencing, videotape, and mail.

Tuition/Fees: $225 per credit for independent study.

Indiana Institute of Technology
Extended Studies Division
1600 East Washington Boulevard
Fort Wayne, IN 46803
219-422-5561, ext. 310
888-666-TECH
E-mail: merchant@indtech.edu (Sarah Merchant)
URL: http://www.indtech.edu

Campus Visits: None.

Areas of Study: Business Administration/Finance (Accounting) (A), Business Administration/Management (A/B), Business Administration/Finance (Accounting) (B), Business Administration/Human Resources (B), Business Administration/Marketing (B).

Admissions: Open to those 23 or older who have significant work experience and a high school diploma or GED.

Program Features: Indiana Institute of Technology is a private college, founded in 1930. The college first offered extended studies in 1982. Courses are delivered via surface mail.

Tuition/Fees: $193 per credit.

Indiana University
Division of Extended Studies
School of Continuing Education
Owen Hall 001
Bloomington, IN 47405-5201
812-855-2292
800-334-1011
E-mail: bulletin@indiana.edu
URL: http://www.extend.indiana.edu

Campus Visits: None.

Areas of Study: General Studies (A/B), Healthcare Accounting (C), Labor Studies (C/A/B).

Admissions: Applicants without a high school diploma or GED may be admitted provisionally and admitted regularly after successful completion of at least 12 Indiana University credits with a 2.0 GPA. Transfer students with cumulative GPAs below 2.0 are admitted provisionally.

Program Features: Indiana University is a comprehensive, government-supported university founded in 1820. The college has offered independent study since 1912. More than 18,000 students enroll in independent study each year.

Tuition/Fees: $89.45 per credit.

Iowa State University of Science and Technology
Professional Agriculture
Off-Campus Degree
206B Curtiss Hall
Ames, IA 50011-1050
800-747-4478
E-mail: holson@iastate.edu (Helen Olson, Advisor)
URL: http://www.exnet.iastate.edu/pages/ece

Campus Visits: Summer workshops of 2 to 5 days may be required.

Areas of Study: Professional Agriculture (B).

Admissions: Inquire directly.

Program Features: Iowa is a comprehensive, government-supported university, offering a variety of on-campus majors and degrees.

Tuition/Fees: $107 per credit.

Ivy Tech State College
Distance Degree Admissions
7999 US Highway 41 South
Terre Haute, IN 47802
812-299-1121
E-mail: darney@ivy.tec.in.us (Don Arvey)
URL: http://ivytech7.cc.in.us/distance-education

Campus Visits: None unless an ASSET entrance exam is required.

Areas of Study: Accounting (A), Business Administration (A), Design Technology (A), Restaurant Management (A).

Admissions: Open.

Program Features: Ivy Tech State College, founded in 1966, is a part of the two-year state college system of Indiana. Courses are offered online and require internet access.

Tuition/Fees: $66.50 per credit (Indiana residents); $123.50 (others/pending).

Jones International University
9697 East Mineral Avenue
PO Box 6512
Englewood, CO 80155-6512

303-784-8045
URL: http://www.international.edu
E-mail: info@international.edu

Campus Visits: None.

Areas of Study: Business Communication (B), Business Communication Skills, Communication Management (C), Communication Technologies (C), Business Technologies (C), Early Reading Instruction (C), Oral and Written Communication Skills (C), Organizational Communication (C), Practical Communication Technology Tools for Managers (C).

Admissions: Applicants to bachelor study should hold an associate's degree or its equivalent with a 2.5 transfer GPA. Internet access is required.

Program Features: Jones International University is a private college founded in 1996 to offer competency-based courses via the internet.

Tuition/Fees: $200 per credit.

Kansas State University
Non-Traditional Study
Division of Continuing Education
221 College Court
Manhattan, KS 66506-6002
913-532-5687
800-622-2KSU
E-mail: info@dce.ksu.edu
URL: http://www.dce.ksu.edu

Campus Visits: None.

Areas of Study: Animal Sciences and Industry (B), Interdisciplinary Social Science (B).

Admissions: Open to applicants who have at least 60 credits or an associate's degree with a 2.0 grade average.

Program Features: Kansas State University is part of the publicly supported educational system of the state of Kansas. The Animal Sciences degree focuses on the processing and management of food production such as chicken and poultry ranges, dairy farms, and breeding operations.

Tuition/Fees: $90 per credit plus fees.

Lesley College
Adult Baccalaureate
29 Everett Street
Cambridge, MA 02138
617-349-8300
E-mail: info@mail.lesley.edu
URL: http://www.lesley.edu

Campus Visits: The Intensive Residency Option requires degree seekers to attend either a nine-day residency at the beginning of each semester or one, eighteen-day residency each academic year.

Areas of Study: Arts (B), Creative Writing (B), Psychology (B), Holistic Studies (B), Humanities (B), Management (B), Individualized (B), Liberal Studies/Arts and Sciences (B), Social and Behavioral Sciences (B).

Admissions: Open.

Program Features: Lesley is a comprehensive private college founded in 1909. The Adult Degree Program began offering alternative degrees in 1953.

Tuition/Fees: $260 per credit.

Liberty University

External Degree Program
School of Lifelong Learning
Box 11803
Lynchburg, VA 24506-1803
800-228-7354
E-mail: n/a
URL: n/a

Campus Visits: A one- to two-week campus residency may be required each summer.

Areas of Study: Business Administration (B), Business/Accounting (B), Business/Finance (B), Business/Management (B), Business/Marketing (B), General Studies (A/B), Psychology (B), Religion (A/B).

Admissions: Open to those 25 or older. Applicants should adhere to Christian beliefs.

Program Features: Liberty University is a private, Christian college founded in 1971 by the Reverend Jerry Falwell. Courses are delivered via videotape.

Tuition/Fees: $180 per credit.

Marywood College

Office of Distance Education
2300 Adams Avenue
Scranton, PA 18509
717-348-6235
800-836-6940
E-mail: disted_info@ac.marywood.edu
URL: http://www.marywood.edu

Campus Visits: Two campus visits of one to two weeks each are required in the spring and summer of each year to earn a degree.

Areas of Study: Office Administration (C), Comprehensive Business Skills (C), Accounting (B), Business Administration/Financial Planning (B), Business Administration/Management (B), Business Administration/Marketing (B), Individualized (B), Professional Communications (C).

Admissions: Open to those 21 or older who live at least 25 miles away from Marywood.

Program Features: Marywood is a comprehensive, private Catholic college, founded in 1915. Distance learning has been offered for the past 20 years. Degrees and courses meet CPA (Certified Public Accountant) eligibility requirements in Pennsylvania. An individualized degree major may be designed by those who already hold an associate's degree.

Tuition/Fees: $266 per credit.

Mercy College

MerLIN Distance Learning
Office of Admissions
555 Broadway
Dobbs Ferry, NY 10522-1189
800-MERCY-NY
914-674-9227
E-mail: Admission@MerLIN.Mercynet.edu
URL: http://MerLIN.MercyNet.edu

Campus Visits: None.

Areas of Study: Business (B), Computer Science (B), Direct Marketing (C), Liberal Studies (B), Psychology (B).

Admissions: Computer, modem, and internet access required.

Program Features: Mercy College is a comprehensive, private college, founded in 1950.

Tuition/Fees: $285 per credit.

Moody Bible Institute

Center for External Studies
820 North LaSalle Boulevard
Chicago, IL 60610-3284
312-329-8019
800-955-1123
E-mail: nstorms@mbi.moody.edu
URL: n/a
Campus Visits: None.

Areas of Study: Biblical Studies (C/A/B).

Admissions: Open to Christians, 17 years or older, who have high school equivalency and are members of an evangelical Protestant Church.

Program Features: Moody is a private college, founded in 1886, providing Bible and ministry training for Christians of all ages. An independent study program was launched in 1901.

Tuition/Fees: $110 per degree credit; $30 per CEU.

Murray State University

Center for Continuing Education
1 Murray Street
Murray, KY 42071-3308
502-762-6971
E-mail: n/a
URL: http://www.murraystate.edu

Campus Visits: A one-day seminar may be completed in April, August, or December.

Areas of Study: Administrative (Business) Sciences (B), Applied Science and Technology (B), Communications (B), Human Services (B), Humanities (B), Social Sciences (B), Natural Sciences (B).

Admissions: Applicants must have a high school diploma or GED, have a 2.0 transfer GPA, and be willing to assume primary responsibility for their learning.

Program Features: Murray State University is a government-supported college offering a variety of on-campus programs. The Bachelor of Independent Studies (BIS) is the only degree awarded at a distance. Applicants to the BIS program develop individual learning contracts with faculty to undertake studies and complete special projects as needed.

Tuition/Fees: $79 per credit.

New Hampshire College

Distance Education Program
2500 North River Road
Manchester, NH 03106-1046
603-645-9766
Email: leewil@nhc.edu (Dr. Lee Williams)
URL: http://www.dist-ed.nhc.edu

Campus Visits: None.

Admissions: All applicants must have access to a computer and modem. Courses are offered online via the internet.

Areas of Study: Accounting (C), Computer Programming (C), Human Resource Management (C).

Program Features: New Hampshire College is a private institution founded in 1932. The distance program operates as an extension of on-campus offerings. Distance-learning courses are offered online via the internet.

Tuition/Fees: $149 per credit average.

New Jersey Institute of Technology

Distance Learning
Guttenberg Information Technologies Center, Suite 5600
University Heights
Newark, NJ 07102-1982
800-624-9850
973-642-7015
E-mail: dl@njit.edu
URL: http //www.njit.edu/DL

Campus Visits: None.

Admissions: High school diploma or GED minimum. All applicants should own computers with internet access as well as VCRs.

Areas of Study: Computer Science (B), Information Systems (Computers) (B), Webmaster (C).

Program Features: The New Jersey Institute of Technology, founded in 1881, is government supported and operates as part of the state university system of New Jersey. Some courses utilize computer conferencing, e-mail, and CD-ROM tutorials. Some courses use mailed videotapes of classroom lectures.

Tuition/Fees: $516 per 3-credit course, plus $136 fees (New Jersey residents); $1,071 per 3-credit course, plus $136 fees (nonresidents).

New School for Social Research

Admissions
Distance Instruction for Adult Learners (DIAL)
68 Fifth Avenue
New York, NY 10011
212-229-5880
E-mail: dialexec@dialnsa.edu
URL: http://www.dialnsa.edu

Campus Visits: None.

Admissions: Applicants should have completed 60 semester credits or have an associate's degree prior to applying. All applicants must own or be able to access a computer and modem. Courses are offered online via the internet.

Areas of Study: Liberal Arts (B).

Program Features: The New School for Social Research is a private college, founded in 1919. The New School has offered a Bachelor of Arts in Social Science and the Humanities (General Studies) since 1944. The Distance Instruction for Adult Learners (DIAL) program offers learners a chance to complete their bachelor's online.

Tuition/Fees: $570 per credit.

New York Institute of Technology

The On-Line Campus
PO Box 9029
Central Islip, NY 11722-9029
800-222-NYIT
E-mail: olc@iris.nyu.edu
URL: http://www.nyit.edu/olc

Campus Visits: None.

Admissions: Courses are offered online. Applicants must have computer and modem.

Areas of Study: Behavioral Science/Criminal Justice (B), Behavioral Science/Psychology (B), Behavioral Science/Sociology (B), Business Administration/Management (B), Hospitality Management (B), Interdisciplinary Studies (B), Telecommunications Management (B).

Program Features: The New York Institute of Technology is a private, comprehensive college that supports one of the first online college programs in the United States. Applicants begin studies by taking a 1-credit course to learn how to attend courses offered via computer conferencing.

Tuition/Fees: $345–$393 per credit.

Northamptom Community College

College-At-Home Program
3835 Green Pond Road
Bethlehem, PA 18020-7599
610-861-4100
E-mail: n/a
URL: http://www.nrhm.cc.pa.us

Campus Visits: None.

Areas of Study: Business Administration/Accounting (A), Business Administration (A), Child Care (C), Liberal Arts (General Studies) (A), Library Technical Assistant (C).

Admissions: Open.

Program Features: Northampton is a publicly supported community college offering a variety of two-year degrees on campus. Courses are offered via mail, e-mail, video, and other means.

Tuition/Fees: Ranges from $63 per credit (local county residents) to $189 per credit (others).

Northern Virginia Community College

Extended Learning Institute
8333 Little River Turnpike
Annadale, VA 22003-3796
703-323-3379
E-mail: nvstovm@nv.cc.va.us (Merrily Stover, Director)
URL: http://eli.nv.cc.va.us

Campus Visits: None unless lab courses are required.

Areas of Study: Business Administration (A), Engineering (A), General Studies (A), Information Systems Technology (A), Liberal Arts (A), Public Administration (A).

Admissions: Open.

Program Features: Northern Virginia Community College is publicly supported and supports 5 campus sites offering more than 150 programs to students in addition to the distance-learning program.

Tuition/Fees: $48.50 per credit (Virginia residents); $162.20 per credit (nonresidents).

Northwestern College

Center for Distance Education
3003 Snelling Avenue North
Saint Paul, MN 55113-1598
651-631-5494
800-308-5495
E-mail: distance.ed.dpt@nwc.edu
URL: http://www.nwc.edu/disted

Campus Visits: None.

Areas of Study: Biblical Studies (C/A/B), Intercultural Ministries (B).

Admissions: Open to Christians with GEDs or high school diplomas. The Intercultural Ministries program is limited to those with two years of prior college experience.

Program Features: Northwestern is a private, nondenominational Christian college founded in 1902. The college's mission is to provide a Christ-centered education. Students are assigned local mentors whom they meet with weekly to complete the degree.

Tuition/Fees: $120–121 per credit; senior, group, and clergy discounts are available.

Northwood Institute

University College—Nontraditional Program
3225 Cook Road
Midland, MI 48640
517-837-4411
800-445-5873
E-mail: carlvw@northwood.edu
URL: http://www.northwood.edu

Campus Visits: Degree seekers attend two three-day seminars.

Areas of Study: Business Management (A/B).

Admissions: Open to those 25 or older who have a transfer GPA of 2.0. Applicants should have good writing skills, experience in the business world, and internet access.

Program Features: Northwood is a private college founded in 1959 to provide business- and career-oriented education for working adults.

Tuition/Fees: $70–$225 per quarter credit.

Ohio University

Adult Learning Services
Tupper Hall 301
Athens, Ohio 45701-2979
740-593-2150
800-444-2420
E-mail: external.student@ohio.edu
URL: http://www.cats.ohiou.edu/~adullear/index.htm

Campus Visits: None.

Areas of Study: Arts or Sciences (General Studies) (A), Individualized/Specialized Studies (A/B).

Admissions: The Bachelor of Specialized Studies is not open to those who already hold a bachelor's degree. Applicants must have a minimum GPA of 2.0 on transfer credits.

Program Features: Ohio University is a comprehensive, government-supported college founded in 1804. More than 5,000 applicants enroll each year through distance learning. The Bachelor of Specialized Studies (BSS) and Associate in Individualized Studies (AIS) allow for self-designed majors. The availability of specialized studies is dependent on faculty availability.

Tuition/Fees: $64 per quarter credit; $40 application fee; $75 annual advisement fee.

Oklahoma City University

PLUS—Competency-Based Degree Program
Petree College of Arts and Sciences
2501 North Blackwelder
Oklahoma City, OK 73106-1493
405-521-5265
800-633-7242
E-mail: plus@frodo.okcu.edu
URL: http://www.okcu.edu/plus

Campus Visits: A weekend orientation is required.

Areas of Study: Business (B), Individualized (B), Liberal Arts (General Studies) (B), Technical Management (B).

Admissions: The program is open to adults who have self-direction. Most applicants have completed some college prior to applying.

Program Features: Oklahoma City University is a private Methodist sponsored college founded in 1904. The PLUS program began serving adult learners in 1976. Distance courses are delivered primarily by surface mail.

Tuition/Fees: Averages $160 per credit plus fees.

Oral Roberts University
Distance Education
School of Lifelong Education
7777 South Lewis Avenue
Tulsa, OK 74171
918-495-6238
800-678-8876
E-mail: slle@oru.edu
URL: http://www.oru.edu/university/departments/alsc_slle

Campus Visits: All degree seekers attend one or two short summer residencies.

Areas of Study: Ministries (B), Elementary Christian School Education (B), Christian Care and Counseling (B), Business Administration (B), Liberal Studies (B).

Admissions: Open to those 22 or older except military personnel who may be younger. A Christian minister's recommendation is required.

Program Features: Oral Roberts University is a private college, founded in 1963, dedicated to Christian values in education.

Tuition/Fees: $105 per credit.

Pennsylvania State University
Department of Distance Education
207 Mitchell Building
University Park, PA 16802-3601
814-865-5403
800-252-3592
E-mail: psude@cde.psu.edu
URL: http://www.outreach.psu.edu/de

Campus Visits: None.

Areas of Study: Administration of Justice (C), Adult Development and Aging (C), Business Administration (C/A), Business Logistics (C), Dietary Management (C/A), Children, Youth, and Family Services (C), Dietetic Food Management (A), Electrical Engineering (C), Counselor Education/Chemical Dependency Counseling (C), Human Development and Family Studies (A), Hotel, Restaurant Management (A), Human Resources (C), Legal Issues for Business (C), Letters, Arts and Sciences (Liberal Arts) (A), Nursing Management (C), Paralegal (C), Retail

Management (C), Small Business Management (C), Turfgrass Management (C), Writing Social Commentary (C).

Admissions: Applicants to the associate's degree must have completed 18 credits with a 2.0 or higher grade average or may enroll in Pennsylvania State independent-study courses, and will be eligible for degree studies after successful completion of 9 credits with a satisfactory grade average.

Program Features: Pennsylvania State is a comprehensive, government-supported university. PSU began offering distance education more than 100 years ago. Courses are delivered using mixed platforms ranging from surface mail to fax, e-mail, internet conferencing, and videotape.

Tuition/Fees: $115 per credit; $195 and up per 3-credit CEU course.

Prescott College
Adult Degree Program (ADP)
220 Grove Avenue
Prescott, AZ 86301
520-776-7116
E-mail: n/a
URL: http://www.prescott.edu

Campus Visits: A 3-day orientation and a weekend Liberal Arts seminar are required.

Areas of Study: Community Development (B), Environmental Services (B), Human Services (B), Individualized (B), Management (B), Teacher Education (B).

Admissions: Open to those with a high school diploma or GED and 30 semester credits of college work. Applicants with less than 30 credits may be provisionally admitted.

Program Features: Prescott is a private college, founded in 1966. Learners who hold a bachelor's and seek only Arizona Teacher Certification are welcome. The Education program is approved by the Arizona State Board in Elementary, Secondary, Special Education, Bilingual Education, and English as a Second Language areas.

Tuition/Fees: $195 per quarter credit.

Regents College University of the State of New York
7 Columbia Circle
Albany, NY 12203-5159
518-464-8500
E-mail: rcinfo@cnsvax.albany.edu
URL: http://www.regents.edu

Campus Visits: None.

Areas of Study: Area Studies (B), Biology, (B), Business (A/B), Business/Accounting (B), Business/Finance (B), Business/International Business (B), Business/Management of Information Systems (B), Business/Management of Human Resources (B), Business/Marketing (B), Business/Operations Management (B), Chemistry (B), Communication (B) (Journalism; or Radio, TV, and Film; or Rhetoric; or Organizational Communication; or Theater), Economics (B), Foreign Language and Literature (B), Geography (B), Geology (B), History (B), Liberal Arts (A/B), Literature (B), Mathematics (B), Music (B), Nursing (A/B), Nursing/Human Resources Management (B), Nursing/Biology (B), Nursing/Psychology (B), Nursing/Sociology (B), Philosophy (B), Physics (B), Political Science (B), Psychology (B), Sociology (B),

Technology/Computer Information Systems (B), Technology/Computer Software (A), Technology/Electronics Technology (A/B), Technology/Individualized (A/B), Technology/Nuclear Technology (A/B).

Admissions: Open to all except professional areas, which require employment or licensing to complete degree clinicals or practicums such as nursing or nuclear technology. A computer and modem will facilitate access to an online support system.

Program Features: Regents College is the adult and distance learning college of the University of the State of New York (USNY). Regents was established in 1970 and awards about 4,000 degrees each year. More than 17,000 learners enroll with Regents each year. An online Bulletin Board System (BBS) is available. Regents offers no courses and operates exclusively as an assessment institution, allowing learners to transfer in courses taken elsewhere or take challenge exams to complete degrees.

Tuition/Fees: Regents offers no courses. Fees are charged to consolidate credits toward a degree and receive advisement on degree completion through alternative options or transfer credits: $650–$750 Enrollment Fee; $325 Annual Student Fee; $410–$440 Diploma and Graduation Fee; $1,100 Special Assessment.

Regis University

Distance Learning
7600 East Orchard Road, Suite 100N
Englewood, CO 80111
303-458-4383
800-805-1385
E-mail: ggrauber@regis.edu (Greg Grauberger)
URL: http://www.regis.edu/rdl

Campus Visits: None.

Areas of Study: Business Administration (C/B).

Admissions: Open to those who have completed 30 credits already with a 2.0 GPA and have three years of work experience.

Program Features: Regis is a private Jesuit university, founded in 1877. The distance degree is delivered using online communications in accelerated 8-week formats.

Tuition/Fees: $213 per credit (Colorado residents); $203 per credit (nonresidents).

Rio Salado College

Distance Learning
2323 West 14th Street
Tempe, Arizona 85281
602-517-8150
E-mail: lindley.john@a1.rio.maricopa.edu (John Lindley)
URL: http://www.rio.maricopa.edu

Campus Visits: None.

Areas of Study: Computer Usage and Technology (A), General Studies (A), Liberal Arts (A), Waste Water Treatment (A).

Admissions: Students over 18 years of age should have a GED or high school diploma or demonstrate the ability to succeed in college by presenting transfer credits. Open to those with computer and internet access. Some courses require a VCR, cassette player, and CD-ROM capability.

Program Features: Rio Salado, founded in 1978, is one of the community colleges of Maricopa County. Courses are delivered via internet conferencing, videotape, surface mail, and other means.

Tuition/Fees: $38 per credit (county residents); $38 per credit plus $25 per credit (others).

Rochester Institute of Technology

Distance Learning Office
91 Lomb Memorial Drive
Rochester, NY 14623-5603
716-475-5089
800-CALL-RIT
E-mail: disted@rit.edu
URL: http://www.distancelearning.rit.edu

Campus Visits: None.

Areas of Study: Applied Computing (B), Electrical/Mechanical Engineering (B), Electrical/Mechanical/Manufacturing Management (B), Emergency Management (C/B), Environmental Management (C/B), Health Systems Administration (C/B), Management (B), Quality Management (C/B), Technical Communication (C/B), Telecommunications (C/B).

Admissions: Applicants to the Engineering bachelor's should hold an Engineering associate's or the equivalent. Applicants to other programs should have some college or transfer credits. A computer, modem, and internet access are required for online coursework.

Program Features: Rochester is a private comprehensive college, founded in 1989. Distance courses are delivered using videotapes, internet conferencing, and phone support.

Tuition/Fees: $240–$263 per quarter credit.

Roger Williams University

The Open Program
One Old Ferry Road
Bristol, RI 02809-2921
401-254-3530
E-mail: jws@alpha.rwu.edu (John Stout)
URL: n/a

Campus Visits: None.

Areas of Study: Business Administration (B), Criminal Justice (B), Industrial Technology (B), Public Administration (B).

Admissions: Open to students who have advanced academic standing in college or the equivalent in military, life experience, ACE (Army Continuing Education)/PONSI (Program on Noncollegiate Sponsored Instruction), or exam credits.

Program Features: Roger Williams is a private college, chartered in 1956 to award degrees. Those who reside near Roger Williams can arrange for many majors through partial classroom and partial independent study in the Open Program.

Tuition/Fees: $1,155 per 3-credit course.

Rogers University
Office of Admissions
Online Campus
1701 West Will Rogers Boulevard
Claremore, OK 74017
918-343-7548
E-mail: admissions@ruonline.edu
URL: http://www.rogersu.edu/online

Campus Visits: None.

Areas of Study: Computer Science (Business Option) (A), Humanities (A), Liberal Arts (A), Business Administration (A).

Admissions: High school diploma or a GED required unless 24 college credits have already been completed. Degree seekers 24 years old or younger, or those with less than 24 college credits may be required to take standardized exams (ACT/SAT) for placement in math and English. Open to those with a computer and modem.

Program Features: Rogers University is a part of the government-supported college system of the state of Oklahoma. Courses are delivered via videotape, online discussion boards, and virtual classrooms on the World Wide Web.

Tuition/Fees: $245 per 3-credit course (Oklahoma residents); $435 per 3-credit course (others).

Saint Joseph's College
Department 840—Admissions
278 Whites Bridge Road
Standish, ME 04084-5263
207-892-7841
800-752-4723
E-mail: n/a
URL: http://www.sjcme.edu

Campus Visits: None for Certificates. A minimum two-week summer residency is required for degree seekers. Clinical requirements in the Licensed Practical Nurse (LPN)-Bachelor of Science in Nursing (BSN) limit enrollment to students residing in Maine and Northern New England.

Areas of Study: American Studies (B), Business Administration/Banking (B), Business Administration/Management (C/A/B), Christian Tradition (C), Health Care Administration (C/B), Liberal Studies (B), Long-Term Health Care Administration (C/B), Nursing (B), Professional Arts/Education (B), Professional Arts/Health Care Administration (B), Professional Arts/Human Services (B), Professional Arts/Psychology (B), Radiological Science (B), Respiratory Care (B), Women's Studies (C).

Admissions: Open to those with a high school diploma or GED. The Nursing, Radiology, and Respiratory programs are restricted to students who have professional licenses or registration status in their fields. The Professional Arts program is open only to health care professionals who are licensed or registered and who have at least 30 college credits.

Program Features: Saint Joseph's is a private Catholic college founded in 1912. The distance learning program was launched in 1976. More than 4,000 learners participate in the distance program each year. The Nursing program is accredited by the National League for Nursing.

Tuition/Fees: $185 per credit.

Saint Leo's College

University Alliance
9417 Princess Palm Avenue
Tampa, FL 33619-8317
888-622-7344
E-mail: degrees@universityalliance.com
URL: http://www.universityalliance.com

Campus Visits: None.

Areas of Study: Accounting (B), Business Administration (B), Computer Information Systems (B).

Admissions: Open to those with internet access.

Program Features: St. Leo's is a private Catholic college chartered in 1899. The college serves more than 8,000 students on sixteen regional campuses. The distance degree is delivered online via computer conferencing with videotape, audio, and textbook supplements.

Tuition/Fees: $290 per credit.

Saint Mary of the Woods College

Women's External Degree Program (WED)
Admissions Office/Guerin Hall
Saint Mary of the Woods, IN 47876
812-535-5106
800-926-SMWC
E-mail: wedadms@woods.smwc.edu
URL: http://www.woods.smwc.edu

Campus Visits: A two-day orientation is required to begin studies. Half-day degree planning sessions are required four times each year at the beginning of each semester.

Areas of Study: Accounting (B), Business Administration (C/A/B), Computer Information Systems (C/B), Education (A/B), English (B), Gerontology (C/A/B), History (B), Humanities (A/B), Human Resources (B), Human Services (B), Management (B), Marketing (B), Math (B), Paralegal Studies (C/A/B), Psychology (B), Social Science (B), Theology (C/B).

Admissions: Open to women with high school diplomas or GEDs. Applicants to teacher education programs must be able to complete teaching internships within a 400-mile radius of Saint Mary's College.

Program Features: Saint Mary's, founded in 1840, is the oldest women's Catholic Liberal Arts college in the United States. The Women's External Degree program (WED) began in 1973.

Tuition/Fees: $252 per credit.

Saint Petersburg Junior College

Veterinary Technology Program
Health Education Center
PO Box 13489
Saint Petersburg, FL 33733
727-341-3653
E-mail: whiteg@email.spjc.cc.fl.us
URL: http://hec.spjc.cc.fl.us/CHIP/VT1.html

Campus Visits: Final lab-exam practicals may need to be taken on campus.

Areas of Study: Veterinary Technology (A).

Admissions: Priority is given to registrants who have already completed general education requirements, are currently employed by a veterinarian, and whose workplace has a vet tech or vets who are AVMA (American Veterinary Medical Association) members. Computer, modem, and internet access required.

Program Features: Saint Petersburg, founded in 1927, is a government-supported two-year community college. The distance education program is delivered online.

Tuition/Fees: $45.84 per credit (Florida residents); $166.95 (nonresidents); $20 per course technology fees.

Seattle Central Community College

Distance-Learning Office
1701 Broadway, 2BE1144
Seattle, WA 98122
206-587-4060
800-510-1724
E-mail: dislrn@central.sccd.ctc.edu
URL:http://seaced.sccd.ctc.edu/central/virtcoll/index.html

Campus Visits: None.

Areas of Study: Liberal Arts (General Studies).

Admissions: Open to those 18 or older with at least a 2.0 GPA or C transfer average.

Program Features: Seattle Community College is part of Washington State's publicly supported junior college system, serving an on-campus enrollment of almost 10,000. Courses are delivered via E-mail, CD-ROM, videotape, and cable.

Tuition/Fees: $260 per 5-quarter credit course (Washington residents); $360 per course (nonresidents); Plus videotape(s) and other course fees.

Skidmore College

University Without Walls
815 North Broadway
Saratoga Springs, NY 12866-1632
518-580-5054
E-mail: uww@skidmore.edu
URL: http://www.skidmore.edu (Click on UWW)

Campus Visits: All learners attend three brief meetings: an admissions interview; an advising session to plan the degree; and a degree plan meeting to approve the final course of study.

Areas of Study: American Studies (B), Anthropology (B), Art (B), Biology (B), Business (B), Chemistry (B), Classics (B), Computer Science (B), Dance (B), Economics (B), English (B), Foreign Languages (B), French (B), Geology (B), German (B), Government (B), History (B), Individualized (B), Liberal Studies (B), Literature (B), Math (B), Music (B), Philosophy (B), Physical Education (B), Physics (B), Psychology (B), Political Science (B), Religion (B), Russian (B), Sociology (B), Spanish (B), Theater (B), Women's Studies (B).

Admissions: Open.

Program Features: Skidmore is a private liberal arts college founded in 1903. The University Without Walls was founded in 1971 and allows learners to design their own degrees.

Tuition/Fees: $2,400 annual fee; $400 per independent study course; $200 final project assessment.

Southern Christian University
EXCEL Distance Degree
1200 Taylor Road
Montgomery, AL 36124-0240
800-351-4040
334-277-2277
E-mail: n/a
URL: http://www.southernchristian.edu

Campus Visits: A three-day orientation seminar must be attended.

Areas of Study: General Studies (B), Ministry (B).

Admissions: Open to motivated students who hold GEDs or high school credentials and have internet access.

Program Features: Southern Christian University is a private college. The EXCEL distance-learning program began in 1997 and uses the internet, videotape, and toll-free phones to deliver courses.

Tuition/Fees: $220 per credit.

Southwestern Adventist University
Adult Degree Program
Keene, TX 76059
817-645-3921
800-433-2240
E-mail: n/a
URL: n/a

Campus Visits: An eight-day campus residency is required to begin. At least one additional three-day seminar is required each year.

Areas of Study: Business Administration/Accounting (B), Business Administration/Management (B), Business Administration/Computer Information Systems (B), Communications/Broadcasting (B), Communications/Corporate Communications (Public Relations) (B), Communications/Journalism (B), Criminal Justice (B), Education/Elementary (B),

Education/Secondary (B), English (Literature) (B), Individualized (B), Math (B), Office Systems Administration (B), Psychology (B), Religion (B), Social Science/History (B), Social Science/International Affairs (B), Social Science/Sociology (B).

Admissions: Open to applicants 22 or older who have never been to college or have been out of college for at least a year.

Program Features: Southwestern is a private Seventh Day Adventist college, founded in 1893. Education programs are approved for Texas teacher certification (elementary or secondary certifications), but learners must complete ten weeks of student teaching in the Keene area. Some educational lab courses may need to be taken on campus also. Course delivery methods include surface mail, videotape, and electronic mail submission.

Tuition/Fees: $293 per credit; $3,616 per semester.

Southwestern Assemblies of God College ─────────────────

School of Distance Education
1200 Sycamore
Waxahachie, TX 75165
888-937-7248
E-mail: info@sagu.edu
URL: http://www.sagu.edu

Campus Visits: Four-day residencies are required to begin degrees. Two-day residencies are required thereafter at the beginning of each semester.

Areas of Study: Accounting (B), Biblical Studies (A/B), Business Administration (A/B), Business and English Education (B), Children's Ministries (B), Christian Education (B), Church Business Administration (B), Counseling Psychology (B), Cross-Cultural Missions (B), Education (A), Elementary Education (B), English (A), English Education (B), Foreign Language (A), History Education (B), Instrumental Performance (B), Management (B), Media (A), Music Education (B), Music Ministries (B), Ministries (B), Piano Performance (B), Professional Development (Individualized) (B), Psychology (A), Secondary Education (B), Social Science (A), Urban Ministries (B), Youth Ministries (B), Vocal Performance (B).

Admissions: Open to those 23 or older.

Program Features: Southwestern is a private, Bible-based college, founded in 1943 and affiliated with the Assemblies of God, Pentecostal church. The School of Distance Learning was founded in 1984. The Teacher Education program is endorsed by the Texas Education Agency (TEA).

Tuition/Fees: $190 per credit.

Stephens College ─────────────────────────

School of Graduate and Continuing Education
Campus Box 2083
Columbia, MO 65215
573-876-7125
800-388-7579
E-mail: sce@wc.stephens.edu
URL: http://www.stephens.edu

Campus Visits: A seven-day or double weekend Liberal Studies seminar is required to begin a degree program.

Areas of Study: Business Administration (B), Education/Early Childhood Education (B), Education/Elementary Education (B), English (B), Health Care (B), Health Information Management (C/B), Health Science (B), Individualized (B), Marketing, Public Relations and Advertising (B), Philosophy, Law, and Rhetoric (B), Psychology (B).

Admissions: Open to adults 23 or older who hold high school diplomas or GEDs. To matriculate, students must pass the initial on-campus Liberal-Studies seminar with a grade of C or better.

Program Features: Stephens College, the second oldest private women's college in the United States, was founded in 1833. The School of Continuing Education was founded in 1971 to provide options for older learners. The Bachelor in Health Information Management may qualify learners to take the Registered Record Administrator (RRA) exam.

Tuition/Fees: $650 per 3-credit course, plus fees.

Syracuse University

Independent Study Degree Program (ISDP)
700 University Avenue
Syracuse, NY 13244-2530
315-443-3480
800-442-0501
E-mail: suisdp@uc.syr.edu
URL: http://www.suce.syr.edu/isdp/main

Campus Visits: One-week residencies are required three times a year at the beginning of each semester: January, May, and August.

Areas of Study: Liberal Studies (A/B), Liberal Studies/Management (B), Liberal Studies/Restaurant Food Service Management (B).

Admissions: Open to those with a college transfer or high school grade average of at least 2.5. Applicants with lower averages may be admitted on a nonmatriculation basis until they demonstrate their academic ability.

Program Features: Syracuse is a private college, founded in 1918, offering a variety of on-campus programs. Independent study programs have existed since 1966. Distance instruction takes place via surface mail, mailed videotapes, electronic conferencing, and E-mail.

Tuition/Fees: $320 per credit.

Texas Tech University

External Degree Program
Box 42191
Lubbock, TX 79409-2191
800-692-6877
806-742-2318
URL: http://www.dce.ttu.edu
E-mail: distlearn@ttu.edu

Campus Visits: None.

Areas of Study: General Studies/Liberal Arts.

Admissions: Open.

Program Features: Texas Tech University is a comprehensive, public, four-year institution. Distance-learning courses have been offered for more than 70 years. Courses are delivered by surface mail and online.

Tuition/Fees: $53 per credit.

Thomas Edison State College
101 West State Street
Trenton, NJ 08608-1176
609-984-1150
800-442-TESC
E-mail: admissions@tesc.edu
URL: http://www.tesc.edu

Campus Visits: None.
Areas of Study: Accounting (C/A/B), Administrative Office Management (C/A/B), Administration of Justice (A/B), Advertising Management (B), African-American Studies, (B), Art (B), Asian Studies (B), Agricultural Mechanization (A/B), Air Traffic Control (A/B), American Studies (B), Anthropology (B), Archaeology (B), Architectural Design (A/B), Art (B), Asian Studies (B), Aviation (A/B), Banking (A/B), Biology (A/B), Biomedical Electronics (B), Chemistry (A/B), Child Development Services (A/B), Civil Engineering Technology (B), Civil and Construction Engineering Technology (A), Clinical Laboratory Sciences (B), Communications (B), Community Services (A/B), Computer Aided Design (C), Computer Science (A/B), Computer Science Technology (A/B), Construction (B), Dance (B), Data Processing (C/A/B), Dental Hygiene (B), Economics (B), Electrical Technology (A/B), Electronic Engineering Technology (A/B), Electronics (C), Emergency Disaster Management (A/B), Engineering Graphics (A/B), Environmental Science (A/B), Environmental Studies (B), Finance (C/A/B), Fire Protection Science (A/B), Foreign Language (B), Forestry (A/B), General Management (A/B), Geography (B), Geology (B), Gerontology (B), Health and Nutrition Counseling (B), Health Sciences (B), Health Services (B), Health Services Administration (B), Health Services Education (B), History (B), Horticulture (A/B), Hospital Health Care Administration (A/B), Hotel/Motel/Restaurant Management (A/B), Human Resources Management (C/A/B), Humanities (B), Insurance (A/B), International Business (A/B), Journalism (B), Labor Studies (C/B), Laboratory Animal Science (B), Liberal Arts (A), Legal Services (A/B), Literature (B), Logistics (B), Management of Information Systems (B), Manufacturing Engineering Technology (A/B), Marine Engineering Technology (A/B), Marketing (C/A/B), Mathematics (A/B), Mechanical Engineering Technology (A/B), Medical Imaging (B), Mental Health and Rehabilitative Services (B), Music (B), Natural Sciences/Math (B), Nondestructive Testing Technology (A/B), Nuclear Engineering Technology (A/B), Nuclear Medicine (B), Nursing (B), Operations Management (C/A/B), Organizational Management (B), Perfusion Technology (B), Philosophy (B), Photography (B), Physics (A/B), Political Science (B), Procurement (A/B), Psychology (B), Public Administration (C/A/B), Purchasing and Materials Management (A/B), Radiation Protection (A/B), Radiation Therapy (B), Real Estate (A/B), Recreation Services (A/B), Rehabilitation Services (A/B), Religion (B), Respiratory Care (B), Retailing Management (A/B), School Business Administration (A/B), Small Business/Entrepreneurship (A/B), Social Sciences/History (B), Social Services (A/B), Social Services Administration (A/B), Social Services for Special Populations (A/B), Sociology (B), Surveying (A/B), Theater Arts (B), Transportation Management (A/B), Urban Studies (B), Women's Studies (B).

Admissions: Nursing bachelor's degrees limited to RNs who live or work in New Jersey. Radiological Technology limited to those with licensing or hospital training in X-ray technology. Bachelor's open only to applicants who hold professional registration or certification: Dental Hygiene, Medical Laboratory Science, Nuclear Medicine, Perfusion Technology, Radiation Therapy, Radiological Science, and Respiratory Therapy.

Program Features: Thomas Edison State College, founded in 1972, is the adult distance-learning division of the state of New Jersey. It operates primarily as an assessment college, allowing learners to transfer in courses taken elsewhere, take challenge exams, and document experience through a structured portfolio process to complete a degree. Some courses are offered with online options.

Tuition/Fees: Students either pay one, annual fee ($2,200–$3,150 per year), or fees per services as follows: Guided Study Courses: $66 per credit (New Jersey residents); $99 per credit (nonresidents). Annual enrollment $440–$780 ($1,350 international students); Technology Fee $50; Credit Transfer Fees from $60–$650 depending on number of credits; $125 Graduation Fee; $42 Portfolio Per Credit Fee.

Touro University International

Internet University
10542 Calle Lee, Suite 102
Los Alamitos, CA 90720
714-816-0366
E-mail: registration@tourouniversity.edu
URL: http://www.tourouniversity.edu

Campus Visits: None.

Admissions: This is a bachelor's completion program. Applicants should have completed the first two years of college or hold an associate's degree. Applicants need internet access and a PC equipped with a desktop video camera and CD-ROM.

Areas of Study: Business Administration/Finance (B), Business Administration/Internal Auditing (B), Business Administration/Management (B).

Program Features: Touro University International is a division of the regionally accredited, private Touro University, located in New York, New York. Courses are delivered via the internet.

Tuition/Fees: $180 per credit.

Troy State University

External Degree Program
PO Drawer 4419
Montgomery, AL 36103-4419
205-241-9553
E-mail: n/a
URL: http://www.tsum.edu/edp

Campus Visits: A one-day campus visit is required to present the final degree project for bachelor's candidates.

Areas of Study: General Education (A/B), Professional Studies (B).

Admissions: Open to those 22 or older. To be admitted unprovisionally, learners must have completed at least 30 quarter hours (20 semester credits) including two English composition courses with a grade of C in both of them.

Program Features: Troy State is part of the publicly supported university system of Alabama. Courses are delivered via the web, e-mail, videotape, and surface mail. Alabama residents may receive some courses via TV.

Tuition/Fees: $52 per quarter credit (Alabama residents); $73 per quarter credit (others); $100 Annual Enrollment Fee.

Union Institute

Center for Distance Learning
440 East McMillan Street
Cincinnati, OH 45206-1925
513-861-6400
800-486-3116
E-mail: dean-cdl@tui.edu
URL: http://www.tui.edu

Campus Visits: Learners must attend a weekend orientation seminar at one of the five Union Study Centers in Cincinnati, Ohio; Miami, Florida; Los Angeles, San Diego, or Sacramento, California. After orientation, learners meet with local advisors and classmates weekly via conference phone calls and computer conferencing. Weekend seminars may be required at the first of each new semester.

Areas of Study: The most popular majors are Business (B), Criminal Justice (B), Education (B), Psychology (B), and Individualized (B). Any major not facility-dependent or regulated by professional licensing (e.g., Bachelor of Science in Nursing) may be accommodated through Union's individualized learning process.

Admissions: Learners should have previous college experience. Most students are 35 to 55 years old, and have completed two or more years of college prior to applying.

Program Features: The Union Institute is a private college, one of America's original Universities Without Walls, founded in 1964. The Bachelor of Science or Bachelor of Arts is available with more than 50 individualized concentrations.

Tuition/Fees: $248 per credit.

University of Alabama New College

External Degree Program
Box 870182
Tuscaloosa, AL 35487-0182
205-348-7037
E-mail: info@exd.ccs.ua.edu
URL: http://bama.ua.edu/~iprogs/exd

Campus Visits: Applicants attend a weekend orientation and degree planning seminar.

Areas of Study: Administrative Sciences (Business) (B), Applied Science (Technology) (B), Communication (B), Humanities (B), Human Services (B), Natural Sciences (B), Social Sciences (B).

Admissions: Open to residents of the United States, at least 22 years old, who hold a GED with a minimum score of 50 or a high school diploma.

Program Features: The University of Alabama is a comprehensive, government-supported college. The External Degree program was founded in 1971 to assist adult learners seeking alternative educational opportunities.

Tuition/Fees: $104 per credit; $500 Campus Seminar Fee; $100 Annual Enrollment Fee.

University of California Extension

Center for Media and Independent Learning
2000 Center Street, Suite 400
Berkeley, CA 94704
510-642-4124
E-mail: askcmil@uclink4.berkeley.edu
URL:http://www-cmil.unex.berkeley.edu

Areas of Study: Accounting (C), Business Administration (C), Computer Information Systems (C), Hazardous Materials Management (C), Marketing (C), Telecommunications Engineering (C).

Admissions: Open but prerequisites may apply to selected courses.

Program Features: The University of California Extension is a publicly suppported institution. The university has offered distance-learning courses since 1913. Courses are delivered by mail, e-mail, and online.

Tuition/Fees: $140 per credit average.

University of California Los Angeles Extension

Online Learning Net
924 Westwood Boulevard, Suite 650
Los Angeles, CA 90024
800-784-8436
E-mail: enroll@unex.ucla.edu
URL: http://www.onlinelearning.net

Areas of Study: Business Studies (C), Teaching English as a Foreign Language (C), Teaching English to Speakers of Other Languages (C), Teaching Online (C), Technical Communication/Writing (C).

Admissions: Open but prerequisites may apply to selected courses. Some programs are professional post-Bachelor options for continuing education students. A computer, modem, and internet access are required.

Program Features: The University of California Los Angeles Extension is a publicly suppported institution. Courses are delivered online.

Tuition/Fees: $145 per credit average.

University of Delaware

FOCUS/Distance Learning
212 John M. Clayton Hall
Newark, DE 19716
302-831-1053
800-833-6287

E-mail: ce@mvs.udel.edu
URL: http://www.udel.edu/conted/webfocus.html

Campus Visits: Students attend a week-long campus institute in Newark.

Areas of Study: Human Resources/Hotel, Restaurant, and Institutional Management (B)

Admissions: Applicants should have a 2.5 transfer GPA and experience in the hospitality industry. Eight hundred hours of practicum work in the hospitality industry will be required.

Program Features: The University of Delaware is a government-supported comprehensive university founded in 1921. Courses are delivered on videotape with electronic conferencing.

Tuition/Fees: $177–$510 per credit, plus $90 per course videotape rental fee.

University of Iowa

Division of Continuing Education
Center for Credit Programs
116 International Center
Iowa City, IA 52242-1802
319-335-2575
800-272-6430
E-mail: credit-programs@uiowa.edu
URL: http://www.uiowa.edu/~ccp/gcs

Campus Visits: None.

Programs: Liberal Studies (B).

Admissions: Restricted to those who hold an associate's degree or its equivalent with 62 semester credits and a transfer grade point average of 2.5 or higher.

Program Features: The University of Iowa is a government-supported comprehensive college. The distance-degree program is a joint offering of the three Iowa Regent's universities. It was first offered in 1977 and has graduated 350 applicants. A few courses offer an e-mail lesson option. Other courses use surface mail, videotape, or fax.

Tuition/Fees: $84 per credit.

University of Maryland University College

Bachelor's Degree-at-a-Distance
University Boulevard at Adelphi Road
College Park, MD 20742-1660
301-985-7000
800-283-6832
E-mail: umucinfo@nova.umuc.edu
URL: http://www.umuc.edu/bdaad

Campus Visits: None.

Areas of Study: Accounting (B), Behavioral and Social Sciences (B), Business and Management (B), Communication Studies (B), Computer and Information Science (B), Computer Studies (B), English (B), Fire Science (B), Humanities (B), Management Studies (B), Paralegal Studies (C/B), Technology and Management (B).

Admissions: Open to those with a college transfer GPA of at least 2.0 or a high school diploma or GED. Others may apply for provisional acceptance. Since most of the courses offered by Maryland are junior or senior level, most students have at least 30 college credits or an associate's degree or the equivalent (60 college-level credits) when they apply. The Paralegal Studies program offers lower-level courses so it can usually be completed exclusively through Maryland regardless of transfer credits.

Program Features: The University of Maryland, a comprehensive, government-supported institution, is one of the 11 degree-granting institutions of the University of Maryland system. The distance learning program began in the 1970s. Courses are delivered via computer conferencing, voice mail boxes, and videotapes.

Tuition/Fees: $183 per credit (Maryland residents or active duty military); $222 per credit (others).

University of Nevada—Reno

Independent Study by Correspondence
Division of Continuing Education/050
Reno, NV 89557-0081
702-784-4652
800-233-8928
E-mail: istudy@scs.unr.edu
URL: http://www.dce.unr.edu/istudy

Campus Visits: None.

Areas of Study: General Studies (B).

Admissions: Open.

Program Features: The University of Nevada is a comprehensive government-supported university. The independent study division has operated for more than 50 years. Courses are delivered via print and e-mail.

Tuition/Fees: $70 per credit.

University of Oklahoma

College of Liberal Studies
1700 Asp Avenue, Suite 226
Norman, OK 73072-6400
405-325-1061
800-522-4389
E-mail: cls@ou.edu
URL: http://www.ou.edu/cls/prospects/internet.html

Campus Visits: A five-day introductory seminar is required. At least one additional one- to two-week seminar is required each year.

Areas of Study: Liberal Studies (B).

Admissions: Open to those with an associate's degree or 60 college credits who have a computer, modem, and internet access.

Program Features: The University of Oklahoma is a comprehensive government-supported university. The Bachelor in Liberal Studies via Internet Guided Independent Study provides for interdisciplinary study in the Social Sciences, Natural Sciences, or Humanities. Students work with advisors to write learning contracts.

Tuition/Fees: $67.50 per credit (Oklahoma residents); $209.50 per credit (nonresidents).

University of Phoenix Center for Distance Education

4605 East Elwood Street, 7th Floor
Phoenix, AZ 85040
602-921-8014
800-366-9699
E-mail: kbburkho.oramail@apollogrp.edu
URL: http://www.uophx.edu/center

Campus Visits: None.

Areas of Study: Business/Accounting (B), Business Administration (B), Business/(Computer) Information Systems (B), Business/Management (B), Business Marketing (B).

Admissions: Bachelor applicants should have at least 24 credits from a regionally accredited college and be at least 23 years of age with work experience. Those without 24 college credits will be required to take an introductory sequence.

Program Features: The University of Phoenix is a private, for-profit college founded in 1976 for working adults. The Center for Distance Education (CDE) offers distance learning via surface mail, phone, e-mail, and fax. Courses are accelerated, designed to be completed in five weeks rather than the traditional six–sixteen weeks.

Tuition/Fees: $318 per credit.

University of Phoenix Online

Online Programs
100 Spear Street, Suite 200
San Francisco, CA 94105
415-541-0141
800-388-5463
E-mail: KLBertne.Oramail@apollogrp.edu (Kevin Bertness)
URL: http://www.uophx.edu/online

Campus Visits: None.

Areas of Study: Business Administration (B), (Computer) Information Systems (B), General Studies (A), Management (B), Marketing (B), Project Management (B).

Admissions: Applicants must be at least 23 years old, have a high school diploma or the equivalent, be employed, and have a computer and modem to access online courses.

Program Features: The University of Phoenix is a private, for-profit college founded in 1976. The college supports campus programs in Phoenix, Arizona and across the nation. Learners meet online weekly via Phoenix's private electronic mail and conferencing service. Classes are accelerated and last only five to six weeks.

Tuition/Fees: $375 per credit.

University of South Florida

Bachelor of Independent Studies Program

4202 East Fowler Avenue, SOC 107
Tampa, Florida 33620-8100
813-974-4058
E-mail: bis@luna.cas.usf.edu
URL: http://www.cas.usf.edu/bis/index.html

Campus Visits: Up to three two-week seminars are required on campus depending on transfer credits. One day is required on campus to present the final thesis.

Areas of Study: Independent Studies (Liberal Arts) (B).

Admissions: The program is open but 80 percent of applicants already have an associate's degree and are working on bachelor's completion. The majority of degree seekers are Florida residents.

Program Features: Florida State University—Tallahassee, the University of Florida—Gainesville, and the University of North Florida—Jacksonville, all participate in the Independent Study degree program through the coordination of the University of South Florida. Degrees are awarded by the University of South Florida.

Tuition/Fees: Varies with seminars attended.

University of Southern Colorado

Division of Continuing Education
2200 Bonforte Boulevard
Pueblo, CO 81001-4901
719-574-3312
800-388-6154
E-mail: coned@uscolo.edu
URL: http://www.uscolo.edu/coned

Campus Visits: None.

Areas of Study: Paralegal (C), Social Science/Business (B), Social Science/Economics (B), Social Science/Criminal Justice (B), Social Science/History (B), Social Science/Political Science (B), Social Science/Sociology (B), Social Science/Psychology (B).

Admissions: Open.

Program Features: Southern Colorado is part of the extensive government-supported Colorado State College system. The Southern Colorado campus offers one degree by independent study: the Bachelor of Science in Social Science, with specialties in various Social Science areas.

Tuition/Fees: $70 per credit; $125 enrollment fee; $85 annual advising fee.

University of Wisconsin Extension

Independent Study
104 Extension Building
432 North Lake Street
Madison, WI 53706-1498
608-262-2011
800-442-6460
E-mail: ilearn@admin.uwex.edu

Campus Visits: None.

Areas of Study: Accounting (C), Business (C), General Business (C), General Studies/Liberal Arts (C), Individualized (C), Personnel Management (C), Purchasing (C), Small Business (C).

Admissions: Open.

Program Features: The University of Wisconsin system is publicly supported. The Extension's independent study program offers self-designed 30-credit certificates and more than 550 courses. More than 12,000 students study through independent learning each year.

Tuition/Fees: $110 per credit.

University of Wisconsin—Platteville
Extended Degree in Business Administration
510 Pioneer Tower
1 University Plaza
Platteville, WI 53818-3099
608-342-1468
800-362-5460
E-mail: edp@uwplatt.edu
URL: http://www.uwplatt.edu/~edp

Campus Visits: None.

Areas of Study: Business Administration/Finance (B), Business Administration/Human Resources (B), Business Administration/General Business (B), Business/Management (B), Business/Marketing (B).

Admissions: Applicants must be at least 22 years old. Applicants with lower than 2.0 transfer GPAs will be considered if more than five years have passed since the last college was attended.

Program Features: The University of Wisconsin system maintains a range of distance degree programs and support services for state residents. The Business Administration program has been offered via distance learning through Platteville since 1979. Courses are delivered by mail and the World Wide Web.

Tuition/Fees: $89.25 per credit (Wisconsin residents); $103 per credit (Minnesota residents); $317 per credit (others); $100 annual fee.

Upper Iowa University
External Degree
PO Box 1861
Fayette, IA 52142-1857
319-425-5252
888-877-3742
E-mail: extdegree@uiu.edu
URL: http://www.uiu.edu

Campus Visits: None.

Areas of Study: Business (A/B), Business/Accounting (B), Business/Management (B), Business/Marketing (B), Business/Human Resources (B), Public Administration (B), Public

Administration/Law Enforcement (B), Public Administration/Fire Sciences (B), Human Services (B), Social Science (B).

Admissions: Those who have graduated from an accredited high school or who have passed the GED are almost always granted admission. Admission is normally granted to anyone with a 2.0 college transfer GPA.

Program Features: Upper Iowa University is a comprehensive private institution, founded in 1857. The distance-learning department was launched in 1973. Courses are delivered via surface mail, video, and e-mail.

Tuition/Fees: $145 per credit.

Vermont College of Norwich University
Adult Degree Program (ADP)
Montpelier, VT 05602
802-828-8500
800-336-6794
E-mail: vcadmis@norwich.edu
URL: http://www.norwich.edu/newcollege

Campus Visits: New college students attend a 2-week seminar on-campus each semester. Adult Degree Program Students, who are older, attend 1 week residencies twice a year.

Areas of Study: Arts (B), Business and Management (B), Counseling and Psychology (B), Historical, Social, and Cultural Studies (B), Teacher Education (B), Environmental Studies (B), Holistic Studies (B), Individualized (B), Women's Studies and Gender Studies (B), Writing and Literature (B).

Admissions: Open to those with a computer, internet access, and strong motivation.

Program Features: Vermont College is a nontraditional private college founded in 1819. Distance learners work with their advisors to design fifteen-credit, independent study clusters each semester.

Tuition/Fees: $4,250–$4,500 per fifteen-credit semester.

Vincennes University
Degree Completion Program
1002 North First Street
Vincennes, IN 47591
812-885-5900
800-880-7961
E-mail: tyoung@vunet.vinu.edu
URL: n/a

Campus Visits: None.

Areas of Study: General Studies (A), Law Enforcement (A), Business (A), Social Science (A), Behavioral Science (A).

Admissions: Open.

Program Features: Vincennes is a publicly supported junior college with a full line of majors and degrees available for on-campus learners. The associate degrees offered by Vincennes are general study degrees that provide a solid foundation for continuing toward a bachelor's in any major area.

Tuition/Fees: $83.35 per credit.

Washington State University

Extended Degree Program
PO Box 645220
Pullman, Washington
800-222-4978
509-335-3557
E-mail: edp@wsu.edu
URL: http://www.eus.wsu.edu/edp

Campus Visits: None.

Areas of Study: Social Science/Anthropology (B), Social Science/Business Administration (B), Social Science/Criminal Justice (B), Social Science/History (B), Social Science/Human Development (B), Social Science/Political Science (B), Social Science/Psychology (B), Social Science/Sociology (B), Social Science/Women's Studies (B).

Admissions: Applicants should hold an associate's degree or college transfer credits. Applicants must have at least 27 semester transfer credits (40 quarter credits) with a grade average of 2.0.

Program Features: Washington State University is part of the government-supported university system of the state of Washington. Courses are delivered using print, videotape, CD-ROM, e-mail, and the World Wide Web.

Tuition/Fees: $90 per credit for print-based correspondence; $163 per credit for internet and interactive courses (Washington residents); $245 per credit for internet and interactive courses (nonresidents).

Weber State University

Distance Learning
4005 University Circle
Ogden, UT 84408-4005
801-626-6785
800-848-7770, ext. 6785
E-mail: dist-learn@weber.edu
URL: http://www.wsuonline.weber.edu

Campus Visits: None.

Programs: Clinical Laboratory Science (B), Health Information Management (B), Health Promotion (B), Health Services Administration (B), Radiological Sciences (B), Respiratory Therapy (A/B).

Admissions: ACT required for those under 25. The Laboratory Science program requires an associate's degree and 3 years of employment as a lab technician. The Respiratory Therapy program is open only to Registered Radiological Technologists or the equivalent. Students must have the appropriate work access to clinical labs for lab studies.

Program Features: Weber State, founded in 1898, is a government-supported comprehensive university. Some courses are delivered online. Others use videotape, audiocasettes, and tutorials on computer disks.

Tuition/Fees: $95–$182 per credit.

West Virginia Wesleyan College

Outreach Education
59 College Avenue
Buckhannon, WV 26201
304-473-8430
E-mail: outreach@wvwc.edu
URL: n/a

Campus Visits: A weekend seminar on-campus is required at the beginning of each semester.

Areas of Study: Nursing (B).

Admissions: Open to RNs who have completed a diploma or associate's degree in Nursing.

Program Features: West Virginia Wesleyan is a private comprehensive college, founded in 1890, affiliated with the Methodist Church. The program is accredited by the National League for Nursing.

Tuition/Fees: $250 per semester credit.

Western Illinois University

Non-Traditional BA Program
Horrabin Hall 5
1 University Circle
Macomb, IL 61455-1390
309-298-2496
E-mail: IS-Program@wiu.edu
URL: n/a

Campus Visits: None.

Areas of Study: Liberal Arts (B).

Admissions: Open.

Program Features: Western Illinois University, founded in 1902, is one of the comprehensive, government-supported colleges of the State of Illinois system. Courses are delivered via video-tape, surface mail, and online. Applicants who live in Illinois may also view local cable television broadcasts.

DIRECTORY OF DISTANCE EDUCATION AND TRAINING COUNCIL ACCREDITED DISTANCE DEGREES

The Distance Education and Training Council (DETC) has been accrediting colleges that offer courses by correspondence for over seventy years. DETC schools offer vocational courses in subjects ranging from air-conditioner repair and auto mechanics to engineering technology. DETC-accredited institutions that offer associate, or bachelor's degrees, or certificates with no campus visits are listed below.

A complete annual directory of all schools offering DETC-approved courses is available for free from the DETC, 1601 18th Street NW, Washington, D.C. 20009-2529. Phone 202-234-5100. For those with internet access, the DETC provides a free course catalog online at http://www.detc.org.

American Academy of Nutrition
1212 Kenesaw
Sequoyah Hills Center
Knoxville, TN 3719-7736
800-290-4226
URL: http://www.nutritioneducation.com

Applied Nutrition (A)

American College of Prehospital Medicine
365 Canal Street, Suite 2300
New Orleans, LA 70130-1135
800-735-2276
URL: http://www.acpm.edu

Emergency Medical Services (C/A/B)

American Health Information Management Association
919 North Michigan, Suite 2300
Chicago, IL, 60611-1683
312-787-2672
URL: http://www.ahima.org

Medical Record Technology (C)

American Military University
9104-P Manassas
Manassas Park, VA 20111
703-330-5398
URL: http://www.amunet.edu

Military Studies (B)

Andrew Jackson University
10 Old Montgomery Highway
Birmingham, AL 35209
205-871-9288
URL: http://www.aju.edu

Communication (B), Business (B), Criminal Justice (B)

Berean University
1445 Boonville Avenue
Springfield, MO 65802
417-862-9533
URL: http://www.berean.edu

Bible/Theology (A/B), Church Ministries (A/B), Bible/Christian Counseling (B), Bible/Christian Education (B), Bible/Missions/Evangelism (B)

California College for Health Sciences
222 West 24th Street
National City, CA 91950
619-477-4800
URL: http://www.cchs.edu

Allied Health (A), Business (A/B), Business/Accounting (A/B), Business/Economics (A/B), Business/Finance (A/B), Business/Management (A/B), Business/Marketing (A/B), Early Childhood Education (A), EEG Technology (A), Medical Transcription (A), Respiratory Technology/Therapy (A/B)

Cleveland Institute of Electronics
1776 East 17th Street
Cleveland, OH 44144
800-243-6446
URL: http://www.cie-wc.edu

Electronics Engineering Technology (A)

Grantham College of Engineering
34641 Grantham College Road
PO Box 5700
Slidell, LA 70469-5700
504-649-4191
URL: http://www.grantham.edu

Computer Engineering Technology (A/B), Computer Science (A/B), Electronics Engineering Technology (A/B)

Griggs University
PO Box 4437
12501 Old Columbia Pike
Silver Spring, MD 20914-4437

301-680-6570
URL: http://www.griggs.edu

Ministry (C/A), Religion (B), General Studies (B), Religious Education (B), Church Business Management (B), Business Management (B)

ICI University
6300 North Belt Line Road
Irving, TX 75063
800-444-0424
URL: http://www.ici.edu

Religious Studies (A/B), Bible/Theology (B), Missions (B)

ICS Center for Degree Studies
925 Oak Street
Scranton, PA 18515
717-342-7701
URL: http://www.icslearn.com

Accounting (A), Applied Computer Science (A), Civil Engineering Technology (A), Electrical Engineering Technology (A), Electronics Technology (A), Industrial Engineering Technology (A), Mechanical Engineering Technology (A), Management/Marketing (A), Management/Finance (A), Hospitality Management (A)

National Institute for Paralegal Arts and Sciences
164 West Royal Palm Road
Boca Raton, FL 33432
561-368-2522
URL: http://www.nipas.net

Paralegal Studies (A)

The Paralegal Institute
2933 West Indian School Road
Drawer 11408
Phoenix, AZ 85061-1408
602-212-0501
URL: n/a

Paralegal Studies (A)

World College
Lake Shores Plaza
5193 Shore Drive, Suite 105
Virginia Beach, VA 23455-2500
757-464-4600
URL: http://www.cie-wc.edu

Electronics Engineering Technology (B)

DIRECTORY OF STATEWIDE AND SPECIALIZED SITE-BASED DISTANCE PROGRAMS

STATEWIDE DISTANCE LEARNING SITES ONLINE

University of Alaska Center for Distance Education and Independent Learning
http://uafcde.lrb.uaf.edu

Information on Alaska's courses and degrees are offered to residents statewide via CD-ROM, site-based videoconferencing and interactive TV, independent study by mail, and the internet.

California Virtual University
http://www.california.edu

Online database of distance courses and degrees offered by accredited colleges in California. Includes site-based distance programs delivered statewide via videoconferencing, cable, interactive TV, and satellite, as well as courses delivered to your home via videotape, surface mail, and the internet.

Colorado Consortium for Independent Study
http://www.colorado.edu/cewww/

Lists courses and degrees offered by Adams State College, Metropolitan State College, and several University of Colorado campuses to college and community distance-learning reception sites across Colorado.

Connecticut Distance-Learning Consortium
http://www.ctdlc.org

A collaborative catalog of the courses and degrees offered through distance-delivery means by twenty-seven Connecticut higher education institutions.

Florida Virtual University
http://www.flcampus.org/

One-stop web catalog of distance-learning courses offered primarily to state residents at ten of Florida's public universities and twenty-eight of its community colleges.

Illinois—University of Illinois Online
http://www.online.uillinois.edu

Degrees and courses offered via all distance-delivery means to residents of Illinois.

Indiana College Network
http://www.icn.org

A partnership of Ball State University, Indiana State, Indiana University, Ivy Tech State College, Indiana's private colleges, Vincennes University, and the University of Southern Indiana. The network delivers college courses to specially equipped interactive television (ITV) sites at high schools, community colleges, and extension locations statewide. Phone: 800-ICN-8899.

Iowa State University—Iowa Communications Network

http://www.exnet.iastate.edu/Pages/ece

Iowa State University offers off-campus and extension distance courses. Includes courses and degrees that are delivered in-state via two-way audio and video at reception sites at high schools, corporations, community colleges, and military bases. Phone: 515-294-6222.

Kansas—Fort Hays State University Virtual College

http://www.fhsu.edu/virtual_college/

Degrees and courses offered via interactive TV at school, local corporations and military sites across Kansas. Phone: 785-628-4291.

Maine—Education Network of Maine

http://www.enn.maine.edu

A listing of associate's and bachelor's degrees from publicly funded colleges that are offered at interactive TV sites across Maine.

Michigan Virtual University

http://www.mivu.org

The newly founded Michigan Virtual University serves as a master catalog and clearinghouse on distance course programs and options in Michigan.

Minnesota Virtual University

http://www.mnvu.org

An online gateway to higher education and lifelong learning in Minnesota. Includes programs for resident and remote learners. Covers higher education (state and private), community education, vocational training, and corporate training.

State University of New York—SUNY Learning Network

URL: http://www.sln.suny.edu/sln

Catalog for distance learning programs operating within the State University of New York system. Includes site-based, interactive videoconferencing programs operated at SUNY reception sites. Phone: 518-443-5331. E-mail: helpdesk@sln.suny.edu.

North Carolina—Carolina Courses Online

http://www.fridaycenter.unc.edu

Distance learning courses delivered by the University of North Carolina system. Includes web-based courses, video courses, and site-based teleconferencing courses. Phone: 919-962-1134. E-mail: stuserv.ce@mhs.unc.edu.

Oregon Network for Education

http://www.eou.edu/one

Online catalog that lists distance-learning courses and programs from Oregon postsecondary institutions. Includes options from Eastern Oregon State College and options delivered via interactive TV broadcasts, ED-NET 2, or ED-NET 3, a regional access computer conferencing system that serves Oregon campus sites. E-mail: Jhart@eou.edu (Joe Hart, Director).

Pennsylvania Virtual University
http://business.ship.edu/vu

A distance-delivery collaboration of several colleges in Pennsylvania.

University of South Dakota Statewide Educational Services
http://www.usd.edu/swes

Listings of degrees offered at interactive TV and videoconferencing sites across South Dakota. Phone: 800-233-7937.

Texas—University of Texas Telecampus
http://www.uol.com/telecampus

The Telecampus is a support unit for distance-learners at the University of Texas System statewide. It includes links to many distance learning resources within the University of Texas System, the state of Texas, and beyond. Phone: 512-499-4292 or 888-TEXAS16. E-mail: telecampus@utsystem.edu.

Utah Electronic Community College and Education Network
http://www.utah-ecc.org
http://www.uen.org

Central online distance-learning sites for the state of Utah. UECC is the Utah Electronic Community College, a five-institution partnership offering courses and degrees. UEN is the Utah Electronic Network, a statewide television and satellite reception network for delivery to rural areas and high schools.

Vermont State Colleges—Johnson State College External Degree
http://www.jsc.vsc.edu

The external bachelor's is open to Vermont residents or those living along Vermont's borders. Learners attend Sunday seminars and meet with mentors at regional sites across the state. Courses are delivered online and through interactive TV reception sites statewide. Phone: 800-635-2356, ext. 1290.

University of Wisconsin—Distance Education Clearinghouse
http://www.uwex.edu/disted/home.html

An excellent master site with directories to all types of distance-learning resources. Special section on site-based distance-learning programs offered through the University of Wisconsin and the Wisconsin two-year community and technical college systems.

REGIONAL AND SPECIALIZED DISTANCE-LEARNING NETWORKS ONLINE

Community Colleges Distance-Learning Network
http://ccdln.rio.maricopa.edu

A consortium of courses and degrees online from community colleges across the nation including Cuyahoga Community College, Dallas Community Colleges, Foothill/DeAnza Community Colleges, Kern Community College, Kirkwood Community College, Miami-Dade Community College, Rio Salado College, and Sinclair Community College.

Community Colleges—PBS Cable TV—Going the Distance Associate Degree
http://www.pbs.org/als/gtd

A directory to more than 170 community colleges in thirty-eight states that offer PBS telecourses on local cable TV networks. Call PBS Adult Learning Services at 800-257-2578 for a referral to a college near you that carries PBS telecourses.

Western Governors University
http://www.wgu.edu

A cooperative formed in 1997 by the governors of the Western States to allow states to share courses and resources through distance-learning means. Offers online courses with plans to offer publicly accessible, competency-based degrees fully online.

Southern Regional Electronic Campus
http://www.srec.sreb.org/

A cooperative arrangement among colleges across the fifteen southern states. Contains online links to more than 1,000 courses and 25 college degree programs available via distance-learning means in the Southern region, many of them site based.

The Midwest Common Market
http://www.cic.uiuc.edu/CMCI/cmci_homepage.htm

A listing of links to distance-learning collaborative offerings in the Midwest.

CANADIAN DISTANCE-LEARNING RESOURCES ONLINE

Canadian University Distance Education Directory
http://www.schoolnet.ca/vp/CAUCE

Online directory of accredited Canadian distance-learning programs, most of them site based, maintained by the Association of Universities and Colleges of Canada (AUCC).

Network for Ontario Distance Educators—NODE
http://node.on.ca

Distance-learning resources and a searchable database of distance-education courses at fourteen universities and twenty-four colleges in Ontario.

TeleEducation New Brunswick
http://teleeducation.nb.ca/distanceed

Distance-learning resources in New Brunswick and the best database of college courses offered online worldwide.

GLOSSARY

Accreditation An independent review process undertaken to ensure that a college offers what it says it offers, operates under sound fiscal policies, and abides by commonly agreed upon high standards of academic excellence.

ACT American College Test. A college entrance exam often required for students who enter college directly from high school but rarely required of older students.

Assessment College A college that specializes in awarding college credits based on assessment procedures, such as testing.

Associate's degree A two-year degree that covers the freshman and sopho-more years of college. Associate's degrees require the completion of about 20 courses or 60 semester credits or 90 quarter credits.

Audit To take a course for fun or personal enrichment rather than for academic credit that can be used toward a degree. Tuition is generally lower for audit courses than for the same course taken as a degree course. Auditors often attend the class and read materials and participate in classroom discussions but are not required to take examinations or submit papers. Auditors are not usually graded on their efforts. Their attendance in a class is simply noted as an "audit" on their academic transcripts.

Bachelor's degree A four-year degree. Bachelor's degrees require the com-pletion of about 40 courses or 120 semester credits or 180 quarter credits. Also referred to as the baccalaureate degree.

Certificate A short, concentrated course of study in a single subject area.

CEU Continuing Education Unit. Refers to nondegree educa-tional activities undertaken to enter or maintain standing in selected professions. One CEU is equal to 10 contact hours of learning.

Challenge exam	Any exam taken by a student in an effort to challenge the need for that student to take a formal course in the same subject. CLEP, the College Level Examination Program, is one such program.
CHEA	Council for Higher Education Accreditation. The non-governmental agency that oversees recognized college accrediting agencies.
Concentration	A formal cluster of courses all taken in the same subject area within a degree, for example twelve courses all taken in the area of psychology. The concentration may also be called area of concentration. Some colleges also use this term to indicate the major area of a degree. For example, a student might earn a bachelor's degree with a concentration or major in psychology.
Credit for experience	Any of a number of programs that allow adult learners to earn college credit for their life and career experience. Includes challenge exam programs and academic portfolio programs.
Degree mill	Any college that issues a degree based on one's ability to write a tuition check rather than on one's ability to complete rigorous educational activities.
DETC	Distance Education Training Council. An accrediting agency that oversees non-residential colleges and training institutions that offer distance-learning programs.
Distance-Learning	Any type of learning that takes place with the instructor and student located physically at a distance from each other. Distance learning may be delivered on the internet, by cable TV, by satellite, by videotape or by mail-based correspondence.
EFC	Expected Family Contribution. Refers to the amount a student is expected to contribute toward his or her own education as reflected on the Student Aid Report (SAR) each year.
FAFSA	Free Application for Student Aid. The form students must complete each year to determine if they are eligible for financial aid.

Full-time study	The completion of four or more classes per semester or academic quarter. Also defined as at least 12 semester credits or 15 quarter credits of class work per academic term.
GPA	Grade Point Average. Colleges assign numerical value to letter grades (A = 4.0; B = 3.0; C = 2.0; D = 1.0; F = 0.0). The GPA is the mathematical average of these numerical values. For example, a student who takes two courses and receives an A in one (4.0), and a C in the other (2.0), would have a 3.0 or B GPA. To determine overall GPA add all numerical grade values, then divide this number by the number of courses completed.
Graduate school	Any post-bachelor's program of study. Master's and doctorate's are common graduate degrees.
Grant	Money awarded by schools, the government, or private agencies to cover educational expenses such as tuition and books. Grants are free money. They need never be paid back.
Major	A formal cluster of courses all taken in the same general subject area within a degree, for example 12 courses all taken in the area of psychology. The major may also be called "area of concentration." For example, a student might earn a bachelor's degree with a major in psychology.
Matriculate	To take classes toward a degree.
Minor	A formal cluster of courses all taken in the same general subject area within a degree, for example four courses all taken in the area of management. For example, a student might earn a bachelor's degree with a major in nursing and a minor in nurse management.
Part-time study	The completion of two or less classes per semester or academic quarter. Also defined as 6 credits or less of class work per academic term.
Portfolio	Academic collection of materials submitted for review by a faculty committee to determine if older students are eligible for college credits based on their life and career experience.

Prerequisite	Any course that must be taken prior to attempting another course. For example, Algebra I is usually a prerequisite course for Algebra II.
Provisional acceptance	When a student is admitted temporarily with the provision that something else must occur later to make the admission permanent. For example, a student might be admitted to a college provisionally because he or she has a low GPA. The provision might be that the student can attend the university provided he or she earns a certain GPA during their first semester of study. Failure to meet the provision may result in academic dismissal.
Quarter	A term of study that is ten weeks long.
Regional accreditation	Accreditation by any one of the six regional boards that are recognized as college accreditors by the Council on Higher Education Accreditation. Regional accreditation is the most widely recognized type of college accreditation in the United States.
Registrar	The official who oversees class registrations and keeps official academic grade transcripts.
Remedial courses	Classes taken to bring skills up to a college level. For example, students who have poor math skills may be required to take Remedial Mathematics to prepare for college-level study in math.
SAT I	A college entrance exam commonly required for students entering college right out of high school but rarely required for older adults entering college.
Scholarships	Money awarded by schools, the government, or private agencies to cover educational expenses such as tuition and books. Scholarships are free money. They need never be paid back.
Semester	A term of study that is fifteen weeks long.
SAR	The Student Aid Report. A report issued by the government each year that details how much aid a student will be eligible to receive at any one college. The results of the SAR are based on data that the student provides each year on the FAFSA.

Student loan	Any of a number of special low-interest loans designed to pay for educational activities.
Transcript	A permanent, official academic record from high school or college. Transcripts list all classes taken and the grades received in each of these classes.
Transfer student	Any student who begins their studies at one college and then transfers to another college to complete their studies. For example, a student might complete his or her freshman year of college at City College of New York, then transfer to New York University for her sophomore year.
Undergraduate	The first four years of full-time studies undertaken in an effort to earn an undergraduate credential such as a certificate, associate's degree or bachelor's degree.

BIBLIOGRAPHY

The College Board. *The Official Handbook for the CLEP Examinations.* Washington, D.C.: The College Board, 1988.

Daniel, John S. *Mega-Universities and Knowledge Media.* London, England: Kogan Page Limited, 1998.

Distance Education and Training Council. *DETC 1998–1999: Directory of Accredited Institutions.* Washington, D.C.: DETC, 1989.

The Education Resources Institute. *Life After 40: A Portrait of Today's and Tomorrow's Postsecondary Students.* Boston, Massachusetts: The Education Resources Group, 1996.

Blazey, Mark, Richard B. Fischer, and Henry T. Lipman. *Students of the Third Age: University/College Programs for Retired Adults.* Washington, D.C.: American Council on Education, 1992.

Clark, Thomas A., and John R. Verduin, Jr. *Distance Education: The Foundations of Effective Practice.* San Francisco, California: Jossey Bass Series in Higher Education, Massachusetts: 1991.

Harvard 1997–1998 Extension School Catalog. Cambridge, Massachusetts: Harvard Printing, 1997.

Lamdin, Lois. *Earn College Credit for What You Know.* Chicago, Illinois: Council for the Advancement of Experiential Leaning, 1992.

Mandel, Alan, and Elena Michelson. *Portfolio Development and Adult Learning.* Chicago, Illinois: Council for the Advancement of Experiential Learning, 1990.

Matthews, Anne. *Bright College Years: Inside the American Campus Today.* New York, New York: Simon & Schuster, 1997.

McMenamin, Brigid. "The Tyranny of the Diploma." Forbes, 28, Dec. 1998, p. 104–109. Merrian, Sharon, and Rosemary Caffarella. Learning in Adulthood. San Francisco, California: Jossey Bass Higher Education, 1991.

Phillips, Vicky. *College with Knowledge: The Smart Way to Earn Your Degree Through Distance Learning.* Waterbury, Vermont: Lifelong Learning Publications, 1996–1999.

Phillips, Vicky, and Yager, Cindy. *Best Distance Learning Graduate Schools: Earning Your Degree Without Leaving Home*. New York, New York: The Princeton Review/Random House, 1989.

Rudolph, Frederick. *The American College and University: A History*. Athens, Georgia: University of Georgia Press, 1990.

Russell, Thomas. *The No Significant Difference Phenomenon*. Raleigh, North Carolina: North Carolina State Publications, 1999.

Tyson, Laura D'Andrea. "Why the Wage Gap Just Keeps Getting Bigger." *Business Week*. Dec. 14, 1998.

University Continuing Education Association. *Lifelong Learning Trends*. Washington, District of Columbia: UCEA, 1998.

Vermont Student Assistance Corporation. *Scholarships for the College Year 1999–2000*. Winooski, Vermont: VSAC, 1998.

Vogelstein, Fred. "How High Can It Go?" *U.S. News & World Report: America's Best Colleges: 1999*. Aug., 1999, p. 82.

ABOUT THE AUTHOR

Vicky Phillips, a pioneer in the field of adult education and distance learning, has helped over 17,000 adult learners understand and excel at the back-to-college process. From 1989 to 1996, she designed and directed America's first online counseling center for distance learners for the Electronic University Network on America Online. She served as Director of Academic Services for Antioch University's San Francisco campus in the 1980s, and has authored educational courseware for companies such as Simon & Schuster's Computer Curriculum Corporation. She has served as a media expert on adult education and training for CNN Financial News, *U.S. News & World Report, Fortune, Money, Kiplinger's Personal Finance, Family PC, Business Week,* and other enterprises. She is a Phi Beta Kappa, summa cum laude college graduate who holds a master's in Psychology. She has taught psychology for the Electronic University Network, Antioch University, and the Community College of Vermont. Today, as CEO of her own company, geteducated.com, she serves as an internal consultant to companies and colleges that incubate and develop new products and services for the online adult education and training markets. Ms. Phillips is the publisher of the free electronic newsletter, the *Virtual University Gazette,* as well as publisher of the *Virtual University Business Digest,* and the *Virtual University Dean's Digest.* She is co-author with Cindy Yager of *Best Distance Learning Graduate Schools: Earning Your Degree Without Leaving Home,* also from The Princeton Review/Random House.

She may be reached via the contact information below.

geteducated.com
170 South Main Street
Waterbury, Vermont 05676 USA
vicky@geteducated.com
http://www.geteducated.com

NOTES

NOTES

NOTES

NOTES

NOTES

NOTES

NOTES

NOTES

NOTES

NOTES

NOTES

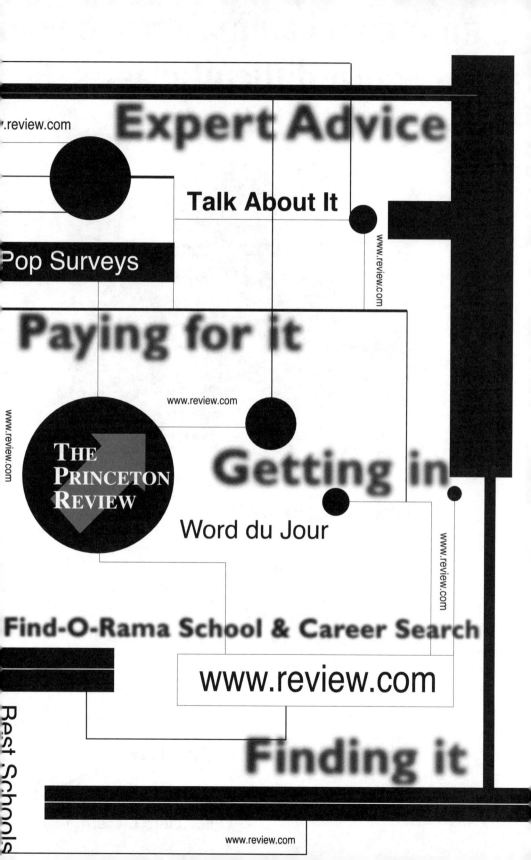

tutor.com can make even your most difficult classes elementary.

Find a tutor in 3 easy steps:

Find.
Log onto our website: www.tutor.com

Connect.
Sign up to find a tutor who fits all your needs

Learn.
Get tutored in any subject or skill

Visit www.tutor.com

Find. Connect. Learn.

FIND US...

International

Hong Kong
4/F Sun Hung Kai Centre
30 Harbour Road, Wan Chai,
Hong Kong
Tel: (011)85-2-517-3016

Japan
Fuji Building 40, 15-14
Sakuragaokacho, Shibuya Ku,
Tokyo 150, Japan
Tel: (011)81-3-3463-1343

Korea
Tae Young Bldg, 944-24,
Daechi- Dong, Kangnam-Ku
The Princeton Review- ANC
Seoul, Korea 135-280,
South Korea
Tel: (011)82-2-554-7763

Mexico City
PR Mex S De RL De Cv
Guanajuato 228 Col. Roma
06700 Mexico D.F., Mexico
Tel: 525-564-9468

Montreal
666 Sherbrooke St.
West, Suite 202
Montreal, QC H3A 1E7 Canada
Tel: (514) 499-0870

Pakistan
1 Bawa Park - 90 Upper Mall
Lahore, Pakistan
Tel: (011)92-42-571-2315

Spain
Pza. Castilla, 3 - 5º A, 28046
Madrid, Spain
Tel: (011)341-323-4212

Taiwan
155 Chung Hsiao East Road
Section 4 - 4th Floor,
Taipei R.O.C., Taiwan
Tel: (011)886-2-751-1243

Thailand
Building One, 99 Wireless Road
Bangkok, Thailand 10330
Tel: (662) 256-7080

Toronto
1240 Bay Street, Suite 300
Toronto M5R 2A7 Canada
Tel: (800) 495-7737
Tel: (716) 839-4391

Vancouver
4212 University Way NE,
Suite 204
Seattle, WA 98105
Tel: (206) 548-1100

National (U.S.)

We have over 60 offices around the U.S. and run courses in over 400 sites. For courses and locations within the U.S. call 1 (800) 2/Review and you will be routed to the nearest office.